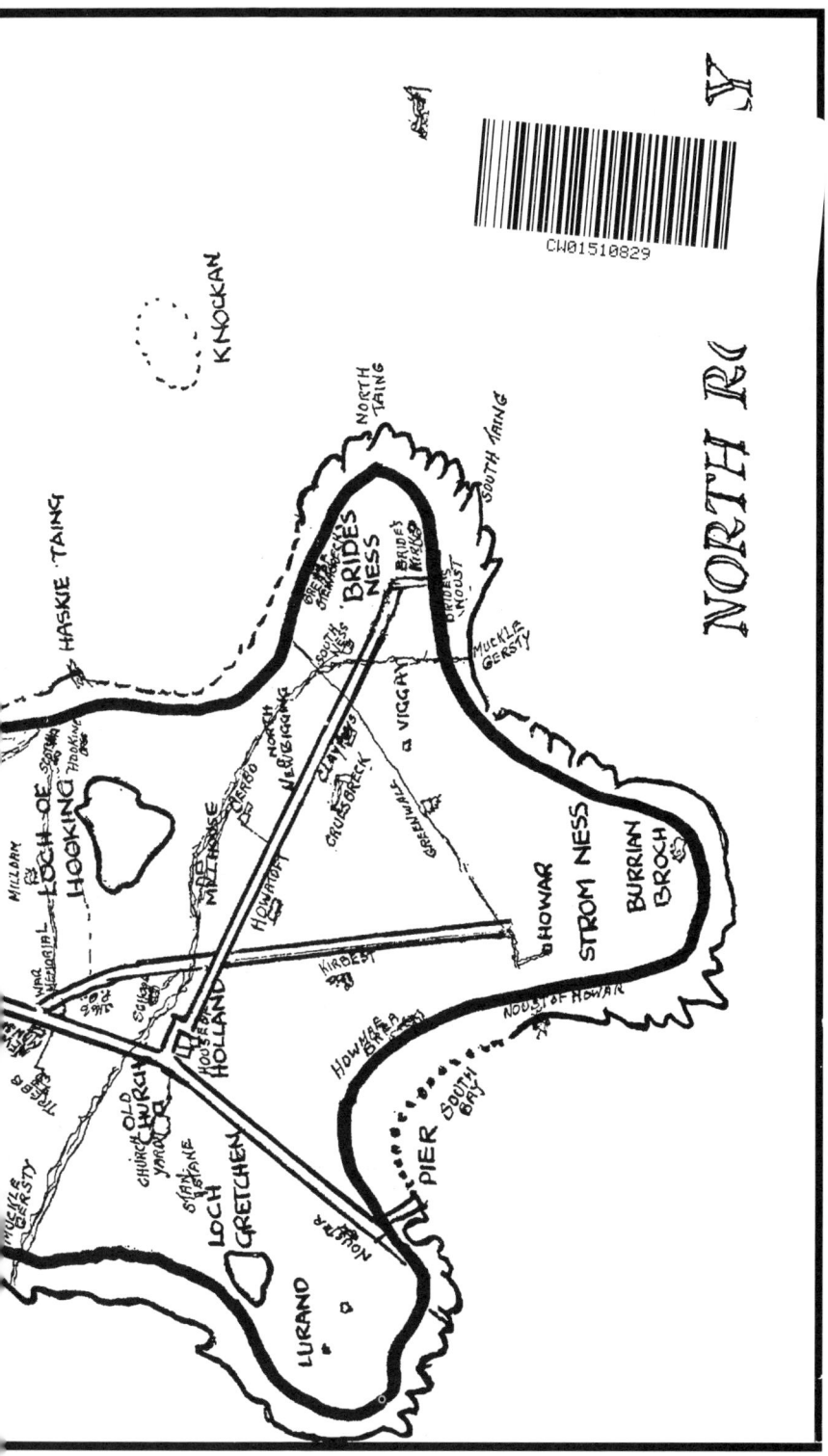

NORTH R(

KNOCKAN

CW01510829

A Window on North Ronaldsay

A Window
on
North
Ronaldsay

by

Peter A. Tulloch

Printed and published by The Kirkwall Press,
"The Orcadian" Office, Kirkwall
First printed 1974
Reprinted 1995

ISBN 0 9526174 0 4

Contents

Introduction and Acknowledgements

Generation follows generation, and life is seldom long enough to do all the things we plan.

As a growing boy and then onwards into manhood, I often listened to two North Ronaldsay men discussing the need to compile a history of their island. Both of them, Mr John Muir, once of Midhouse and then residing in Edinburgh, and my father Peter Tulloch, Garso, grew more and more enthusiastic about the subject each time Mr Muir visited his birthplace, but being well on in years, neither of them was spared to see the fulfilment of his desire.

I naturally became trustee of the rough notes that I had made during these discussions. These had also been supplemented by other conversations with my father, who had a very retentive memory for former island events and people. The quest gradually widened to include everybody who might add to the story of my island, and I am grateful to them all.

Of those who are no longer spared to see the result, I would especially mention with thankfulness Mr Thomas Tulloch, Seaside; Mr William Swanney, Veracott; Mr George Seatter, Howar, and Mr William Scott, Roadside.

Others who provided information and who will, I hope, derive pleasure from seeing how their verbal contributions have enriched the whole, are Captain William Tulloch, once of Upper Breck; Mr John Swanney, Nether Linnay, and Mr John T. Swanney, Claypows.

More years went by and it was only after I retired from the near seven-day-week routine of working in North Ronaldsay, and moved to Kirkwall, that I found the leisure to sort out the accumulated material. At this stage I received much valuable help, which I gratefully acknowledge, from several sources; especially from Lord Birsay; Mr John Sanderson, a director of Alginate

Industries Ltd., and the staff of the Orkney County Library, who were invariably helpful and obliging throughout my whole search.

With my written material ready for typing, I asked for and was readily given the help of a friend from my school-days in North Ronaldsay. Mr John W. Muir, now resident in Glasgow, took on the task and also carried out a correspondence with various sources from which valuable background information was obtained.

His untiring efforts in gathering information about island shipwrecks brought him into contact with the curators of state archives in most of the Northern European countries, and with the National Archives and Records of the United States of America. This correspondence brought to light several early shipping losses on the island which would otherwise have been missed. I am indebted for such help.

I would also offer my very sincere thanks to Mr. Ernest W. Marwick, the popular Orkney writer and broadcaster, who has used up so much of his time checking typescript and in giving advice on any point on which I felt uncertain. Mr Norman King, M.A. gave me expert and much appreciated help in putting the work into its final form and in preparing it for the press. Mr John Shearer, ex-Director of Education, kindly read over the galley proofs. Mr Ian MacInnes, Art Teacher, Stromness Academy, has very kindly drawn the two-page artistic map of the Island. My grateful thanks are due to them all.

I am indebted also to Mr Stewart Davidson and the printers for their helpfulness and advice, and to "The Orcadian" Office staff; for their courtesy. Any typing that needed to be done locally was carried out by Miss Hazel Ogg and Miss Janice Spindler, both of Kirkwall, and their assistance deserves mention.

In conclusion, I would apologise heartily to anyone who may have been inadvertently omitted from my list of helpers. I can only hope that *A Window on North Ronaldsay* may have successfully gathered into a single volume much of the scattered and unpublished information on the island.

PETER A. TULLOCH.

A Window on North Ronaldsay

. . . a profile of people and places from the dyke-enclosed island of North Ronaldsay . . .

Islands can range from continental proportions right down to a mere sea-girt platform which is little more than a stepping-stone set in the ocean. North Ronaldsay comes rather close to the lower end of this classification. Yet, its size and topography are just right for bringing out that characteristic which can be best summed up by the coined word 'island-ness.'

Almost any stance enables the viewer to get an uninterrupted view of the sea on three sides. An easy climb up the central brae at Holland House raises the sea on all sides and may show ships to the nor'ard, the east'ard, the south'ard, and the west'ard. Sometimes there may also be seen a small aeroplane coming in to land at the island airfield, or a larger one passing overhead on its way to Shetland.

From this it will be realised that North Ronaldsay is a small, low island situated on the edge of an important shipping lane. The actual location of Dennis Head lighthouse is Lat. 59 degrees 23 minutes North, Long. 2 degrees 23 minutes West.

While these co-ordinates provide exact information for the skilled navigator, it may be helpful to state that many maps of Scotland show North Ronaldsay and the other islands of the Orkney and Shetland groups as an inset in the Moray Firth instead of in their true position northwards of the Pentland Firth. It must, however, be added that this misplacement is not done to mislead the unwary, but to give the cartographer a more compact layout and larger scale than would otherwise be possible on the standard rectangular sheets used for mapmaking.

A simple way of finding and remembering the position of this most northerly island of Orkney is to draw a straight line northwards from Thurso to Kirkwall and continue it until North Ronaldsay is reached. From the scale of the map the distance from Thurso to North Ronaldsay will be seen to be about sixty-four miles, and Kirkwall will be near the middle of the line.

Visitors from across the Pentland Firth have the choice of entering Orkney by either air or sea. British European Airways fly a daily service from Edinburgh (Turnhouse Airport) to Kirkwall via Aberdeen and Wick, and also from Glasgow (Abbotsinch Airport) to Kirkwall via Inverness and Wick. Travellers by sea have less choice than formerly, but can still connect almost daily with a ferry across the Pentland Firth. This route, operated in conjunction with British Railways, sails between Scrabster (port of Thurso) and Stromness, Orkney. There is also a twice-weekly service between Aberdeen and Kirkwall in which the vessels arrive at Kirkwall on Wednesday and Saturday. This sea transport is operated by the North of Scotland Orkney and Shetland Shipping Company Ltd., a subsidiary of the P. and O. Line.

All communication between Kirkwall and the North Isles of Orkney is operated by the Orkney Islands Shipping Company along with Loganair. This again provides anyone visiting North Ronaldsay with a choice of making the last lap of the journey by either air or sea, but the latter is now very much reduced, being restricted to a once-a-week direct trip by the motor vessel *Islander* which generally does the run on Friday. Booking is also necessary as this cargo ship carries only a limited number of passengers.

Before 1971, the island could also be reached by means of a ferry boat based on and run from Sanday. This boat was owned and sailed by Henry Thomson, who held the postal contract for carrying letters and parcels from the Black Rock jetty to Nouster pier. These and any passengers for North Ronaldsay had been brought from Kirkwall to Kettletoft pier at the southern end of Sanday by the Orkney Islands

Shipping Company's vessel *Orcadia*, which still provides sea transport between Kirkwall and Sanday, Stronsay, Eday and Westray on Wednesday, Thursday and Saturday. Loganair, using small aeroplanes of the "Islander" type which carry up to eight passengers, have flown a regular service to North Ronaldsay since 1967. The plane leaves Grimsetter Airport near Kirkwall on Monday, Wednesday and Friday, taking about 24 minutes for the flight. So far only letters and passengers are carried, parcels being dispatched from Kirkwall by the Friday steamer.

The Loganair Service may also be hired for special charter flights to North Ronaldsay, but it must be pointed out that there is no hotel and visitors to this 'Northmost Isle of Orkney' are advised to arrange their accommodation well in advance of the required date.

Having fixed the island's position and listed the alternative ways of getting there, it is time for me to return to a more detailed examination of the factors which have attracted and held a human population for at least four thousand years.

The island forms part of the fifty-mile-wide channel that separates Orkney from Shetland and strong tides surge through this passageway as well as through the North Ronaldsay Firth on the opposite or south side where the distance to the nearest land in Sanday is only about three miles. The main set of these tides is in a north-westerly direction during the ebb-tide and in a south-easterly direction during the flood-tide. The combination of rapid currents and a shallow, uneven seabottom can sometimes result in the island being ringed by broken water. These rosts are always more extensive and widespread when there is a strong gale blowing in the face of the tide at its swiftest.

Under such conditions, the driving spindrift can almost obscure the land, and it is understandable that shipwrecks were frequent in the days of sail, more especially before the present lighthouse came into operation in 1854. Shipping losses have gradually been reduced since then. Nowadays the powerful lantern, effective fog-signal, radio-beacon, and radio-telephone link make Dennis Head lighthouse one of the best equipped on the British seaboard.

The dividend derived from this modern warning system is very obvious, for there have now been no strandings during the last fourteen years, while the previous record of losses over the preceding two centuries adds up to around seventy ships, or an average of one total wreck every three years.

The low sloping beaches, which occasionally alternate with sandy bays and comparatively flat rocks dipping gently into the sea with fishing crags, give variety to the outline on the north and west sides of the island. The shallow water and rock pools act as a forcing-frame that brings on all sorts of seaweed which spread outward like under-water meadows and forests. Nourished by the rapidly flowing tides, this abundance of marine vegetation has always been an important factor, both as an anti-erosive agent and as a provider of raw material that contributes towards the self-supporting economy of the island.

The seaweed provides another indirect benefit by supplying cover and suitable feeding-grounds for crabs, lobsters, and other crustaceans. Dried seaweed and tangles were also used as a 'make-do' fuel until into the present century. During the Spring and early Summer when the stock of imported coals had run low, it was no uncommon occurrence to see the housewives doing their rougher cooking on a fire which was mostly made up of dried dung and dried tangles.

Up to comparatively recent times, seaweed was also collected and carted on to the fields as manure for most of the cultivated crops. As this fertiliser cost nothing but the labour of applying it, large quantities were used, perhaps 2,000 to 3,000 tons every year. The kelp industry accounted for, at least, an equal amount of tangles and ware most years. The burned ash of the air-dried seaweed was shipped to Grangemouth or Newcastle and the cargoes seldom fell below 150 tons, and reached some 300 tons in exceptional years.

Yet another demand on the seaweed arises from the keeping of a communal flock of native sheep which live almost exclusively on it. There are over two thousand of these seaweed-eaters living on the beaches. They are confined to a narrow margin of beach-head and foreshore by a stone dyke which encircles the island. With very little grass growing on the seaward side of this dyke, each animal would be likely to require a ration of at least 5 lbs. of seaweed every day of the year, so this would add up to a consumption by the flock of around 2,000 tons.

Thus it will be seen that this natural resource of seaweed had, in terms of fuel, manure, kelp, and sheep-fodder, to provide over 8,000 tons per year in former times. Such an enormous harvest of tangles and ware could not have been handled without a large island population, and, indeed, there was no scarcity of manpower until after the 1914-18 war.

In this connection, it is necessary to stress that kelp-making used up far more man-hours than either farming or fishing during the eighteenth, nineteenth, and early part of the present century. A full explanation of how this came about must, however, await the appropriate place. Both the story of kelp making and that of seaweed-eating sheep are so characteristic of North Ronaldsay that they require lengthy chapters to themselves. So, too, do agriculture and fishing. The wealth of fish to be found in the surrounding seas may indeed have been the attraction which held the first people who settled on the island. There is in any case plenty of evidence of the enormous quantity of shell fish eaten in bygone days. Accumulations of discarded limpet and other shells still mark the sites of these early clusters of habitation and these can, in some instances, alter the contours, breaking up the surrounding flatness by a number of slight mounds.

Other links with the distant past are equally deserving of examination. The ruined Broch of Burrian, now far eroded by the sea, and the solitary Standing Stone, posted like a sentinel midway between Gretchen Loch and Rinar's Hill, present a double question mark. Along with island relics, such as the Burrian Cross, and the presence of prehistoric burial cists, they invite speculation about the men and women who lived there long before any Viking ever set foot on what these Norsemen called Rinansay.

Why, for instance, did this small island, lacking any natural harbour, attract such different races as are indicated by the ornaments, the tools, and the weapons which have been dug up? Was it the white sands of Linklet and Nouster Bays that invited the 'coracle-borne-newcomers' at a time when much of the British Isles was still unoccupied?

Perhaps a sea swarming with fish and a low unforested island, giving no cover to either human or animal enemies, presented the promise of a home that no wanderer of that period could resist. The need for building some form of shelter would keep the newcomers busy throughout the short northern summer. Winter storms would then prevent any further move for another seven or eight months, and when spring came round again the community would probably realise that they would be safe from other sea-borne interference for most of the year. So after weighing up the advantages and disadvantages they would decide to stay.

As the centuries went by and trading began to be carried on throughout these Orkney and Shetland waters, the winter storms continued to be an active agent in influencing the way of life in North Ronaldsay. Shipwrecks were of frequent occurrence and records show that a particular March day, the 11th March, 1826, saw three ships ashore on the island at the same time.

" The *Ida* barque of Stettin (Master Schurer), the *Henrietta Wilhelmina* brig of Stettin (Master Thurlow) and the *Neptunis* galiot of Stettin (Master Bradenahl) all bound from Dantzig for Liverpool wrecked on the north-east end of North Ronaldsay. All crews were saved, although very heavy seas were running at the time. It is expected that some of the cargoes may be salvaged in a damaged condition."

This must have been a stirring day in the island, with three wrecks and three shipwrecked crews to accommodate and feed until the weather improved sufficiently for the stranded men to come together for their return home.

In connection with these nautical subjects, the beaches and foreshore with their round-the-island dyke and population of seaweed-eating sheep have a unique attraction. The variation of the shore formation—a geo here and a boat noust there, followed by a stretch of rocks further on, with perhaps a pair of selkies swimming round the point of a taing will captivate the interest and maintain the urge to keep on exploring the whole thirteen miles that go to make up this unusual sheeprun.

This walk round the island is an experience which is familiar to every boy who is born and brought up in North Ronaldsay. The numerous beach features are often named so as to preserve something of their story. The actual names may either be of pre-Norse or of Old Norse derivation. Others may again be directly linked with some shipwreck which has taken place at the particular spot. These can, for instance, show where survivors of a stranding were mustered in such a name as 'Crewgather,' or the nature of the cargo of an ill-fated vessel as in 'Iron Geo,' or fix the nationality of the seamen using the place such as where the 'Geo o' Denmark' probably marks the place used for boating the salvaged materials from the wrecked *Kron-prinsen* out to the smaller ships anchored in Linklet Bay waiting to transport the money and other valuables back to Denmark.

At one stage of this self-imposed trek-round-the-island, the stravaiger would come to the roofless remains of a building that had formerly been used for storing the grain, meal, butter, and other goods that had to be given to the island laird as rent for the farms and crofts. One of the gables and most of the upper storey of this old building are missing. Nature, using wind-blown sea-sand and bird-carried seeds, has planted and grown a window box of white and red flowers on what was once a prison sill! The indistinct initials, scratched on the nearby masonry may, perhaps, be the handiwork of the three young men who were locked-up there overnight to await a ship. They had been pressed into service as the island's quota of fighters for the Napoleonic Wars.

Like those who preceded and followed them, these three were part of a stream of young men 'going to the wars.' Whether 'these defenders of their country' are rounded up by a press gang, volunteered or were mustered by some form of disguised conscription like the Derby Scheme, or Kitchener's hypnotic stare, some would be unlikely ever to return and settle down in their birth place again.

So 'going to the wars' makes another subject that is worthy of a chapter to itself. The window-box already mentioned is now forming a part of the island-encircling-sheep-dyke, and also suggests a name for the book, as well as being a centre piece for the book jacket.

The fleet of Norse Longships which sailed to fight against Scotland and failed to bring off victory at Largs may not have had much aid in either ships or men from Rinansay or any of the small islands of Orkney, but this defeat, in an indirect way, was to bring centuries of hardship and oppression to the Norse settlements of Orkney and Shetland.

Later overlordship by Scotland soon brought rule from Edinburgh instead of Bergen. The Scottish Feudal and the Norse Udal systems of government were allowed to operate at the same time, causing great confusion and always working to the detriment of the islanders. This misrule was perpetuated by a succession of rulers from the Scottish nobility in which the Stewarts and their kin vied with each other in carrying out such extortions as the use of forced labour that went unrewarded by payment in cash or kind.

This long period of misrule would, in the case of North Ronaldsay, likely be enforced by the lawman, rather than directly by the Stewarts themselves. It, however, had the same deteriorating effect and eventually forced all the more independent and high-spirited members of the community to leave their birthplace in search of greater freedom. So Scottish Overlordship and Migration must add another two chapters.

Primitive methods of agriculture, with crude farming systems such as the run-rig division of land, were still prevailing well into the nineteenth century.

Traill's representative, 'Ald Scart' is, however, credited with having introduced and completed the land-squaring by 1832, a date well in advance of most other places in Orkney. With each holding thus having the major portion of its land in one main block, the enclosure of fields and other improvements soon followed. Better rotation of crops, more enlightened legislation, and the fixing of fair rents, were other agricultural advances which took place from the later half of the nineteenth century onwards. This again gives plenty of material for another two chapters, one on Primitive Agriculture, and the other on Developing Agriculture.

So do Island Schooling, and Island Storytelling. The comparative isolation of North Ronaldsay did not, as might be thought, prevent the island children from getting educational instruction until this became compulsory in 1872. The island was lucky in having a 'compulsive teacher' as early as the first quarter of the nineteenth century. As might be expected, all his pupils did not appreciate their good fortune, for William Fea, while acknowledged to be an excellent instructor of both Bible Subjects and the Three Rs, left behind a reputation of being rather prone to drive home his lessons by a liberal use of the tawse. So naturally the brighter pupils came on fast while the backward ones gave up the struggle. Yet, while the methods of teaching have changed, it would be difficult to find better handwriting than that preserved in the form of signatures left behind by some of William Fea's pupils.

It is also believed that a man at Peckhole taught elementary subjects in the early part of the nineteenth century. There is no way in which the value of this instruction can be directly judged, but records show that at least two North Ronaldsay men had become seagoing captains before the mid-century.

The tradition of storytelling is much older. The Orkneyinga Saga tells how an Icelandic verse-maker on his way to Earl Rognvald's court became storm-stayed in the island for a whole winter. Evidence of how well this 'spinner of yarns' laid the foundations of his art may still be seen in the crowd of men and boys who gather together to while away the long winter nights with stories new and old.

Another sort of yarn used to be spun by the women folk who collected together to card and spin the wool of the native sheep. This 'carding match' usually consisted of a meeting of a dozen or more women at the same house, and the scraping of the wire-toothed hand-cards seldom failed to be punctuated by scraps of feminine talk about courtships or impending weddings. As one of the island worthies put it, "the younger women were more interested in the 'matc' than in the 'carding.' "

Maltmaking and brewing is another local custom which formerly helped to break up the long winter season. The Yule festivities usually lasted for more than a week and led up to a house-to-house visit by the island menfolk on New Year's Eve, generally reckoned according to the Old Style calendar, twelve days later than the New Gregorian one, which in this connection was not fully recognised by the islanders until near the present century.

The nature of these house-to-house festivities is shown by the words of the New Ye'rs Sang, one verse of which runs:

> " Guidwife gae t' your barming vat
> An' draw us aff a skeal o' that.
> or draw us ane, draw us twa
> An' we'se be merrie, or gae awa'.
> Draw us twa, draw us three
> An' aye the merrier we will be."

This song is also said to have been sung by the revellers as they danced around the Standing Stane on Old New Year's Night in former times. As this lone watcher is thought to belong to the same period as the Standing Stones of Stenness and Ring of Brogar, it may have been in position for four thousand years and have been the centre for pagan ceremonies for many centuries before the Celtic missionaries arrived on the scene. Anyway, these missionaries are thought to have brought Christianity to the island and set up chapels at Bride's Kirk, Cross Kirk, and at St Olaf's Kirk. They are also sometimes credited with naming the island after their founder St Ninian. This name is supposed to have been corrupted to Ringan, making it Ringan's Isle. There does not, however, seem to be much support for this beyond the unearthing of the Burrian Cross by Dr. Traill in 1870.

So, like Island Education, Religion and Churches must also be examined in greater depth. Each will require a chapter to itself.

Whatever may have happened to the pre-Norse occupants of the island, there is ample evidence that both North Ronaldsay and Sanday attracted the spearhead of the Viking colonisation of Orkney. Together with the Fair Isle and Westray they figure prominently in the family feuds that raged around the Earls of Orkney. The rivalry, especially that between Earls Paul and Rognvald, who eventually became the victor and ruled the islands as Earl Rognvald, gave plenty of scope for what were called 'the well landed Norse families' to take a hand in this power-game. Outstanding among these behind-the-scene counsellors was Ragna the Wise of Rinansay and her son Thorstein the Strong.

The story of North Ronaldsay would, however, be incomplete without some attempt at an appraisal of depopulation and the present day trends that might influence local events. In making such an attempt, one fully realises that prophecy must always be a risky business, and that most forecasts either prove to be wrong or in need of considerable modification in the light of actual developments.

One does, however, seem to be on fairly solid ground in criticising the tendency for more and still more houses to become unoccupied while their land goes to the enlargement of the surviving crofts. While this change certainly makes for more viable working units, it still retains the serious disadvantage of a very scattered layout of the various fields belonging to the same crofter: something akin to the run-rig problem that was tackled by 'Ald Scart' in 1832. Perhaps another attempt at land-squaring is overdue?

With the number of powerful tractors now being

used, it is inevitable that fewer people will be needed for working the land. While this helps to bring about a higher standard of living it also creates another problem, for any reduction of population below the present level would make it difficult to maintain essential services or keep the island-encircling-dyke in sheep-tight condition.

Should the present population of under 130 fall below the critical hundred-mark this would also be likely to bring a review of the State-aided amenities. If this were to become an immediate threat, could anything be done to attract fresh blood? The nearby island of Fair Isle, which is admittedly less fertile than North Ronaldsay, has tried this without achieving any great success. But all the 'newcomers 'to Fair Isle were from the South whereas the previous population of Orkney and Shetland crossed the sea from the North-east.

In a rapidly changing world where international decisions may quickly alter life at the fringe, it may on the other hand be some economic, or political plan, still to be implemented, that will raise or lower the population of this island which has often held more men and women during former times than it could well support.

2

Walking Round the Island

. . . a stroll round the island, in which the topography and seascape help to bring alive events from past and present . . .

A look at any sizeable map of North Ronaldsay will show that the island has over twelve miles of coastline, but lacks any natural harbour. Closer examination will also reveal that a large number of geos break up the rocky parts of the beaches. These thirty-odd creeks have tell-tale names such as the Geo of Denmark, Hindoo Geo, or Iron Geo and Meal Geo, showing that ships of many nationalities, and with a variety of cargoes, have been wrecked along this coast.

Other names like Roofed Geo and the Cellar of Hamar Geo, descriptive of ground features, make a strong appeal to go exploring, a command to fold away the map and begin a twelve miles' hike of the actual shore.

There is never any problem about where to start, for the numerous stiles and beach gates make it easy to enter this circular strip of beach-head and foreshore that lies outside the island-encircling sheep dyke. Neither is there any problem about the best direction to take, for the tall lighthouse at the north-east corner of the island invariably attracts visitors, irrespective of whether they alight at the island airfield, or step ashore at the pier.

Recalling my own experiences on these walks along the shore, I always set out by climbing over the stile leading to the Stuian o' Garsowick. Our house was close to the sheepdyke, and I had become aware of the interesting world that lay on the other side long before I started school. There, moored in the pool left by the ebbing tide, were the skiffs and yawls used for inshore fishing, with the ends of their mooring ropes made fast to either heavy stones, or weighty pieces of metal such as old anchors. The beach-head, or part above the high-water mark, seldom failed to have untidy piles of creels and all the other gear belonging to the lobster men.

This disarray made an ideal playground, and growing, strengthening limbs soon discovered new footholds for climbing over the boulders and other obstacles in order to go further afield.

Eastwards, the next stretch of beach goes under the names of Skoo Helzie Banks and Summer Ayre, but any idea that these two later names for the original ones of Purgatory and Paradise indicate a sudden transformation must be discouraged. The whole stretch is heavily strewn by boulders and makes difficult going.

This part, especially the Bigging, includes a section of the island in which pre-Norse as well as Norse settlements have been located. Evidence of the former rests on the fact that this was the area in which the first Bronze Age burial cists were unearthed near Cross Kirk in 1872. Traces can still be seen of this burial ground, which is thought to date back to the time of Celtic missionaries. Of the Bigging, once consisting of five houses, only Senness, Sholtisquoy and Westhouse are still in existence, although Senness alone is now occupied.

It has already been mentioned that fishing played a vital part in providing food for these early settlers, and it follows that a nearby landing place, usable at any stage of the tide, would become a deciding factor in any agreement about the location of their dwellings. So Swin Geo and Boat Geo, both on this Helzie Banks stretch, would almost certainly have needed as an approach route the ancient roadway that links the Bigging to the Beachhead by the most direct way.

Swin Geo has also become recognised as the starting and finishing place for anyone visiting the Seal Skerry, and it was from there that Dr. Rae, as guest of Mr Traill, was taken to see the seals and scarfs (cormorants) that make their home on this off-shore rock. While there is no record of what this Arctic explorer may have thought about the selkies and scarfs, there is still a lingering memory of what Mr Traill was told on one of his visits to the skerry.

Old Tammie o' Seaside, who was still at Senness at that time, had arranged to act as boatman for a Traill picnic to be held on the skerry. Traill and his guests had for some reason delayed long beyond the time fixed for departure, and Tammie, who had been a sailor in his younger days, gradually became more and more annoyed at the unpunctuality. To make matters worse the injury sustained when he fell from the rigging, leaving him with a permanent stiffness of the knee joint, was also protesting more than usual. So, by the time the party turned up, Tammie had made up his mind how to voice his displeasure.

"By George! Time and tide wait on none. There's no such thing as Traill tide on the skerry."

Other features of this first furlong in the trek towards the lighthouse include a fishing crag, just beyond Savegoe Point. Then, after Boat Geo and Swin Geo, come Clett Geo and Finning Geo, followed by another fishing crag. These are flat rocks, the outer edges of which drop perpendicularly into the sea, allowing the fish to come right up to the face. These were the places where former generations fished for 'cuithes' using a 'wand' and homemade fishing line of twisted horse hair, the hooks baited with flies of goose feathers, or with limpets, depending on how far the season had advanced.

Another beach feature a little further on bears the Old Norse name of Skate Holter. Beyond this lie Ires Taing, the Bay of Ires Taing, and the Rocks of Ires Taing. Seawards, and separated by the Sound, is the off-shore Seal Skerry, which is just visible in parts at high tide, but can rise for a length of more than a quarter of a mile during a spring ebb-tide. It has a considerable colony of seals which use it as a breeding place. There is also a colony of cormorants or shags, which are reputed to have been in residence since 1700. Evidence of shipwrecks can also be seen in the form of rusty skeletons, but the details of these wrecks belong to a chapter on this particular subject.

Passing along the Sound shore, one sees an almost

continuous array of tangles laid out to dry. These are piled on rough stone foundations, or sometimes on the nearby sheepdyke. In former times they were burned into kelp at the spot, but are now only air-dried before being shipped to Alginate Industries Ltd. for processing at their works. There are several other interesting things which are worthy of notice as the coast reaches its furthest north point at the Lurands of the Sound.

Nearer to the beach head is Trolla Vatn, the three-acre freshwater loch which carries an Old Norse name but it does not seem to have any tradition to justify such a sinister description as 'loch of the trolls.'

The already mentioned Lurands of the Sound is a flat rocky ridge nearly reaching the east end of Seal Skerry. Most of it can be seen at low water, when it is visited by the native sheep in search of food. The turn of the tide, however, brings a danger in the form of an outflow liable to sweep the animals to their death.

From the Lurands of the Sound the coast bends inwards, leaving an off-shore rock called the Skerry of Linay, and then juts out again at the Point of Sinsoss. There it turns south-eastwards to form Versa Geo and Couls Geo before continuing to the Point of Skiver.

Inland, all along this route crue after crue line the shore. Most of these small circular enclosures were formerly used for raising cabbage plants, or for growing cabbage seed.

The coastline is now indented by the Bay of Skivar and Saythe Geo. The latter was used as a landing place for the survivors of torpedoed ships in both world wars, and is still a boat noust of the local lobster fishers. Nearby stands the Old Beacon. This now unlit tower was built in 1789, and served as a lighthouse for sixteen or seventeen years, before it was replaced by the Start Point lighthouse in Sanday. This Old Beacon has been left standing in order to provide an additional daylight mark to ensure that there can be no confusion between Dennis Head lighthouse in North Ronaldsay and the aforesaid one in Sanday.

The projecting rocks at the Old Beacon are known as the Kirk Taing, and further on the coastline bends inwards in an approximately southward direction

towards Dennis Head. All this part of the coast has been
the scene of many shipwrecks, and it is interesting to
note that although the name of one of the vessels which
was stranded in the bight between these headlands has
long been forgotten, the place where the "Biscuit and
Butter" ship came ashore is still remembered.

Beyond Dennis Head, the coast bends back in a
north-westerly direction for about half-a-mile, indented
by Mel'r Geo, Iron Geo, the Geo of Bewan, and the Geo
of Rue. The west side of the Geo of Bewan extends as a
stone jetty for landing lighthouse stores. There is also a
boat noust nearby which was formerly used as winter
quarters for the island's herring boats.

The beach between Kirk Taing and Dennis Head is
locally known as 'Between Taings' and the top of it
forms one side of Dennis Loch, which has an area of
almost six acres, and is frequented by many water
birds. From the Geo of Rue, the coast continues in a
westerly direction to, and beyond, Scottigar Taing,
where another beach head loch with an area of just
over an acre lies inland from the Taing. It is known as
Scottigar Loch.

A little further westwards and slightly inwards, the
ground rises into a small knoll called The Hoin, which
is said to be of pre-Norse origin. The next beach
features are the Skerry of Senness, the Noust of
Sandback, the Skerry of Longer, and Snash Ness.
These cover a distance of about three-quarters of a
mile, and the Noust of Sandback, with what was
latterly an old kelp store for the three northern
districts, is worthy of mention. Like the old store near
Howar, which has already been mentioned, this
building may also have been used for storing the grain
from the northern part of the island while it was
awaiting shipment from the Linklet Bay anchorage.
What can be said with greater certainty is that it was
used to shelter shipwrecked crews engaged in attempts
to lighten and refloat their stranded ships.

It is also reputed to have been used as a mortuary
for the sailors who perished when the "Lena" was
wrecked. In this connection one of the islanders, Robert
Tulloch of Phisligar, is said to have been locked in with

the corpses during the hours of darkness, probably to ensure that the dead were not disturbed by wandering dogs or beach mice. This was looked upon as a nerve-wracking experience, but Robert seems to have suffered no ill effects from the ordeal.

Inwards from Snash Ness a long Tumulus suggests an ancient burial place, but this feature has not been excavated. After this the coast takes a more southerly direction, and another quarter-of-a-mile brings a change in the nature of the beach. The rocky shore suddenly ends, and is replaced by a stretch of fine white sand, which carries the descriptive name of 'Sandsheen.'

As the high-water mark has already been followed for a distance of four miles, and the next section of beach borders the Linklet district, this seems to be the right place for giving some more details about the 'Easting' or 'Nort'-end' district.

Before the middle of the eighteenth century there were only eight crofts, or holdings, in this district. Five of these were at Senness, Bigging, and the other three, Scottigar, Sandback, and Conglabist lay along the southeast side of the 'toonship' At this time the sheepdyke crossed from the north side of the 'Easting' at Summer Ayre to a point just west of Scottigar Loch, beyond which there were no houses. As the demand for kelp began to increase, the need for workers also grew, and it became the laird's policy to create new crofts by pushing the sheepdyke further out into Dennis Ness.

In its new position, the sheepdyke then extended from a point about five chains eastward of its original position, and ran in a direction which brought in another thirty-six acres before it reached the opposite side of the district at the Geo of Rue. This new enclosure allowed four crofts to be added, Grind, Dennishill, Vincoin, and Rue. The concentration on kelp making became so complete that there was one season in the 1850s when the factor and kelp-grieve mobilised the three toonships of Linklet, Aby, and the Easting for a combined effort in which the whole remainder of Dennis Ness was spread with drying seaweed.

This steady increase of kelp workers soon brought

about yet another rebuilding seaward of the sheepdyke to take in an additional forty-eight acres, and bring it to its present position. By this time there were three cottar houses and 14 crofts on the Easting, averaging only a dozen acres each, which is much too small to make a viable unit.

Such overcrowding continued until well into the twentieth century when a few became vacant through some families dying out, and others leaving the island. Some of the vacant ones were then divided out to provide enlargements for the rest. Of recent years, this reduction has accounted for five of the crofts and all three of the cottars' houses, leaving only nine occupied houses. Of these, five have only one person each, two have two persons each, and the remaining two have three, or four people in the household.

Many of the house names, and also the names of beach or other ground features, are of Norse origin. Examples of these Norse house names which can still be found in the Easting are: Bigging, Bist, Breck, Garth, Grind, Quoy, and Vin, while Clett, or Klett, Ness, Noust, Skoo, Taing are representative of ground features. Tradition also claims that the island was once divided into three parts by the marches of Matches' Dyke and the Muckle Gersty. Although both these partitions lie outside the present boundary of the Easting, it was also thought that Upper Breck, standing on the second highest brae in the island, may have been the home of one of the families who then shared the island. It is also interesting to find that The Bigging is mentioned in the Orkneyinga Saga.

When resuming the walk from Sandsheen southward along the shore of Linklet Bay, one discovers that the distance between the sheepdyke and the foreshore widens out to leave a stretch of flat ground which is called The Links. This area of about fifty acres is grazed by the native sheep, who keep the grass so short that it resembles the greens of a golf course. Like the Dennis Ness hill land this too was formerly used for drying seaweed, and later on as a nine-hole golf course by the laird of the island. Still more recently it served as a football pitch for the island's team, but depopulation has also rung down the curtain on that, leaving the Arctic Terns to scream their defiance at anyone who dares to invade their territory in the nesting season.

Apart from this and the bordering stretch of dazzling white sands which extend along the water's edge for over two-thirds of a mile, the only other features are a freshwater stream, issuing from Ancum Loch, and a slightly raised earthen mound which also runs to the eastern side of this loch, and restarts again on the northwestern corner to continue to a point opposite the Celler of "Himera Geo." This ridge is said to be the remains of Matches' Dyke, the ancient division referred to in a previous paragraph.

The coast becomes rocky again past the mill burn which flows out of Hooking Loch. This stream was formerly dammed in order to provide the power for a mill until it went out of use at the beginning of this century. There is also a boat noust near by, which was sometimes used as a landing place for passengers and goods before the present pier was built at the south end of the island.

At this stage of this circular tour the boundary between the eastern side of Linklet Toon and Ness Toon is crossed, and this makes an appropriate place to add a brief general description of the former.

Linklet, the central district of the island, consists of fifteen holdings which vary in area from as little as seven or eight, to thirty acres or more. Two houses at Cauldhame and South Gravity are no longer occupied. Four other crofts have only one occupant. Some of the others house two or three, while the remainder have four persons, or over. This makes Linklet Toon the most populous district of the island at present.

Sangar and North Manse are the only crofts created during the nineteenth century. The Sangar Swanneys left Ancum and built Sangar so that a Tulloch from Senness might take over the tenancy of Ancum. At about the same time the Scotts moved from Quoybanks to a partly-built house at North Manse which was also given some of the lands of Veracott to make the extended croft a reasonably sized unit.

Both Veracott and Linklater are mentioned in the 1653 Attested Rentals of North Ronaldsay in the portion which is devoted to this part of the island. There were also a few more houses and crofts in being until around the middle of last century or later. These included North Holm, Clatter Ha', Coo Mire, and West Hill.

This district is also rich in prehistoric relics, many of which were unearthed only when an East-West Roadway was made in 1905. This roadway skirts the lower slope of Finyarhouse Brae and the cutting revealed a variety of Bronze Age ornaments. Other finds suggested that a systematic search would probably uncover underground dwellings dating much further back. Stone cists containing human remains were also found in a field near by in 1874.

The United Free Church with Manse is sited in this district, but this denomination is now re-united with the Church of Scotland so that one minister can conduct all the services required by the community. Its central position continues to make this building the most convenient place for worship, and the Manse is also used in the new role of house for the island doctor. The island Post Office, licensed grocer's shop, and Co-operative shop at Trebb, are just outside the Linklet boundary, making them part of Hollandstoun.

Norse influence is indicated by many of the house names such as Breck, Garth, Holm, Ha. What is thought to have been a very old Dam, situated below the present house of Milldam, was responsible for that name.

On resuming the walk along the beach, one notices next the Geo of Haskietaing, followed by the protruding Taing itself. Beyond this, the shore once again becomes more sandy than rocky until Hastie Geo is reached. This stretch, of about two-thirds of a mile, is also a ware and tangle beach, and an island Links extends nearly all this way. It provided a good drying green for the kelp makers of former years, and it is still used by those who collect tangles for Alginate Industries Ltd.

Onwards from Hastie Geo, the coast bends in a south-easterly direction to the North Taing of Bride's

Ness. It then takes a more or less southerly direction to the South Taing, where it again changes to a westerly direction past Meil Geo, before turning inwards in a north-westerly incline to the sandy inlet of Bride's Noust. This boat noust provided summer quarters for the North Ronaldsay Ferry which formerly carried the mail and passengers to Sanday, a service which was later operated by a boat harboured on the Sanday side of the North Ronaldsay Firth.

On the landward side another two prehistoric mounds have been passed, the first at the Brae of Stennabreck, and the second at the site of Bride's Kirk. Seawards, if the weather happens to be rough, the Reef Dyke can be seen as a stretch of broken water, beginning opposite the North Taing and extending for about half-a-mile south-eastwards of Bride's Ness. This submerged danger has been the scene of many shipwrecks.

With approximately half of the circular walk now covered, and the southern end of the old boundary, known as the Muckle Gersty, also about to be left behind, the coastline of Busta Toon is approached, and a brief summing up of Ness Toon is called for.

This district contained eleven crofts, or holdings, until well into the present century, but seven of these are now unoccupied, and the present population of the whole toonship is only about half a dozen people. The size of these holdings ranged from six to forty acres, but the distribution of the land belonging to the now unoccupied crofts has raised those which still remain to a more economic size.

In the nineteenth century this toonship supported even more houses, such as West Newbigging, Myres, Oback, and one or two of which the names are now forgotten. Hooking was only enlarged to its present size in the early part of last century, when a Tulloch from Senness moved there and got part of the lands of Peckhole. Bridesness was built by the Cutts after they had been evicted from the croft of Dishar, but this happened later in the nineteenth century. Claypows, on the other hand, was constructed in the early part of that century by a Peter Swann, who returned to the

island after having served as a Master of Arms in the
Royal Navy. The Myers became vacant after its last
occupant Benjamin Tulloch moved to Westness when
the Walls family left there to emigrate to Australia.
This took place about the middle of last century, and
the roof of Myers was removed to re-roof the Water Mill
which had been damaged by fire in 1853.

The next stretch of beach borders the south-east,
south, and west sides of Busta Toon. This southmost
district of the island has a coastline of about one-and-
three-quarter miles, comprising the Geo of Hann, Kist
of Burrigar, and Ship Geo before the Point of Burrian is
reached. The remains of the Broch of Burrian, which
have been partially excavated and examined by the late
Dr. Traill, are also situated at this point. The ruin lies
so close to the water's edge that Winter storms have
washed part of it into the sea.

As the shore turns westwards Clett Sweyn, Scarfie
Geo, Long Labor, and Round Labor will be passed
before the coast again turns in a north-westerly
direction to Blue Clett and the Boat Noust of Howar.
This landing place has been the scene of two fatal
boating accidents, one in 1873 and the other in 1895. It
is also the location of an old storehouse which was used
in the days when rents were paid in grain and other
farm produce, but is now remembered as the place
where three islandmen were imprisoned while awaiting
the ship which was to take them on the first stage of
the campaigns against Napoleon.

From the Boat Noust of Howar, the rocky coast
continues in a northerly direction to Hindoo Geo.
Becoming more broken with sandy patches, it then
sweeps north-westwards to form the South Bay. Taking
the shape of a wide U, this beautiful sandy bay leaves
Busta Toon and enters Holland Toon at about its mid
point. But a reference to Howmae Brae, and a general
summing up of Busta Toon is again necessary before
entering a new district.

Busta Toon district had nine holdings and crofts
until well into this century, but four of these are now
unoccupied, and the five remaining ones support only
nineteen people. Howar is the largest holding in the

district with an area of 75 to 80 acres. Some of the
former small crofts had a mere 6 or 7 acres, but most of
these are now vacant and their lands divided among
those who remain, thus increasing the average acreage.
In the eighteenth and early part of the nineteenth
centuries, the lands which have now been brought
together to form the farm of Howar existed as several
separate crofts, some of the old names being Disher,
Fletties and Stromness. Other names shown in the
1653 Attested Rentals of North Ronaldsay for the Busta
district are Burgar, Boustay, Hargar, and Howan, all of
which have also been incorporated into one or other of
the fields which now make up the farm of Howar.

The only definite record of what befell the people
who were moved out of these houses is confined to those
from Dishar, Stromness and Flett. The Swanneys of
Flett were moved to Nether Linnay. The Thomsons of
Stromness were given the croft of Quoybanks, when its
former occupants, who had already come from
Dennishill, acquired the half-formed croft of North
Manse to build up. The Cutts from Dishar had to break
out uncultivated land at Bridesness and make a new
croft there. In this connection, it is perhaps worth
recording that one of the Cutt girls, who was endowed
with 'good looks,' had the luck which eventually
compensated her for the insecurity and upsets of her
childhood. Diana Cutt had not been long away from her
island home when she became the wife of Mr
Armstrong of the Newcastle-Upon-Tyne firm of
shipbuilders.

Kirbest, another Busta Toon farm, is also made up
of what was formerly small crofts, two of which were
Owerland and Winderless, but the Bu of Kirbest was
probably well established long before either of these
houses was built. Students of Norse history are mostly
agreed that it was the home of Ragna (Ragna the Wise)
and her son (Thorstein the Strong) in the early part of
the twelfth century—years before St Magnus Cathedral
of Kirkwall had even been planned.

Yet this very old house of Kirbist is of 'only
yesterday' compared with the underground Stone Age
dwellings at the nearby Brae of Howmae. This

extensive area was partially excavated and catalogued by the late Dr. Traill. It is also fully described in the Inventory of the Ancient Monuments of Orkney and Shetland (H.M.S.O.). So, taken all round, no one coming from Busta Toon, or from any of the Six Districts which make up the island of North Ronaldsay, could wish for a better archaeological heritage than their birth place has provided.

The next stretch of coastline bordering the district of Hollandstoon extends from about a furlong west of Howmae to Roofed Geo, a distance of nearly two-and-a-quarter miles As the last portion of the South Bay is passed, the shore becomes more rocky and juts out south-westwards to make Twinyas Point. The features encountered in rounding this headland are Scarf Skerry and Scarf Geo, where the island pier is located. This pier was built in 1902 but underwent extensive repairs and was also extended in 1964-5.

Westwards of the pier, the main features are Ire's Taing, Sand Geo, Kiln Geo, and the Lurand. The coast then turns sharply towards the north and continues in approximately the same direction for the remainder of Hollandstoon's western side. But before the walk northwards this seems an appropriate place to say that this south-west corner of the island, like the north-east, and the south-east corners, has also got offshore shoals to trap any ship which 'cuts-the-corner' too finely. Twinyas Rocks lie nearby with only eleven feet of water, and Masewell Rock about a mile southwestwards suddenly raises the seabed from fifty feet to less than thirty feet and causes a tide race with the north-west ebb tide. A local boat was sunk and three lives lost near this danger point when a cargo of peats was being transported from Eday for landing at Sand Geo.

As one resumes the northward trek along the west side of the island, one comes on Moo Geo, which is followed by a rocky coast all the way to Gerona Geo. This is also the western end of the Muckle Gersty, which runs in a south-easterly direction right through the middle of the present Hollandstoon district. Gersna Geo is of interest in another way, for it is the place where the sheepdyke runs right up to a cliff-edge with deep water so as to make a natural obstacle blocking off part of the hill-land and foreshore as a private sheep run for the farm of Holland.

Another run of shore features brings such unusual names as Little Moo Geo, Doo Geo, the Skeld of Gue, Clett Rous, Gue, and the Craw Stane of Gue, before Roofed Geo, another deep-water geo, allows the sheepdyke to reach the cliff-edge and makes the northern end of Holland's private sheep run.

As this is also the end of the coastline bordering Hollandstoon, a brief survey of this district is called for, before the walk around the remainder of the west and north beaches is resumed.

Hollandstoon district contains the Laird's House, the three-hundred-acre farm of Holland, the old Parish Church and Manse, the island Churchyard, the School and School House, as well as five crofts and a small Glebe belonging to the Parish Church. In the early part of last century, Hollandstoon comprised as many as a dozen more small crofts, but some of the tenants were compulsorily ejected so that these Udal fragmentations might be re-assembled into one sizeable farm. Some of the names of these former crofters' and cottars' houses were: Backakeldy, Wester Holland, Lyers Breck, Nether Trebb, Sander be South, Skelper Ha, and Var House. It is probable that the three men who were drowned off Sand Geo were among the tenants of these crofts, but knowledge of what befell the others is confined to the movements of the Cutts of Lyers Breck, who went to Cauldhame, and the Tullochs of Var House who settled at Phisligar. Other Cutts, Swanneys and Tullochs were sent to Eday and their holdings incorporated into the new farm of Holland.

It is thought that the brae on which the Parish Church is built is likely to have been the Rinar's Hill, where Torf Einar slew Halfdan Highleg and erected a cairn in the early part of the tenth century. It could also have been the Ward Hill from which Thorstein the Strong relayed Dagfin's false alarm, which had a demoralising effect on the summoned followers of Earl

Paul, and eventually helped Rognvald to win the Earldom of Orkney.

Another link with the past, a far distant past, can be seen in the form of a Standing Stone. This solitary sentinel is located in the Sander Park of Holland. Near by there is a small freshwater pond which is called the Loch of Gretchen. At the other end of the time scale, Hollandstoon's most recent innovation is an airfield. The inter-island aeroplane uses the northmost field of Holland as a landing strip for its flights to and from the island.

As the next half-mile of coastline borders the western side of Linklet Toon, which as a district has already been described, it now only needs a list of shore features to complete the stretch to Aby Toon.

Northward from Roofed Geo there is, firstly, the Geo of Antabreck, followed by the Geo of Veracott, Hamar Geo, the Cellar of Hamargeo, with the western end of the ancient boundary of Matches' Dyke, and then Inglass Geo, before Linklet Toon is left behind.

Another two miles of coastline have to be covered before the whole thirteen mile circuit of the island is completed, and these shores form the north-west and north sides of the Aby Toonship. The shore features encountered on this walk are the Bay of Rysageo and Staff's Geo, which has within it, below tide level, a rock called The Staff. A little further on, and well above high-water mark, either a very severe storm or the melting of glacier ice has left behind a large boulder. This precariously perched mass is called the Grey Stane.

From there the shore turns in a more northeasterly direction towards a long chasm bearing the name Savegeo, and the far side of this rock-bound inlet flattens out into an extensive rocky plateau. This north-west corner, like the other three corners of the island, has its own off-shore shoal. The Altars of Linay, submerged rocks which are exposed at low water spring tides, are located about a quarter of a mile north-west of the high water mark at Hoe Skerries. Their proximity to a main shipping route has often resulted in shipwrecks.

The shallow bay of Linds Wick provides a good ware and tangle beach, but the boulder-strewn ebb has prevented it from ever becoming a popular boat noust. The action of cross tides, helped by the backwash of severe storms has, however, thrown up a semi-circular sort of breakwater which on a superficial examination gives the impression of being a man-made effort at harbour making. This feature is known as Grithamy Dyke.

Nearby comes another inlet, the side of which is, or has been, used as fishing crags bearing the Old Norse names of Suliber and Wheeber. It then continues along the shores of what is known as Back of the Quoy, to jut out towards the Point of Trinley beyond another fishing crag. The Green Skerry, which is an elevation of this rocky ebb near the extreme point, is cut off at high water, but dries at low tide.

After the Point of Trinley the coastline bends southward past the Rock of Hangie and Red Banks. Then comes a deep depression in the ebb formation which forms a salt-water basin when the tide is out. It is called Pool, and could probably be made into a salt-water farm for lobsters and other shellfish, without expensive alterations being required. The southward sweep of the coast then changes to a more easterly direction as it reaches the tangle and ware shores at Ground End.

This is also the demarcation between Aby and the Easting. Another furlong or so further on lies the tangle and ware beach of Garsow Wick, which for some reason was allocated to the crofters of Aby for kelp making, and for gathering the seaweed needed as manure. As Garsow Wick was also the starting point of this round-the-island tour, your self-appointed guide has only to complete his task with a brief survey of Aby Toon, as has already been done for the other five districts of the island.

At present (1972-73) Aby has only seven occupied holdings, and two of these are cultivated by relatives to whom the land has been allocated as the sitting tenants are no longer able for the task. As the two crofts concerned are the last two small ones left, the remaining five are all of thirty acres, or more. Westness, which is generally considered as part of Aby, rather than the Easting, is actually a more or less self-contained holding with its own triangular piece of ground and beaches which go to make the Trinlay headland. Ancum, and the former old house of Nether Linay, are included in the 1653 Attested Rentals of North Ronaldsay. This list also mentions Tougar, which probably became Longar, but that, too, is now one of the vacant holdings.

There were several more houses in this district during the last century when such crofts as Mid Linay, Nether Cott and Piggy were still occupied. Of these, Nether Cott was added to Upper Cott, Mid Linay to Upper Linay, and Piggy became part of Brigg. As for the subsequent movements of the tenants, the Cutts of Nether Cott died out, and the Thomsons of Mid Linay moved to Dennishill after its first occupants, the Scotts, built another house at Quoybanks.

Norse influence is evident in the names of many features and ground divisions of Aby Toon. These include such words as: Cutty-Vat-E-Garth, Kringle-A-May (a circle), Lens Wick, Sander, Skroo, and Tifta Loos. There are also some prehistoric remains such as the Old Brae of Ancum, which is largely composed of a huge midden of limpet shells, while the Skroo Brae is full of burned stones. Tifta Loos too, has continued, since it was first cultivated, to produce a never-ending supply of loose stones, some of which are of considerable size.

3

Links with the Past

*. . . speculating on the Broch, Mounds, Standing
Stone, and other Relics of prehistoric time...*

Evidence that North Ronaldsay has had a human
population As long ago as the Stone Age is plentiful in
different parts of the island. Partial excavations and
accidental finds show that people of the Stone Age, the
Bronze Age, and the early Iron Age, have all left behind
some fragments of their handiwork. These preserved
relics, be they a crude flint weapon, or a fourteen-feet-
high monolith, act as a constant stimulus for all those
who like to contemplate and speculate on the
unrecorded past.

In a flat island such as North Ronaldsay, any site
which has been continuously occupied for century after
century tends to raise itself into a slight mound. Any
excavation for road construction, or other digging into
these man-made knolls, always shows a soil which is
largely made up of limpet shells. The West Brae of
Holland, the Brae of Breck, the Old Brae of Ancum,
Finyar House Brae, and The Hoyne, are all examples
where the kitchen-middens left behind by a long
succession of human occupants have, in a way,
preserved a part of its story.

There, layers of fish bones, shells, and broken or lost
weapons support other layers of bones from larger
animals, and simple flint tools. Nearer the surface, still
further layers might, and sometimes have, revealed the
bones of domestic animals, bits of pottery, and articles
and ornaments made from bronze. In other words, man
has always left some indication of his development from
the fishing-hunting stage onwards through the period
of land cultivation and the keeping of domestic animals,
and still onwards towards the gradual acquirement of

the knowledge and skills that have enabled him to overcome many of his early problems.

The slow change of contours so far dealt with have all been a by-product of life, but death too can take an indirect hand in throwing up a recognisable mound. There is one such tumulus near the croft of Niven, which is 140 feet long and over 100 feet wide. If, as is generally thought, it marks the burial place of warriors who may have been slain in some fiercely-fought but unrecorded battle, the dimensions of their common grave would surely justify a proper examination of this site.

More is known about Howmae Brae, and Stenerbreck Brae, as both of these were partially excavated and catalogued by the late Dr. Traill, in 1870 and 1883 respectively. As full accounts are published in the Proceedings of the Orkney Antiquarian Society, and the articles found are on show at the National Museum of Antiquities of Scotland, Queen Street, Edinburgh, all the details are readily available.

It is understandable why Dr. Traill concentrated on these two sites rather than on those which have been mentioned earlier. Both Howmae and Stenerbreck show more visible indications of the presence of sunken dwellings. These are thought to belong to the late Stone Age, or Early Bronze Age period, and have, like Skara Brae, been buried by wind-blown sand.

The whole area of Howmae is tunnelled by these underground buildings, and people crossing this part of the links on a still, frosty night are always aware of the echo produced by their footsteps. It is also claimed that the farm of Kirbist, which is thought to occupy the site of Ragna's and Thorstein's Bu and is built on the edge of this area, may be sited on the top of an underground passageway which connects with Howmae. This assumption is based on the experience that the voices of school children who happen to play around the Howmae underground dwellings can be heard coming up through the farm kitchen floor as well as entering by the windows and door.

The Standing Stone, or Stan Stane in local dialect, is the only monolith which can still be seen. Whether it may have once been an out-marker in association with a Stone Circle, which is thought to have stood on Tor Ness hill, is unknown. There is, however, some evidence that such a stone ring may have once stood on this Tor Ness plateau, and it is also interesting to note that the Ordnance Surveyors set up their Trigonometrical Station in the centre of this piece of flat ground when they made a map of the island.

This lone sentinel stone is set in what is called the Sander Park of Holland, in a position about midway between Holland House and Gretchen Loch. It is over thirteen feet high, three to four feet wide, and from a base about four inches thick narrows slightly upwards. The sloping top of the stone is typical of the other Orkney monuments of this time, such as the Standing Stones of Stenness, and the Ring of Brogar. There is also a round hole, placed above eye-level, but the diameter is such that no courting couple are ever likely to have vowed everlasting fidelity by clasping hands within the aperture.

Yet, both tradition and records insist that the Standing Stone did, in fact, retain an importance by remaining the meeting place where community decisions were made, and mass celebrations were held. In this connection, the Reverend William Clouston, minister of the Cross and Burness Parish of Sanday, writing in the late eighteenth century, states that he had seen "fifty of the inhabitants assembled there on the first day of the year, and dancing by moonlight with no other music than their own singing." Could it be that the words and tune being used at that time (before 1794) were those of the traditional New Ye'r's Sang? The words and verses of The Valkyries, or Fatal Sisters, in the original Norse language, were still remembered at or beyond this time as another minister discovered when he read Thomas Gray's translation for the congregation!

There is no general agreement about the original purpose of these Standing Stones. Some archaeologists think that they may have been erected to mark some outstanding event; others think that the circles and rings may have been used as temples for sun worship, and the offering of sacrifices to ensure the fertility of animals and crops. Another, and perhaps the largest section, think that the primary object of the stones was to provide a community timepiece: a huge sundial designed to mark the changing seasons, give the time of day, and indicate such events as an eclipse of the sun or moon.

Such ambitious objectives are beyond the scope of a solitary stone, but it is possible, as has been hinted already, that the Standing Stone may have once been part of the circle and outlying markers which go to make up such a sundial.

The Broch is another ancient erection, close to the sea, on the most southerly headland of the island. Old records claim that there are traces of a similar building having been sited at the extreme north end of the island, near Trolla Vatn loch. While there is no entirely satisfactory answer to the questions of who the builders may have been, or of the original purpose of these towers, there is no lack of theories on the subject. Various inquirers, by using a formula like Kipling's ". . . What and Why and When, And How and Where and Who . . ." have brought back some feasible explanations.

Set against the time-scale of the prehistoric period, the Broch is a late-comer, which might be said to occupy a place on the threshold of recorded history. Research into the purpose and source of the Broch seems to indicate that they were designed for defensive purposes, and were unlikely to have been used as permanent living quarters when times were peaceable and settled.

These forty to fifty feet high towers were a forerunner of the Norman castle, and are thought to be a development of a building tradition which the Picts brought to northern Scotland from their ancestral home in Brittany and the shores of the Bay of Biscay. But the acceptance of this view still leaves plenty of room for different ideas as to why these buildings were mostly confined to the northern counties and islands of Scotland. What set of circumstances could have been responsible for the very unequal distribution which gave Orkney 108 Brochs, while only 7 were built south of Scotland's waist at the Forth and Clyde inlets?

As most of these Orkney Brochs are sited so as to look out over the sea, it seems a reasonable hypothesis to assume that some water-borne enemy had been in the habit of making frequent raids on the islands. This would naturally result in an urgent campaign to find some deterrent, some counter-measure. The communal memory of defensive towers would almost certainly suggest a crash building programme, in which all the available manpower would be directed to the erection of more and better Brochs.

Who could this enemy have been? Were the Norse and other European raiders already paving the way for a permanent occupation? Perhaps they were, but another enemy, which would also account for all the river-mouth and other Broch positions throughout the whole North of Scotland, suggests itself.

The Roman conquest of Britain, including Southern Scotland, following the defeat of Galgacus at Mons Graupius, would set up a pressure that tended to force the Pictish tribe northwards. This regrouping would, in its turn, result in a fairly dense Pictish settlement of the more fertile parts, and of the places where fishing was good. These relatively peaceable conditions would, however, come under a different sort of indirect threat once the Romans organised their newly conquered territory, and sealed off the whole of Northern Scotland by Antonine's Wall c. A.D. 146.

Luxury-loving Rome required more and still more slaves, and it would never do to collect these within her occupied but well-governed territories. Fortunately the foreign parts outside Antonine's Wall presented a profitable source of such domestic labour, and Rome's seafaring allies, the Phoenicians, who had their ships around the Roman British coasts, would always find it profitable to add a few young Picts to their cargo.

The Broch of Burrian, which is locally known as the Castle of Burrian, was, as has already been mentioned, excavated by the late Dr. Traill in 1870. He carried out a systematic search of the site and found various relics which showed that this particular one had been

occupied after Christianity had been introduced into
the island. Although this is a useful pointer regarding
the time when it was still considered to be a safe
retreat, it still fails to settle whether it was
missionaries from St. Ninian at Whithorn (c. A.D. 400)
or from St. Columba at Iona (c. A.D. 563) who brought
the New Faith to this remote island?

Whatever the answer may be, it is reasonable to
assume that the Castle of Burrian would still have been
a conspicuous landmark at the time when one-eyed
Torf Einar spotted his rival Halfdan Longlegs crawling
ashore somewhere in the vicinity of the tower. It is
likely that the building would still have been in a fairly
good state of preservation at that time (c. A.D. 910-920)

This leaves ample reason for curiosity as to why
Halfdan did not try to barricade himself within the
Broch, and also poses the question of what changes this
might have given to the island story.

4

The Norse Colonisation

. . . brings important Norse families to North Ronaldsay . . .

The keels of Viking longships are almost certain to have crunched the wet sands of Linklet and Nouster beaches for centuries before there was any permanent Norse settlement of the island. The belief that these hit-and-run raids soon led to the permanent occupation of the two island Brochs as strongholds by these pirates can, I think, be discounted. The absence of any natural harbour, where these prowling galleys could be held in readiness for the chase, and the Saga's avoidance of any mention of nests of pirates having had to be cleared out, suggests that these towers had lost their importance before the Norse colonisation of North Ronaldsay began.

Island history begins with Torf Einar's and Halfdan Longlegs' fleets meeting and fighting in the North Ronaldsay Firth. These two rivals were engaged in a combat to decide who was to be the Earl of Orkney and Shetland; for the sixty islands of the former and hundred islands of the latter were too few for a peaceable co-existence between these sworn enemies.

In any case, North Ronaldsay was brought right into the centre of this naval battle, and the Saga's terse description of this encounter and what happened afterwards seems to show that both men were at sea searching for each other, and that each hoped to take his enemy by surprise. In this, neither contender seems to have succeeded, for the eventual battle would hardly have been staged in the narrows of this firth from deliberate choice.

It begins to appear that the encounter took place on the evening of a summer day after the rivals had met head-on, as one sailed eastwards, and the other westwards through the firth. It also seems reasonable to assume that it happened during slack-water, for how else could this tidal stream have been sailed through in opposite directions at the same time? Two other deductions may be made in the brief saga paragraph. The weather must have been settled, and the cold northern sea warmed by a long spell of fine sunny days, for Halfdan Longlegs to survive the six or seven hours between the time he jumped overboard from his sinking ship and the time he swam ashore. Equally, without a bright, rising sun in a clear sky the one-eyed Torf Einar could hardly have spotted his enemy crawling ashore at a distance of over three miles.

Another question, already suggested in the chapter entitled "Links with the Past," seems worth asking: What prevented the fugitive from putting up a stiffer resistance by barricading himself in the Broch of Burrian, which must at that time have still been in a reasonable condition? If he had been able to hold his pursuers at bay for a time, there might have been the possibility of secret allies coming to his assistance. Some historians even go as far as to suggest that had Halfdan been victorious, his father, the King of Norway, would probably have been ready and willing to overlook his son's part in murdering Torf Einar's father, the Earl of More.

It could have been a suspicion of this that motivated Torf Einar to slay Halfdan as well as the professed object of avenging his father while at the same time offering a suitable sacrifice to Odin. But whether North Ronaldsay, and the other islands of his Earldom, would have been better ruled if the fortunes of war had been reversed is doubtful. Time has judged Torf Einar, and left behind the verdict that this thrall-mothered son of Rognvald Earl of More governed his lands wisely. The Saga account also ensures that the sacrificial slaying of Halfdan is recorded in Torf Einar's own verse. So, like the flash of lightning which illuminates a whole countryside on a dark night, this violent episode turns attention to Rinansay.

Where, for instance, is Rinar's Hill, and is there any

remaining trace of the Cairn which was erected there about the year A.D. 910? It is generally thought that a seafaring race like the Vikings would give the title of Rinar's Hill to the land feature which would first rise above the horizon as the longships approached the island, and was also the last to sink into the sea as they departed. If this deduction is right, it would seem to raise the Brae of Holland to the dignity of Rinar's Hill, and mean that Halfdan's burial cairn was sited somewhere near to the place where the Old Parish Church now stands.

After this Halfdan-Torf Einar encounter, Rinansay (the Old Norse name for North Ronaldsay) produces for almost another hundred years no further event which was thought worthy of an entry in the Saga. This particular incident follows the usual Saga pattern, where a quarrel developed into bloodshed and a familyfeud, which was eventually ended by a marriage between Helgi of Rinansay and the daughter of Ulf of Sanday.

In the words of the Saga:

'Ulf of Sanday killed Harald of Rinansay, when the latter's son Helgi was away from home. Ulf went to the Jarl (Earl Sigurd the Stout, great grandson of Torf Einar) and confessed what he had done, and the Earl told him that he must make restitution to Haraldis relatives. When Helgi returned home, however, either not knowing, or not caring what the Jarl had decreed, he killed Ulf's nearest kinsman, Bard of South Ronaldsay. The Jarl summoned Helgi, and reproved him, saying, "Had you but waited, you might, with my help, have had the matter honourably settled." Helgi replied that he knew nothing of any settlement the Jarl had intended to make.

'At length Helgi, an adventurous young man, ran away with and married Ulf's daughter, and after her father's death, the young couple succeeded to both Rinansay and Sanday, and the feud was ended.'

After giving this piece of information, the saga-writer turns to other matters. Rinansay does not re-enter the chronicle until almost a century and a half later. By that time Paul II had become joint Earl (in

1129), for his fellow Earl Rognvald was in Norway. He had not held the Earldom for long before he outlawed the great Viking, Sweyn Asliefson of Gairsay, for killing Sweyn Breastrope. This follower had once befriended the Earl, and to make matters worse, the killing was done in the Earl's presence. On second thoughts, however, Paul seems to have had doubts about the wisdom of his decision, or at least thought it advisable to sound out the views of what were called "the best born, and well-landed people in the islands."

With this end in view Paul visited Rinansay, and stayed in the house of Ragna, who had the reputation of being a wise woman. She counselled him to pardon, and make friends with Asliefson, for by doing this "he would secure strength and popularity." But the haughty, quick-tempered Paul was not the sort of person to take advice readily, and his reply quoted here shows him as a man more likely to make enemies than friends. "Thou art a wise woman, Ragna, but thou shalt not rule here."

The wisdom of Ragna's advice was, however, soon brought home to Paul. Rognvald, Kol's son, over in Norway, was a nephew of Earl Magnus who was murdered by Paul's father Earl Hakon. Rognvald had already claimed his half-share in the Earldom. Having already made an unsuccessful attempt to grasp it by force, he was again actively planning new and better ways of winning his rightful heritage.

Rognvald had the reputation of being brave, skilful and a good all-round fighter, but his father, Kol, who was a leading nobleman of Norway, foresaw that even these qualities might be made more effective by linking them to the new religion that was gaining ground at that time. In order to make victory doubly certain, Rognvald was also to make a vow that he would, in the event of victory, build a minster in Orkney to be dedicated to the memory of his uncle, Magnus, a minster of such magnificence that it would be "the wonder and glory of all the North."

Earl Paul also had friends in Norway. These kept him posted with news of what might happen, and he on his part took what steps he could to anticipate a possible attack, or at least to prevent it from having the advantage of coming as a surprise. With the knowledge that such an attack must be sea-borne, and would most likely be launched by way of Shetland, Earl Paul arranged for warning fire-beacons to be set up on the hill-tops of all the North Isles of Orkney so that the alarm might be relayed to his headquarters on the Mainland of Orkney.

As responsible friends of the Earl had been appointed beacon-wardens at each site, the precaution seemed as fool-proof as was humanly possible. But the knowledge of these secret precautions had not been well kept, and once the information came to the scheming Kol, he soon found ways of turning it to Rognvald's advantage. Kol arranged for a fleet of Shetland fishing boats to be rowed toward Fair Isle. When in sight of the island, all the vessels were hove-to on their oars. From this stationary position each of them hoisted its sail slightly, and gradually raised it higher as time went on, so that it caused Dagfin, the beacon-warden, to light his warning bonfire.

In Rinansay Thorstein, the beacon-warden, immediately saw the alarm signal and set his pile alight. In response to this, all the other Orkney beacons were also fired, with the result that Paul's followers were soon streaming to Kirkwall from all the outlying islands. When no enemy appeared, it gradually became apparent that the summons had been the outcome of a trick due to someone's stupidity. In the search for a scapegoat, Dagfin of Fair Isle and Thorstein of Rinansay blamed each other, and the quarrel ended by Thorstein 'the strong' killing Dagfin.

So Earl Paul was confronted by a dissatisfied following who took sides in a general quarrel. His demoralised forces had, however, to be sent back to their respective islands to build new beacons. In the case of Fair Isle, Paul had also to appoint a new warden. And once again, strange as this may seem, the next Fair Islander was no match for the wiles of the resourceful Kol and his son Rognvald.

Presently another stratagem brought a persuasive stranger to the Fair Isle with the tale that he had been robbed by Paul's followers and would be grateful for the islanders' hospitality for a time. While in the island, he gradually gained the people's trust with his friendly advances and acts of kindness. He even became so friendly with the newly appointed beacon-warden that he was allowed to look after the warning system, while Dagfin's successor went fishing. When Rognvald was ready to sail again, this spy had made sure that the bonfire materials were thoroughly soaked with water so that the beacon could not be lit

Remembering what had happened already, the real warden delayed his warning until the identity of the longships could be properly established before a burning peat was tossed into the pile. Rognvald's fleet would consequently be passing the island on their way to Westray by the time the warden rushed up the Ward Hill to raise the alarm. Needless to say his deputy had disappeared, although his handiwork remained evident. It was also apparent that the collection of material for a new beacon would take too long, for by the time it could have been set ablaze the strong ebb-tide would have speeded the square-sailed galleys to their destination. It was obviously too late to bring any assembled force to contest a landing.

Earl Paul was thus confronted by the armed invasion he had striven to prevent, and as if this catastrophe was not enough, fate had brought forward another enemy to endanger this luckless man. Sweyn Asliefson, who Ragna had said was better as a friend than an enemy, must also have had spies who kept him informed about Paul's movements. It so happened that when the Earl continued his opinion-testing visits, and was staying with his friend Sigurd of Westness in Rousay, he took the opportunity to set aside a day for otter hunting on the rocky shores of the island. Neither the Earl nor his attendants returned from this expedition, and there is no doubt that he was kidnapped and carried by sea to Scotland by the sea rover Sweyn Asliefson. It might have been wiser if Earl Paul had taken Ragna's advice after all.

At any rate, this new development gave Rognvald, who was soon to be made Earl Rognvald, his heritage without further bloodshed. It also had the effect of bringing Rinansay into the picture again, for it was not long before Ragna was using her powers of persuasion on the new Earl. This time, however, it was not the Earl who came to see Ragna. She had, instead, to present herself at Rognvald's court, for he had no need to seek advice while his father Kol lived.

Rognvald knew that Ragna and her son, with their lands in Rinansay and Papa Westray, had recently been staunch friends of Earl Paul, his rival, and that they would now need to prove themselves afresh before being fully accepted and trusted as being favourable to the new regime. Ragna, too, was probably aware of how she stood, and may have contrived to bring her Icelandic relation to Orkney as a means of finding a way into Rognvald's good graces.

Be that as it may, Earl Rognvald had not held his Earlship for long before the Icelandic Scald, Hall Thorarinson, came to Rinansay, so that Ragna might introduce and if possible help him to find a place at the Earl's Court. Ragna's son, Thorstein 'the strong,' who had killed Dagfin of Fair Isle, must have been a better fighter than persuader. Sent as the emissary to get Hall accepted as one of the Court Scalds, he had to return empty-handed. Hall's disappointment seems to have been intense, for he used the occasion for some verses on the subject.

Listening to these verses, which might be construed as casting some doubt on the power and influence of her family, Ragna decided that she must see what else might be done to further the interest of her close relation. She would visit the Earl, but with winter almost at hand she would wait until the spring, and use the next six months to think out ways of getting her way with Rognvald.

During this waiting period, it is more than likely that Hall whiled away the long winter nights with activities other than a preliminary planning of his 'Old Meterkey.'

Ragna had completed her plans by the time of the long voar days and settled weather. The Saga record of this event tells how she dressed herself up, and wore a hat, or wig, of red horsehair. Whether this headgear was motivated by information that Rognvald had at some time been attracted by a red-haired woman, or that it was used only in order to make the wearer more noticeable is, of course, left unanswered.

If this unusual head-dress was meant as a gambit, or a preamble to the bout of lighthearted banter that took place between them before settling down to the real business of the meeting, it seems to have served its purpose. The Earl asked where Ragna had got the red mare's tail, and back came the answer that a closer look might show it to be a redhorse's tail. Anyway, Rognvald considered further the advantage of adding another Scald to his 'Hird' and Ragna of Rinansay showed herself to have been persuasive, as well as wise.

With Hall at the Earl's Court, Ragna and her son Thorstein no doubt remained a favoured family, and this assumption is borne out by the fact that Ragna visited Kirkwall again before Rognvald set out on his Crusade to the Holy Land. The Earl took Hall along with him on this mission, and the wisdom of his choice can be seen from the way they co-operated in experimenting with poetical metres. They also produced various verses and rhymes, the best known of which is Hattalykill.

While it is not intended to cover the Norse period beyond this brief treatment of events directly concerned with North Ronaldsay, the writer is fully aware of the difficulty of achieving cohesion and unity by this method. However, any reader who may wish to examine the full background to the Viking colonisation of Orkney and Shetland is advised to read one of the translations of the Orkneyinga Saga, or other books which are entirely devoted to this subject.

Even then, there will still be plenty of puzzling situations to argue about. Two random examples should make clear what is meant. What, for instance, happened to the successors of Thorstein? Can there, as some Orcadians think, be some connection between this old Norse name and the present Orkney name of Yorston? Again, one is left wondering why all the feuds and violence were between the Vikings themselves, without any mention of any opposition from any former inhabitants of the island? This difficulty is 'explained' by certain authorities, who maintain that the Celtic missionaries and the Picts had been driven out by bands of Viking pirates who operated around these islands for two or three centuries before the Norse colonisation took place, but agile side-stepping from an obstacle does not allow a clear path ahead for long.

Purity of race and non-fraternisation between the Norsemen and the Picts is another aspect of this period which cannot stand up to much scrutiny. If, for instance, one gives credence to the tradition that it was the Scandinavian custom to let women but seldom aboard a longship, it becomes difficult to see where the early Norse settlers found female companions.

After allowing for the few determined Viking women like Ragna who, as we have seen, could always get over any man-made taboo to prevent them from getting across the North Sea, it must still be conceded that many of the Norsemen must have won a wife as the result of a raid into Caithness and Sutherland.

It may also be appropriate to mention that it was another sort of Norse raid on Scotland, an unsuccessful attack which was planned to win all the land north of the Clyde and Forth, that weakened and eventually brought about the downfall of Norse power. The autumnal storm which broke over the Firth of Clyde on the first of October, 1263, wrecked so many of King Hakon's ships that Scotland could not have had a better ally than the onshore wind of that particular night.

While it is unlikely that Rinansay could have contributed very much to the expedition of men and ships which set out for Largs, there can be no doubt that, like all the other Orkney and Shetland islands, it was soon to feel the effects of this defeat. After having enjoyed a publicity which was almost in inverse proportion to its size, the small island faded from the Viking story. It was to be almost three hundred years, by which time Scottish rule was firmly established, before a writer known as Jo Ben, who is supposed to have been an itinerant priest, described what he found on a visit there. But his observations must await the next chapter.

5

Scottish Overlordship

... the Stewarts and their Kin ...

Any comparison of Norse and Scottish Rule is
difficult as far as North Ronaldsay is concerned. While
the Norsemen made the island one of their first landing
places in their colonising of Orkney, the Scots tended to
look on it as little more than just another of those
overgrown skerries: a place the pickings of which would
be unlikely to compensate for the hardship of having to
settle in such a remote land.

The Mortons, Sinclairs, Stewarts, and other less
well known members of the Scottish aristocracy,
undoubtedly extracted a little of their income from the
island, but this was invariably collected by
intermediaries, or tacksmen. These carefully picked
underlings not only looked after their masters' interest,
but also made life harder for their sub-tenants by
exacting an extra toll of grain and malt for themselves.

An examination of Earl Patrick's Court Book for
Shetland shows that his justice was on the whole
neither better nor worse than what was dispensed by
those left in power when Patrick's reign was ended.
Bishop James Law, who succeeded the Earl, retained
all the 'money grabbing' manoeuvres of mulching under
both the Udal and Feudal laws, just as his predecessor
had done. But this Churchman, albeit he made full use
of his rigorous kirk session discipline, enforced by such
refinements as 'goging,' 'branking' and 'douking,' did
not stir up anything like the hatred that Orcadians and
Shetlanders reserved for the Stewarts. Why? Maybe it
was because of the Bishop's position in the church, the
dictates of which people almost took for granted as
unassailable.

While North Ronaldsay was considered too remote

and unimportant to attract the direct attention of the Stewart Earls, their interests, as has been implied, are unlikely to have lost anything by being operated indirectly. Some indication of how rents, teinds, and the profits thereof were channelled into the Earl's coffers might be gleaned from an authentic document of this period. This record of the transfer of a Tack to Robert Henderson of the 'vickerage' of North Ronaldsay is authorised by Patrick Earl of Orkney, and drawn up by Cuthbert Henderson N.P., the Treasurer of Orkney. It is signed, witnessed, and dated at Kirkwall on August 1st, 1595 so as to grant:

". . . Mr Robert Hendersoun, eldest son of the deceased William Hendersoun, Treasurer of Orkney, of the vickerage of Northrounoldsay, with the rents, teinds, and profits thereof, during his lifetime, and the lifetime of his heir, or heirs succeeding, and for nineteen years thereafter, for the yearly payment of 20 merks . . ."

This yearly payment of £13 6 8d. (Scots) for what must have been a comparatively small division of the island land helps to show the large amounts of butter, grain, malt, and fish-oils that had to be collected before a tacksman's commission became profitable. All Debts and Duties were paid in kind or produce and measured by the Pundlar and Bysmar for weight, by the Can and Barrel for capacity, and by the Cuttel or Alin, a wooden rod of the length of the Scottish ell, for length. All these old Norse measures were interfered with to such an extent that, during the 49 years of Stewart reign by Earls Robert and Patrick, the resultant lower readings had the effect of increasing the amount of island produce needed for discharging the tack by as much as 250 per cent.

Another pointer to the conditions which prevailed in North Ronaldsay, just before the Stewart phase, has been provided by Jo Ben. This scribe appears to have been trained for the priesthood, and may have been sent to Orkney to make a reconnaissance of the islands so that his superiors could have an up-to-date report on how the inhabitants fared regarding religious instruction. At any rate, there was a Scottish family,

Bellenden by name, who had already settled in the isles. They held lands and were soon so well established that they filled various important posts, including that of Principal Sheriff of Orkney during the time of Earl Patrick Stewart.

Jo Ben's Description of Orkney is written in Latin. The varying translations available indicate that the author in his section on North Ronaldsay found the islanders in need of better instruction. However, the island itself is shown as very fertile, growing much oats and barley which was made into bread. The summer also helped to provide a more varied diet through the addition of milk and small fishes. He goes on to describe how the North Ronaldsay men caught and killed 'selchis' on a small islet to the north of the island, known as 'Selchskerry,' where the seals were plentiful. Jo Ben implies that he accompanied the boatmen who, armed with strong hempen nets and clubs, caught as many as sixty seals on that occasion.

Other observations made by Jo Ben indicate that the islanders were well fed and clothed as a result of these seal-hunting trips to the Seal Skerry. The island's main disadvantage, of having no fuel, had also been largely overcome by using dried seaweed and dried animal dung. Winter lighting was also well provided for by burning the oil obtained from fish livers and from seal blubber. Mention is also made about the island's freedom from rats, which when brought there by wrecked ships, perished as if they had been poisoned.

Two other indirect references to island conditions prevailing in North Ronaldsay during the latter part of the seventeenth century come from letters dealing with the banishment of the Rev. Alexander Smith to the island in 1668, and from an account of the island as found by the Rev. James Wallace, minister of Kirkwall, when he visited North Ronaldsay around 1693.

The Rev. Alexander Smith was exiled to North Ronaldsay in 1668 for holding conventicles after the passing of the Conformity Act of 1662. On being put ashore in this remote spot, he immediately set about making himself useful to the inhabitants. Writing to Sheriff Blair, who was the official responsible for arranging his transportation and detention, Smith writes:

"... The poor people have received me wt. much joy." He then expresses his intention of preaching to them "... wt. out the least mixture of anything that might smell of sedition, or rebellion." Continuing, he implores Sheriff Blair:

"... Sir, I desire that the 'rotten hearted' old man gett not liberty to vex these poor people, who are not pleased vt. his dead ways." (A request that the local Bible Reader be removed from his post and replaced by someone better fitted to preach the gospel).

Further light on this matter is shed by the Rev. Alexander Smith's reply to an inquiry by a Mr Andrew Taylour. This letter takes the following lines and seems to have been sent to, and been forwarded by, Sheriff Blair. Taylour writes, "... Withall being desirous to know, or 'Dywe in Mr Alexander Smith his intension he making himself ready to preach next Sabbath and challenging the place where."

To this, Alexander Smith made reply that he was not resolved to go to the church, but only to conduct family worship, seeing that the Church was the King's house, while he, himself, was His Majesty's prisoner.

This correspondence on the Smith banishment helps to establish two aspects of island life at that time. It confirms that North Ronaldsay was thought to be a more difficult place to escape from than Shetland, where Smith had already been outlawed, but from which he had somehow managed to return to the Scottish Mainland. Yet, this isolation had not prevented the island from having a Church that was being regularly used by some sort of Scripture Reader.

The insight into life and customs which are preserved as a result of the Rev. James Wallace's visit to North Ronalsha', as he calls it, is what might be expected from someone who, as minister in Sanday before going to Kirkwall, would have gained an intimate knowledge of the place. He manages to give a fuller description, and better assessment of local farming and fishing, than could have resulted from the brief visit of Jo Ben a century and a half earlier.

Considerable progress is indicated. Better fuel in the form of peat imported from Eday had, at least, partially removed the dependence on dried seaweed and animal dung, while improved cultivation allowing for more cattle and sheep had brought an economy that was less reliant on seal hunting. In Wallace's own words:

". . . the most Northern-Island in this Country, call'd North-Ronalsha, which is a little fruitful Isle, but both it and Sanda' have no Moss Ground, but are obliged to bring their Peits and Turfs (which is the only fuel they have thorough this whole Country) a great way off, from the next adjacent Island, Eda."

He also has something to say about the state of agriculture in his time.

". . . Their Corn Land is everywhere Parked, and without these in-closures their Sheep and Swine, and some of their Cattle go at random, without a Herdman to keep them. The most ordinary (usual) Mannour they have for their Land, especially in places near the Sea, is, Seaweed, Sea Ware, as they call it."

After describing how this ware, which is used to manure the cultivated fields, has to be carried from the beaches in 'cassies' or baskets made from straw, this minister shrewdly observes, ". . . but methinks 'is the greatest slavery in the World, for the common People . . ."

Continuing in a more cheerful vein, Wallace writes about Orkney as a whole. "Here is a good store of Sheep and Cows, which tho' they be little, yet yield abundance of Milk. Their Ewes are so fertile, that most of them have two at a birth, some three. I myself saw one that had four all living and following the Dam.

"Their Horses are but little, yet strong, and can endure a great deal of Fatigue, Most of which they have from *Zetland* and are call'd *Shelties*. There are great Herds of Swine and rich Warrens . . . well stor'd with Rabbits."

Of the sea, and fishing, he writes:

". . . Many *Ottars* and *Seals* are to be had every where, and oft times *Spout Whales* and *Pellacks* run in . . . (become stranded) . . . In the Sea they catch Ling, Keeling, Haddock, Whiting, Mackrel, Turbat, Scate,

Congre-Eels, Sole, Fleuks, &c. and sometimes they catch Sturgeon.

". . . Herring swim through these Islands in great plenty, but the People are not so frugal, or have not the way, to catch them. Some years ago, many Ships from Fife frequented this Country for the catching of Herrings; but the Seamen having been in the year 1545 at the Battle of *Kilsyth,* they were there almost all Killed; since which time that Trade failed; tho' the Hollanders, to our eternal Reproach, fail not to keep it up to their great advantage."

Of the exports of Orkney, as a whole, he writes: ". . . The chief products of this Country, and which are Exported yearly by the Merchant, are Butter, Tallow, Hides, Barley, Malt, Oatmeal, Fish, Salted Beef, Pork, Rabbit Skins, Ottar-skins, White Salt, Stuffs, Stockings, Wool, Hams, Writing Pens, Downs, Feathers &c."

We have looked at the period before, during, and immediately after the Stewart phase, through three different pairs of eyes, and the evidence seems to show that the Udal, or Norse system of land holding may have lingered longer in 'Rinansay' than anywhere else in Orkney. In "The Rentale of King and Bischoppis lands of Orkney, 1595," published by Sheriff Alexander Peterkin in 1820, the rental divisions of the island almost correspond with the Ancient Marches made by Matches' Dyke and the Muckle Gersty, but now named Sailness and Sand: Nesbusta and Sand: and Linklet

How far each of these divisions may have been subdivided and splintered by four centuries of the Udal system of providing equal shares for the Udaller's family must be left to the reader's imagination! While the Udaller may have been a freeman, and not a serf, there must have been times when he felt more like a starving man, once he became too civilised to take part in the raiding of southern lands. It even seems a reasonable deduction that Udalism had run its course by the time that Earl Robert Stewart made Margaret Bonar the first feuar of the island, towards the end of the sixteenth century.

The next century saw the earldom lands

incorporated in the Crown of Scotland and North Ronaldsay farmed out to various tacksmen, before it was mortgaged to the Earl of Morton by Charles I in 1643. Some light on the division of the land and names of the island houses during the time of Oliver Cromwell's occupation of Scotland has been preserved in the form of a document that claims to be "Attested Rental of North Ronaldsay" (1653) .

"David McLellan of Woodwick has Three pennylands of Busta: 2 penny-land of Howan and Hargar: ½ penny-land of Stromness and Burgar: 1 pennyland of Howar and ¼ penny-land (1 Farding) Kirkland in Boustay: Towmail of Nouster: Fletties Towmail, and Piggar: Towmail of Newbigging: 4 penny-land of Sander be South, and 1 penny Kirkland there: Towmail of Kelday: Kirkland of Orbiness: Towmail of Brestan: Towmail of Trib: 18 penny-land of Linklater: Towmail of Sugarhouse, and Veracott: 24 penny-land of Sabines and Hutchum: Towmail of Nether Linay: Four Selkie Nets for Sailness: 1 penny-land Kirklands of Tougar: Vaultness of Ankum: Drawn Teinds of North Ronaldsay: Mill of North Ronaldsay:—

Total £1185: 1: 9d. Deduct Superior Duties £350..................................	£835	1	9
Margaret Graham, relict of William Henryson has..............................	253	6	8
The Earl of Morton has Superior Duties..	427	13	1
Total	£1516	1	6

16/2/1727 Archibald Nisbet of Carfin sold his Orkney lands to Mr James Traill. Besides North Ronaldsay and Woodwick, these included several panels of land in the West Mainland.

With that brief note on the transfer of ownership, this would seem to be the time to leave the Stewartship era and begin a new chapter of island history. Undoubtedly it would have been the right moment to introduce such a change if there had not been a romantic link between the Stewart and Traill families which deserves mention. This link is a portrait of Mary Queen of Scots, attributed to Farini, and called 'The Orkney Portrait.'

There is still a lingering memory of the time when either the original, or a very good copy of this painting hung in Holland House, which has been the island home of the Woodwick and North Ronaldsay Traills for over two centuries. This half-length picture of Queen Mary had changed hands and been added to the Duke of Sutherland's collection by 1912, when the "Old Lore Miscellany of Orkney and Shetland" devoted a Note to the history of this painting, adding an explanation of how it came to be copied.

". . . it was in the possession of William Traill of Westness and Woodwick (born 1797) until 1833, and, perhaps a number of his predecessors also. Its originaL history was not well known to the owner himself, but when Henry Glassford Bell published his 'Life of Mary Queen of Scots' (the first of many modern studies) in 'Constable's Miscellany' of 1828, the portrait was thought worthy to be reproduced as its frontispiece. The description appended hinted that the picture might have belonged to some of the family of Robert Earl of Orkney, and led its descent through a maze of owners, some rather visionary, Haleros, Baikies, Stewarts and others, until it came (though how is not distinctly mentioned) into the Woodwick family.

"In 1833 an attempt was made to sell the portrait, when according to Malcolm Cowan it had got into the hands of a different pedigree, derived from Jean Kennedy, first wife of George Traill. The discrepancy and dubiety of the offer was, however, speedily pointed out by Mr John Whitford Mackenzie (cf. 'Mary Queen of Scots, the Orkney Portrait' in the Library of the Scottish National Portrait Gallery, Edinburgh). The same year it passed into the possession of the Duke of Sutherland at Dunrobin Castle.

"The picture, whatever its origin is, however, a very pretty, if 'late 'portrait of the Queen, and undoubtedly belonged to the Orkney family of Traill of Woodwick. "

6

Overcrowding and Misrule

. . . Feudal v. Udal . .

Udal Law ordains that a Udaller's land must be divided among all the members of his family upon his death.

This arrangement, primarily designed for pioneering conditions, must by its nature have run into difficulties immediately a community became fully settled. North Ronaldsay could, for instance, have had the size of its holdings reduced from the reputed first division of only three farms to about eighty 'run-rig bits of ground' to support four hundred people. So it would seem to be a reasonable assumption that the Udal Laws had come under suspicion of lacking 'divine inspiration' before the Orkneys were annexed by Scotland.

Then again, the circumstances under which Norse responsibility for the economic welfare of Orkney and Shetland was shed by King Christian I of Denmark must convey an impression that this monarch looked upon these Northern Isles as a liability rather than an asset as far as Crown income was concerned. How else can the Marriage Agreement, that offered a Dowry of 60,000 Florins of the Rhine, be equated with the state of a Dano-Norwegian treasury which could only scrape up 2,000 Florins, or one fifth of the promised first instalment, when king James III of Scotland and Margaret of Norway were married, only a year after the agreement had been signed?

This transfer of Orkney to the Scottish Crown does not appear to have had much immediate effect as far as the islanders were concerned. The former Earl's property was rented out to tackmen who collected scats, rents, and other duties in much the same manner as had been done under Norse rule. The Scottish

Parliament in Edinburgh were prepared to wait while their representatives on the spot, such as Bishop Willaim Tulloch, Bishop Andrew, and Henry, Lord Sinclair had all been given an opportunity to show what their particular 'mixture' of Udal and Feudal Laws might channel into the Scottish Treasury.

In 1567, Lord Robert Stewart arrived in Kirkwall to take up the role of "feuar of the lands and lordship of Orkney and Zetland and sherif principal of the samyn." On checking the records regarding the income which might be raised from the earldom lands, he immediately decided to introduce his own version of feudalism. Aided by such lawyers as Henderson, Dishington and Fermour, Robert Stewart might be said to have scrutinised both the Feudal and Udal laws, picking out and combining anything that might be expected to increase his revenue.

Subjected to this hotch-potch of laws which left -the tackmen free to extract a bit extra for themselves, the islanders gradually became despondent. Without any prospect of fairplay and justice, all pride in their work disappeared. The butter in which they paid part of their rent and taxes deteriorated in quality until it was said to be unfit for consumption.

It is understandable that such a climate of apathy would operate against the keeping of any detailed records covering this period, and this certainly seems to have been the case as for as North Ronaldsay is concerned. Apart from a 1595 document, showing the transfer of the Tack of the island from Cuthbert Hendersoun to Mr Robert Hendersoun, and a 1653 Attested Rental of North Ronaldsay, no other direct record of the sixteenth and seventeenth centuries has survived.

The early eighteenth century did, however, bring two events which had an important bearing on the future of the island. North Ronaldsay changed hands in 1727, after the former owner, Archibald Nisbet, had found his estate unprofitable and had been forced to borrow so heavily that he became insolvent. His main creditor, Mr James Traill, an Edinburgh lawyer, who may have also had faith in the prospects of the kelp industry which was starting in Orkney, bought the island for £2,222.

James, the new laird, administered his estate through the medium of his brother-in-law, David Traill of Elsness, who acted as factor. This collaboration seems to have worked well from the new proprietor's point of view, for the "Traill Correspondence" of that time indicates that the islanders had been encouraged to grow more grain, of which they were able to sell some for malt and meal, over and above what was required in order to discharge their rents, tithes and other duties that were paid in kind. James Traill's faith in the future of kelp was also well founded. In 1795 the Rev. William Clouston said that kelp-making was bringing into the county approximately £15,000 each year, and the Rev. George Barry estimated the total income for the fifty years between 1740-1790 as £370,000 sterling, and that as much as one tenth of the Orkney kelp was made in North Ronaldsay.

This new industry might have been thought to be exactly what was needed at the time, but it encountered considerable opposition from the very beginning. The dried tangles and ware had to be burned, and the smoke, or 'kelp reek' as it was called, was thought to drive the inshore fish out to sea. There was a suspicion too that it had an adverse effect on growing crops, and the domestic animals. Worse still, it was certain to produce abortions and cause infertility in both animals and people. Kelp-making also required so much manpower that the traditional work of fishing and cultivating the land had to take second place whenever any large-scale stranding of seaweed took place.

Although most of these objections were either unfounded, or only partially valid, all the Orkney lairds had earned the description of being 'mesterful men' by the time they had persuaded their tenants to make kelp. Having fixed the amount of kelp to be made, the absentee landlord would sometimes leave his factor and kelp-grieve full freedom in the method employed to raise this quota. Under such an indirect system, the laird's deputy often resorted to measures which kept the tenantry in constant fear of eviction. To disobey some relatively unimportant, and often unfair, request could easily lead to a row in which the factor would always score by having the offender 'warned out' and replaced by a more amenable tenant. Although the landlord's deputy was mainly concerned with increasing the yearly export of kelp and with collecting the butter, malt and meal in which the rents and tithes were paid in kind, he often interfered in other ways. Fishermen might not only be recalled from the sea, but might also have their catch confiscated for the benefit of the factor himself, who was just as liable to commandeer a tenant's store of wood and flagstones for his own use. Again, in the absence of a direct heir, or where some misfortune had left a widow, who was considered unable to cultivate the croft and produce her quota of kelp, the land would most probably be appropriated for the enlargement of either the laird's or the factor's own farm.

Rev. George Barry's account of this period, showing the effects of kelp-making on the economy of Orkney, is given in the Old Statistical Account of the Parish of Kirkwall, Vol. VII. The concluding paragraphs of this report state:

". . . Since the year 1780, there has been such a failure in the crops, that Orkney has been sometimes almost visited by a famine; and if the people had not had the produce of this beneficial article (kelp) to depend on, many of the poor, in all likelihood, would have starved; while the lairds, instead of being able to help them, would have been stripped of their estates, and reduced to bankruptcy.

"Many other effects, besides preserving the lives and the estates of those connected with it, have been produced by this manufacture. Industry, which was very low, has considerably increased. The lower class of people live much better in point of food, clothing, and houses; since they began to know of what importance they are to their superiors, they are throwing off, by degrees, that servile subjection, under which these islanders were formerly kept, and discovering more and more the spirit of liberty.

"But while we trace with pleasure the advantages which it has produced, candour forbids us to conceal its disadvantages. Owing to the kelp manufacture, every species of provision has greatly increased in price, which makes it difficult for those to live who have only fixed incomes: wages are much higher; agriculture, which in every country is the first and most necessary of the arts, is greatly neglected; and a style of living has been introduced among the proprietors, which their lands can by no means support, and which, if ever this manufacture should fail, must bring certain ruin upon them, their tenants, and their families."

As the President of the Board of Agriculture, instituted only in 1793, Sir John Sinclair of Ulbster was understandably anxious to encourage everything connected with land improvement. While his views might be coloured by this, nevertheless a very accurate, longterm forecast of the kelp industry was contained in the above extract. The President of the Board of Agriculture rightly concluded that a yearly export of almost 3,000 tons of kelp, although very profitable to the Orkney lairds, would also be certain to bring about overpopulation in all the islands where seaweed was plentiful.

While the French wars seem to have delayed the immediate fulfilment of this prediction, it was only sixteen years after Waterloo that North Ronaldsay's population had increased by 138 people, raising the 1787 total of 384 to 522 in 1831. This population increase of 36 per cent also coincided with a shrinking kelp market, thus bringing all the misfortunes that Sir John Sinclair had warned against.

But the islanders, already well inured to hardship, were in one sense fortunate in having a laird, who in addition to being 'a mesterful man'was also a man well accustomed to deal with emergencies. Most of the Woodwick and North Ronaldsay Traills had at some period of their lives held important administrative posts in India, and this particular member of the family was no exception. Unpopular decisions had to be taken and acted upon, lest his island estate should go the way of a 'deserted Indian Village.'

While a full account of these corrective measures rightly belongs to the next chapter, it may not be inappropriate to close "Overcrowding and Misrule" with an extract from "The New Statistical Account of Scotland" Vol. XV, page 109, which states:

"In North Ronaldsay the division of the land into squared farms and the confining of the native sheep to the shore lands took place in 1832, but it was not until later that the run-rig lands on most of the mainland of Orkney were consolidated into separate farms."

7

Migration

. . . overspill to Eday and the other North Isles of Orkney, with emigration to the British Colonies and to the United States of America . . .

The North Isles of Orkney are located far away from the battlefield of Waterloo, but this British victory soon proved itself to be a mixed blessing as far as some of them were concerned. With the English Channel reopened to shipping, the Navy and merchant ships ceased to provide an outlet for the surplus fish and farm produce as had been the case during Napoleon's blockade. Returning seamen and soldiers, who were no longer needed in the forces, had difficulty in finding work. They also helped to push up an already high population at a time when dwindling markets and falling prices had taken the value out of most island products.

Kelp, which could be sold for £20 a ton at a critical period of the French Wars, had declined in price so severely that it was no longer profitable to the laird, or the tenant. The reduction of value of everything that the crofter-fisherman had to sell coincided, therefore, with the decline in demand for kelp.

Confronted with such unpromising conditions, the laird and his factor must have had serious doubts about the wisdom of a policy which gave kelp-making primary importance. The long neglected crofting and fishing could not suddenly be made to provide the food for an overcrowded island. Nothing less than drastic reorganisation could even in the 'long term' bring about improvement. The land would need to grow more grain and be made to support more livestock. The run-rig system of land cultivation would need to be abolished, and the straying, unherded cattle and sheep confined, if any such improvement was ever to be made possible.

Considerable skill and firmness of purpose were needed to bring these aims to fruition. Unpopular decisions like the re-allocation of lands, perhaps held by the same family for several generations, so that the crofts might be merged into larger units were generally resented by the losers in this arrangement. Sub-tenancies especially, where two or three families lived together on the same croft, had to be discouraged. One of the families might have to be 'warned out' and in extreme cases be sent to one of the neighbouring islands where the population density was less than the North Ronaldsay figure of over 130 persons to the square mile.

In taking stock of the island's assets, Mr Traill and his factor must have decided that the wealth of local seaweed might be more profitably used as fodder for the native sheep. The improvement of the sheep-dyke that divided the proposed squared land from the common shore-land would provide a communal farm. All the crofters and farmers would then be given an allocation of sheep corresponding to the size of their individual holdings. This arrangement of combining the island's foreshore with the infertile fringe lands would not only allow extra sheep to be kept, but would also prevent them from straying and damaging the cultivated crops. With more grain and straw becoming available, more cattle and livestock might also be kept.

Buoyed up with this prospect, and kept busy with the improvement of the dry-stone dyke, which had to be made sheep-tight over a length of more than twelve miles and to a height of about six feet, Mr Traill's tenantry, as a whole, lent their support to this effort to make the island more productive. But the year 1832 has left behind a memory of a distinct cleavage of opinion regarding the methods employed to push North Ronaldsay into the forefront of Orkney's agricultural advancement of that time.

It is understandable, however, that such a major island-event as 'land squaring' in the interest of progress would be the excuse for certain injustices. How bitter some of the quarrels must have been can be realised from the fact that they are still being discussed, nearly a hundred and forty years later.

Relatives of families who had been evicted from their homes and forced to start life afresh in one of the neighbouring islands could hardly have been expected to appreciate the merits of enclosures and land squaring. It would also have required a more humane combination than a nineteenth century laird with his factor and kelp-grieve, to produce an acceptable plan deciding which small or badly-cultivated crofts must be taken over and included in the home farm.

Perhaps the grievance which rankled most was the factor's high-handed way of settling disputes when the laird was abroad for years at a time. Any outspoken criticism of these arbitrary decisions could lead to the offending tenant being deprived of his home and livelihood. The evicted person's land might either be used to enlarge the factor's own holding, or be leased to someone who was considered to be more amenable. This new tenant might be either a favourite of the factor, or even someone brought from another island.

The treatment meted out to rebels might help to preserve a 'cowed and easily disciplined tenantry' but could not solve the problems of an overcrowded island with its kelp industry in a depressed condition. More people must somehow be encouraged to leave their home before even improved agricultural methods could reasonably be expected to grow sufficient food for those who remained behind.

We have already seen how the welfare of a small remote island is linked with distant happenings, but it must be equally stressed that those days of gloom were only a prelude to brighter times. The period 1830-50 brought a general expansion of world trade, with the new British Colonies and the United States of America opening their doors to immigration. Nearer home, the laird of Eday needed more workers for his peat industry. Surplus population might either overflow to nearby Eday, or go further afield, where both the dangers and opportunities were greater.

No record of the first mass movement of North Ronaldsay people to Eday seems to have survived. Indirect evidence may, however, be obtained from the census returns covering this period. In 1831 the population was given as 522, and five years later, in

1836, it had fallen to 480. This reduction of 42 people would therefore roughly represent the first overspill to Eday and elsewhere. It is also reasonably safe to assume that this group of prospective peat workers included Muirs, Swanneys, Cutts and Tullochs, names which are still common to both islands.

We can however, be on surer grounds regarding the next two mass movements of North Ronaldsay people to Eday. Both the dates and exact numbers involved have been kept, and have recently been published in a Survey of Eday, which was carried out on behalf of the Orkney Council of Social Service. This shows an influx of thirty-two people from North Ronaldsay in 1851. The group consisted of fifteen men, fourteen women, and three children. It is also stated that they were settled on poor and only partially cultivated land on the west side of Eday. This unattractive area must, however, have been brought under cultivation and made more fertile during the next thirty years, for in 1881 a further group left North Ronaldsay for Eday. Thirteen people were involved in this voluntary overspill, consisting of four men, seven women and two dependents.

These hundred people who emigrated from North Ronaldsay to Eday during the nineteenth century helped to ease a situation which might otherwise have deteriorated into island famine.

Eday also derived benefits from having a growing labour force which helped to ensure a steady supply of peats to the distilleries producing Scotch whisky. The increase of peat output must also have made more of this sort of fuel available for the other North Isles, and the heavily laden boats carrying such 'winter comfort' must have been a pleasing sight for Torf Einar if these Orkney firths are visible from his Valhalla.

And even now in the 1970s, we continue to see interesting sequels to the emigration from one Orkney island to another. None of the North Ronaldsay folk who went to see their relatives and friends sail away to start a new life in Eday could visualise the day when a descendant of a family who went from North Ronaldsay would fly back to take up the ministry of the church. But this is what happened as the 'Islander" taxied to a halt on the landing-ground with the Rev. T. Arthur Tulloch for his induction to the combined island charge.

There seem to have been opportunities at the middle and in the latter part of the nineteenth century for some of the more enterprising men and women to find a new life in places far away from their overcrowded homeland. The same seas which carried the Vikings on a 'voar cruise' might still be crossed by any young man who considered his island too dull or too small. The larger world outside could still provide the excitement, the danger and perhaps the reward. But this new apprenticeship on the sea generally began in a Kirkwall coaster. After a year or two of backbreaking work handling cargoes of coal and kelp, the aspiring sailor would be considered sufficiently experienced to sign on as an ordinary seaman in the deep-sea trade.

For one of the crew of a clipper engaged in the wool or tea trade, voyages to far-away ports with the thrill of strange new sights would be attractive, but advancement beyond 'able seaman' or 'bosun' required a knowledge of navigation as well as seamanship. This handicap of starting without what might be called a formal education did not, however, prevent some of the more ambitious of these young men from rising to the command of the stately ships of their time.

Memories of a Captain Hugh Kelday still linger in North Ronaldsay whenever old men meet and talk about the sea. As one of a large family on a small island croft, he had to make a living as best he could from a very early age. Beginning with local fishing, he went in turn to herring fishing, coastal trade, and, finally, foreign trade. His advancement in each of these different branches of seafaring was equally progressive and resolute. Saving and studying, with the object of winning a command of his own at the earliest possible moment, he soon achieved his desire, and according to all accounts drove his full-rigged ship as hard as he did himself.

Hughie, like most of the record-breaking captains of his time, was always loth to reduce sail. Although the owners of the ship and cargo no doubt appreciated their being 'first in the market' with a new season's crop of tea, the Fates soon tire of a prolonged record of success.

Pressing on as usual, Hughie ran into a tornado and neither he nor anyone else on board was ever heard of again.

Hugh Kelday had a contemporary who became captain of a sailing ship about the same period, a John Tulloch from Veracott. Captain Tulloch must have been either luckier, or perhaps more cautious, for he still holds a very special niche in memory owing to the reputation he acquired by a skilful handling of his ship in the vicinity of his birthplace. He somehow managed to outmanoeuvre the storm that wrecked the Brig "P,ince" in Versa Geo. By heaving-to and taking the south-easter on his starboard bow Captain Tulloch was able to sheer away from the land, while the "Prince," by taking the wind on her port bow, was blown ashore to break up on the rocks below where the present island lighthouse was built, some fourteen years later, in 1854.

With the example of two mid-century master-mariners, it became almost inevitable that many of the next generation should turn to the sea. This urge would also be fostered by the sight of a large number of ships of all rigs which constantly sailed past the island. Sessions of story telling in one or other of the island shops during the long winter nights no doubt helped to paint the picture of an El Dorado where the deserving might win rich rewards.

One particular version of this kind of story has been linked with a North Ronaldsay man who rose to the command of a ship engaged in the Indian trade. In this tale, John Traill, the elder son of Dr. Traill, the laird of North Ronaldsay, held a post in Bombay, where he was approached by a distinguished-looking man with the offer of a free passage to North Ronaldsay. As Traill's home leave was not due for another year, he reluctantly had to refuse. This ship-master did not, however, disclose his identity beyond saying that he had been born on one of the smallest crofts on Dr. Traill's North Ronaldsay estate.

It may have been ten years before John Traill became laird and brought this story back to the island. His lengthy spell of duty in the tropics had by that time injured his health to such an extent that he was never very clear about what had actually transpired at the

Bombay meeting. So it could not be decided whether it had been a Kelday or a Tulloch who had proposed to John Traill the free passage from Bombay to Bridesness. Perhaps the laird even invented the story to encourage more young men to venture further afield and find out what the outside world had to offer!

Anyhow, the attractions of a seafaring life seem to have made themselves felt to an increasing extent as the century advanced. Some of those who took up this calling, and whose names are still remembered in this connection, included William Tulloch, Phisligar; John Tulloch, Ancum; John Muir, Burray; Hugh Muir, Midhouse; John, David and Thomas Thomson, Quoybanks; John and Peter Swanney, Ness Muir. Most of these sailors served part of their time in the well-known clippers of that period, and, engaged in the wool and nitrate trades, logged up many voyages 'around the Horn.'

Only William Tulloch of Phisligar seems to have emulated the example which had been set up by Kelday and Tulloch. This young man passed for mate at the early age of 23 years, but his career was short-lived for he unfortunately contracted a tropical fever in Calcutta and died there.

The rapid opening up of new countries, like Australia, Canada and South Africa, and an even faster expansion in the United States of America had also begun to attract emigrants from the island. When writing home, some of these early colonists tended to paint their new environment and describe their own prospects in an optimistic manner more designed to reassure elderly parents than to give an accurate picture of life 'down under,' on the prairie, the veldt or in the meat town of Chicago. Nevertheless, this sort of enthusiastic correspondence undoubtedly brought out far more younger brothers and sisters than were ever attracted by the advertisements placed by the countries concerned.

Among the more successful of those who settled in Australia was Robert Tulloch of Upper Linnay, who set up and ran an engineering firm in Sydney; and George Seatter, Howar, who became a successful Estate Agent. Peter Muir of Sholtisquoy, as a building contractor, was responsible for constructing many of the government offices and departmental stores in Winnipeg, being particularly proud of the New Parliamentary building erected 1916-20. He was killed in a railway accident at the height of his career.

The United States also on several occasions provided the opportunities that were lacking in a small overcrowded island, and this is best illustrated by noting the heights to which some unknown emigrants climbed in that country. Pride of place goes to Vice-President Wallace, who had North Ronaldsay connections on the maternal side. Others with outstanding achievements in the land of the Stars and Stripes include the Editor of the influential "New York Times," a son of Charlie Thomson of Howar, who emigrated towards the end of last century, and in this century several Congressmen. In more recent times the late John W. Tulloch of Garso built up for himself a very successful decorating business in Washington D.C., while a friend of his, James Watts, whose mother Mary Tulloch of Sandback also hailed from North Ronaldsay, holds an important post in the Rockefeller financial world. As Vice-President of the Chase Bank of Manhattan, he makes frequent trips to the money centres of Europe.

Very few records are available about anyone emigrating from North Ronaldsay before the mid-nineteenth century. Among the first were the Walls, or Waas, families from Westness, who went to Victoria, Australia. They were closely followed by Thomas Muir, Burray, who settled in Queensland, Australia, and also by John Tulloch, Senness, who travelled still further in order to settle in New Zealand. Mary Tulloch, Upper Breck, left her home to settle in Brisbane about the same time.

In another few years, Robert Tulloch, Upper Linnay, with his brothers Adam and Tom, settled in Sydney, where Robert set up his own blacksmith shop that eventually grew into a sizeable iron foundry. The next departure for 'down under' was John Swanney, Holm, who made his home in New Zealand.

Canada and the United States of America had also developed sufficiently to be attractive to would-be settlers by the mid and later part of the nineteenth century. Janet Tulloch of Garso, who was married to a Mr Gore from Sanday, was among the early pioneers who chose Canada. Together with their young family they travelled to Hamilton, Ontario and settled there. Thomas Swanney, Nether Linnay, also went to Canada in search of a new home at about the same time.

The next group of North Ronaldsay people to leave decided on the United States of America. These included Martin Tulloch, Senness; Robert Tulloch, Sandback, and William Thomson, Dennishill, together with Scotts from Kirkwall, who originally came from Westhouse, North Ronaldsay. Most of them settled in Chicago and Detroit.

Several brothers from the Rue family together with Henry Muir from Neven also settled in Toronto and Ontario in the latter part of the nineteenth century.

While Thomas Swanney, North Gravity, along with his wife and family settled in Manitoba about the end of that century.

Three of the largest farmers in North Ronaldsay also sold their holdings in order to try their luck in the New World well before the end of the last century. The Cutt family from Holland went to Canada, while the Tulloch family from Kirbist, and the Thomson family from Howar, both chose California.

Others who went to the United States before the end of the nineteenth century were John Muir, Waterhouse; John and Thomas Tulloch, Purtabreck; Anne and Robina Tulloch, Garso; Robert Thomson, Peckhole; Mina and Marion Seatter, Howar; Thomas Thomson, Dennishill; and Mary Tulloch, Sandback. Canada, too, comes into the picture again. Three of the Muir brothers from Sholtisquoy settled in the land of the maple leaf. Two in Winnipeg, and the other in Alberta. They were followed at the beginning of the present century by William Tulloch, Phisligar; and Thomas Thomson, Bewan; the former choosing Vancouver, while the latter settled in Toronto. William visited his birthplace twice during the 1950's when he presented his relatives with some examples of his exquisite wood carving. Janet Thomson, Quoybanks (Mrs Duffus) along with her husband and large family exchanged life in Scotland for the greater opportunities in the United States, also, during the early years of this century.

With the opening of the present century, Sarah and Adam Tulloch of Upper Linnay set out to join their relatives already established in Sydney. Then Thomas and William Tulloch, also from Upper Linnay, and Alick Swanney from Sangar left their homes to take up prairie-farming in Canada. Three Thomson brothers from Antabreck followed shortly afterwards to settle in Alberta.

This all-male group was in its turn soon balanced by three women; a sister of Alick of Sangar, a sister of the Thomson brothers of Antabreck, and Mary Cutt from Nether Breck. John Cutt, also from Nether Breck, spent a spell at prairie-farming near Moose Jaw, Saskatchewan around this time, but eventually returned to North Ronaldsay.

After an interval of several years some of the older members of the Tulloch family of North Ness left home to join their Seatter aunts who were already settled in Rochester, U.S.A.

Then, after the 1914-18 war, a whole group of ex-service men and others left to go to America and Australia, or to find work and settle in other parts of the world. Of these John A. Tulloch, Sholtisquoy went to join his mother in Alberta, Canada. Of those who had served in the fighting forces, John R. M. Tulloch, M.M., Greenwall; John, Peter and William Cutt, Greenspot; William Laverty, Barrenhall; Robert Tulloch, Cott; and John W. Tulloch, Garso first made for Canada, but soon crossed into the United States, attracted by the better climate and greater variety of opportunities.

Another ex-serviceman to go abroad, in 1921, was John Muir of Burray. John, like his father before him, did not take readily to the prospect of life spent in crofting. Deciding to try some other line, he conferred his rights as the tenant of Burray, together with the stock and other property, to his step-father Thomas Tulloch, and the act remains unique.

The post 1914-18 period also saw several more of the Tulloch family of North Ness leave in order to join those who were already settled in Rochester. This U.S.A. city soon attracted another six cousins of the

rapidly growing group of North Ness Tullochs. Four of
the cousins were Seatters from Howar, and the other
two were Thomsons from South Ness. Three Munro
brothers from the United Free Manse and three Begg
brothers from Holland Farm all left North Ronaldsay
for Rochester and New York. Another young man to
emigrate about this time was Thomas Tulloch, Ancum,
who finally settled in Hamilton.

The next group to go consisted of yet another three
people—Charlotte and James Tulloch of Purtabreck,
and William Cutt of Gerbo. All three joined relatives
who were already established in Chicago.

The late 1920s saw a further exodus of young
people. George Seatter of Howar, with John and Netta
Tulloch, Cruesbreck, set out for Sydney, while an even
larger group, made up of William Thomson, Phisligar;
Thomas Tulloch, Upper Linnay; Scotts of North Manse
and Gunns from Holland Farm, all left for
Saskatchewan, Canada to take up farming. Also around
this time and again in the 1930s several Thomson
sisters of Howatoft left for Canada, and two of them
finally settled in California.

This rapid loss of population during the 1920-30
decade was so marked that a shortage of both
manpower and woman-power had grown into a
considerable island problem, before the 1939-45 war.
This trend has also continued in the post-war years.
John Seatter, Howar, a victor of the North African
campaign, along with his wife and family, left for
Sydney in the 1950s. He was followed in 1964 by his
niece Mary Tulloch, Purtabreck, who has already
returned twice to see her relatives. On her last trip
back to Sydney, she took her aunt Mary Seatter along
with her for a holiday. So emigration still seems to
persist to a lesser degree.

8

Primitive Agriculture

. . . most of the island's food, clothes and other requirements are grown, or made locally, in what might be described as a 'compulsory self-supporting economy . . .'

Traditional methods of cultivation, almost as primitive as those of the Middle Ages, continued in North Ronaldsay until well into the nineteenth century. The patches of crop were all intermingled, and the plough used was still the one-stilted type which merely scratched the soil. Un-enclosed fields allowed the native sheep to roam wherever they wanted. Stray cattle and flocks of geese also damaged the newly sprouted blades of bere and oats.

These crops of bere and barley were grown on the same ground year after year, and the uninterrupted cultivation, carried on without any rest by fallowing, or proper rotation of crops, might, one would have thought, resulted in a rapid deterioration of the soil, but complete exhaustion seems to have been partially prevented by heavy manuring with seaweed. This system of feeding the land with the vegetation of the sea was doubtless due to the abundance of it always washed ashore on the north, east and south sides of the island every winter and voar.

Another reason for this extensive use of seaweed-manure may have been the shortage of dung, as most of the animal droppings had to be wind-dried and used for fuel. It has also been said that the fertilising value of farmyard manure was not fully realised at that time.

This ignorance about the chemistry of the soil did not extend to the field of improvisation. With little or no money in circulation, the land and surrounding seas had to be utilised in a way that would suffice for almost all the needs of man and beast. Even this sort of self-supporting economy demanded a considerable adaptability of the Robinson Crusoe variety. Most of the tools and everyday requirements had to be fashioned from whatever materials could be found at hand.

As both iron and the skill required for making it into farm implements were scarce, ploughs, harrows, and even spades had to be made of wood. The supply of timber could also have presented a difficulty, but what Nature withheld in the way of trees was more than made good by the oak, teak and softer woods which were always being washed ashore as driftwood or wreckage. So, the renewal of a broken plough-stilt, or the re-toothing of a harrow called only for a rudimentary kind of carpentry. The right sort of wood would come from the Baltic, or from Burma, with an even greater certainty than it could be got from a timber merchant nowadays.

Some canvas and cordage could always be expected as a result of the summer fogs and winter storms that caused many shipwrecks before the present lighthouse was lit in 1854. As the sea might also have a bonus of other useful odds-and-ends that might indirectly help with the cultivation of the land, there was always plenty of room for improvisation. Every stage, the ploughing, sowing, and harvesting, called for a variety of home-made equipment that had been fashioned from whatever raw material might be had on the spot.

Straw, for instance, had to be put to many other uses besides the obvious ones of fodder and bedding for the animals. Made into a 'wazzie' or collar, it provided that piece of harness essential for yoking the horse to the plough. Taking the form of a 'flaikie' or soft straw-mat, it might be used to protect the horse's back and sides from being chafed. This irritation was due to the method of carrying seaweed-manure from the beaches to the fields at the time when there were no carts. Each small horse bore a 'clibber' or wooden pack-saddle that supported a wooden creel on each side of the animal. These creels each held about a hundredweight of 'ware' and the bottoms were hinged, so that the manure might be dropped on the land as required.

With a stock of 249 horses, 256 cattle and 1900 sheep, there would be plenty of animal skins and wool to keep the 5 weavers and 4 tailors busy making blankets and clothes for the 420 people who made up the island's population in 1791. The Rev. William Clouston, Minister of Cross, Burness, and North Ronaldsay, gives this information in "The Old Statistical Account." Although he does not list any shoemakers or other workers in leather, it is reasonable to think that there must have been a few who could make simple footwear. Rivlins were in general use, so the wealth of skins would be fully used. It is even probable that narrow strips of skin would be plaited into ropes of different weights and strengths to supplement the halters, leads and tethers made from sow and horse hair.

Other interesting statistics included in this account of North Ronaldsay show that there were 44 farmers, and that 43 of them owned single-stilted ploughs. Mr Clouston gives the average size of the crofts as 8 acres. Rents and tithes were paid mostly in kind, and some 18 chalders, or 288 bolls of bere had to be grown for this purpose each year. Sufficient seed-corn would also need to be put aside to sow next season's crop, and these two requirements must have accounted for a high proportion of the grain which could be raised from the area of little over 300 acres under cultivation at that time.

Under such conditions, it is not surprising that the land was over-cropped and made to produce as great a bulk of grain as possible. With this end in view, the eighteenth and early nineteenth century crofters used so much seaweed-manure that it could scarcely be buried in the furrows. This liberal dosing with ware resulted in the release of various salts which forced an early growth of the crop of bere, or black oats, but completely failed to enrich the soil, or even sustain the growth until the heads of grain were fully filled. So a bulky crop of low quality grain in which the ratio of husk to kernel was high had to be accepted. On light sandy ground the bere might only weigh from 16 to 24 lbs. per bushel, which is under half the weight of well-filled and ripened grain.

Prices of animals and farm produce were also so low that butter and poultry were used to supplement the quota of grain and fish-oil which had to be exported to cover the payment of rent in kind. Hens were reckoned to be worth only 3d. each, and 360 of them had to be found every year. Butter sold at 3d. to 5d. a pound, depending on the quality, and 9 barrels, valued at £22: 10: 0d., had to be handed over as rent before there could be any 'butter on the home-baked bread.'

Even these low prices represented a considerable increase on those ruling in 1720. At that time, a cow could be bought for 10/- and a sheep for 1/6d. By 1791 the price of the former had risen to 50/- and that of the latter to 4/- or 5/-. This increase of 500 per cent in 71 years shows that the upward trend in prices had set in long before the World Wars of 1914 and 1939 had boosted the inflation which enabled a well-fed beast to realise more than £200 when sold at the Kirkwall Auction Mart in 1972-73

All the agricultural implements of this period were of the simplest construction, and made from any local material which could be fashioned into a 'pitby' or substitute for the more advanced labour-saving machinery already in use on the farms in Norfolk and East Lothian. Besides the already-mentioned wooden plough and harrow, tools for sowing, harvesting, threshing, storing, drying and milling, as well as instruments for measuring and weighing the grain, malt, meal or other farm produce, were all essential.

Anything like a full description of these implements and utensils would need at least a chapter to themselves. As this would in any case be unlikely to add anything to what John Firth has provided in his "Reminiscences of an Orkney Parish," I shall omit further comment on it.

When harvest came round, every puckle of grain and inch of straw had to be saved, and this need would always be greatest when a sunless season had resulted in a poor crop. The short stalks and ill-filled heads of grain would then be doubly precious, for failure to gather enough to tide man and beast through the

winter, and also leave sufficient seed-corn for the next
year's crop, could only end in famine, or worse.

Under these conditions the short stalks would
probably be hand-pulled instead of being cut with a
sickle, or 'heuck,' and most of the earth also removed by
hand. If, on the other hand, the season happened to be
a good-growing one, the run-rigs would be reaped by
the quicker method of one-handled scythes, but any
flattened or 'bedded' part would still be shorn with
'heucks.' Whatever method of harvesting might be
suitable, the 'hairst wark' would be laborious, slow and
certain to employ every fit man and woman for at least
six weeks.

The sheaves of that time were always bound, or tied,
with the longest 'band' that could be made. This was
effected by pulling several stalks in two separate
handfuls of bere or oats as the case might be, and
joining them together with a special knot for the
different owners. This completed 'band 'was then laid
on the ground ready for the 'lifter' who placed the
already gathered sheaf across it and bound it together
with one of the twists then in use. This operation was
rendered necessary in the run-rig system, for
neighbours' sheaves were very liable to be blown
together during high winds.

After harvest these sheaves were 'stooked' or set
upright on the stubble. In this operation two or three
pairs were set side by side together, well apart at the
bottom, but leaning inwards against each other at the
top. This triangular set-up allowed the wind and sun to
produce the maximum air-drying of the grain and
straw before the crop was carried home pack-saddle
fashion to be built into the stacks for use as required.
These stacks, locally known as 'screws,' would be
earmarked for particular purposes, such as the one for
'simmons,' the one for 'Yule malt,' or the one reserved
for 'keepin' the animals alive in a backward voar.'

But whatever the purpose of these numerous small
'screws,' every one of them had to be thoroughly 'taiked'
or thatched, and big lengths of strong straw-rope had to
be made for this, and also for renewing the roof
coverings of dwelling house, barn, byre and stable.

These 'simmons' made just as essential a demand on the straw as the seed-corn did on the grain, for winds of 70 to 100 miles an hour were frequent during the winter season, when both roofs and stacks had to be securely anchored in order to prevent their being blown away.

The island's barns of that period provided a place not only for threshing and storing of grain and straw, but also for housing most of the resultant handicrafts based on straw. In the nature of things, threshing must always be a preliminary to any further use of the grain and straw. So, any account of primitive agriculture would be incomplete without a brief description of the 'flail.'

This early form of threshing tool consisted of two hinged wooden poles, the longer one, one-and-a-half inches across, being called the 'hand-staff,' and the shorter one, two inches across, the 'soople.' The former was three-and-a-half feet long while the latter measured about twenty-seven inches. Both poles were attached to each other lengthwise by a band of hide which allowed the 'soople' to rotate around the 'handstaff.' The latter was then swung circular fashion by the flail-man so that the 'soople' would come down flat across the head of an opened-out sheaf lying on the barn floor.

The flail-man would repeat this beating a few times before turning over the sheaf and subjecting the other side to the same treatment. The straw had next to be inspected and if necessary be given a final hand-beating against the 'hand-staff.' Then, with every 'mettin' of grain removed, the straw would be ready for any one of a large variety of uses, such as feeding to the beasts, winding into 'simmons,' or making into such plaited articles as 'cubbies,' 'caisies,' 'flaikies' and 'straw-backed chairs.'

The grain obtained would be gathered into a heap so that it might also be flailed to loosen the beard, or chaff, from the kernel. The corn, or oats, as the case might be, was then ready to 'windoo.' This winnowing would be done by riddling the 'uncleaned' mixture in the draught across the barn floor between two opposite doors. With this air-flow suitably controlled, the 'clean' grain would drop in a heap below the riddle while the bits of broken straw, chaff and other lighter refuse would be blown out of the lee door.

If the season had been good and the grain reasonably plentiful, this 'tail,' or portion nearest the lee door, would probably be set aside for the beasts and hens, while the heavier, well-filled grain directly below the riddle would be reserved for human use as meal or malt.

But, before it could be ground into meal, or processed into malt, it had first to be dried. When the amount was small and needed for immediate use, this might sometimes be done in a metal pot hung over the kitchen fire. The operation demanded the right amount of heat and a constant stirring or turning-over of the heated grain until examination showed very 'puckle' to be crisp and sufficiently shrunk to loosen the kernel from the husk.

The grinding of such small amounts would then be done at home with the aid of a 'hand-quern.' This hand-manipulated machine consisted to two miniature millstones which could be adjusted to produce a 'fine,' 'medium' or 'coarse' output. In the case of malt, only a slight crushing or 'bruising' would be needed as the hot water added during the 'masking' process extracted the 'virtue' of the grain.

With 'quern-ground' meal the husks or 'sids 'had to be removed by repeated sieving, and in the case of oatmeal, the grain-coverings obtained during the cleaning were kept and steeped in water. After several days, the liquid would then be drained off and used for baking into a sort of thin pancake called 'sowen scones.'

Pot-toasted corn or bere could also be made into a crude kind of barley with the aid of a 'knocking stane,' which was essentially a sizeable lump of sandstone having a bowl-shaped hollow on one side. The dried corn was poured into this cavity and gently pounded with a mallet or 'mell." The loosened husks could then be removed by the addition of water, on which they floated and were skimmed off, leaving the cleanedbarley. This laborious process would eventually yield up a small amount of 'knocked corn.' Eaten by itself, or with boiled kale, this made a welcome change to the fish and other monotonous diets of that time.

When larger amounts of either meal or malt were required, the grain would be carried to either the windmill or the watermill on horseback, as neither roads nor carts existed at the period. Roughly a quarter of the finished meal or malt would be claimed by the mill owner and miller as payment in kind for grinding the grain. This levy went by the name of 'mutter,' and all the crofters were under 'thirlage,' the legal term for being under compulsion to send their grain to these mills.

As the amount of 'mutter' claimed was greater when the grain was sent to be milled in an undried state, almost every house had a kiln built on the end of the barn for the drying process. It is also interesting to find that North Ronaldsay is shown as having a mill in 1653. This property is listed as "Mill of North Ronaldsay "in the 1653 "Attested Rental of North Ronaldsay."

Measuring and weighing instruments of the seventeenth, eighteenth and early nineteenth centuries were very primitive. Earlier, of course, inaccuracies were aggravated by the dual Norwegian and Scottish standards obtaining throughout Orkney and Shetland from the time of their annexation by Scotland in the fifteenth century, and later there existed injustices until the latter part of the nineteenth century, when the worst of these were removed by reforms introduced by the British Parliament.

These long centuries of confusion and demoralisation may perhaps be best illustrated by inviting the reader to try and imagine what conditions would become like if the present Government were to insist that both the British and Decimal Systems of Coinage and Measures were allowed to operate at the same time. Would the present-day shopper be able to safeguard his interests if the shopkeeper sold his wares in litres and kilograms, quoting the prices in Sterling?

If you conclude that shopping under such conditions would be something of an ordeal, how much more difficult must it have been for these Islanders, with very little formal education, to check and understand the conversion of the settin and lispund or bushel when all these weights and measures were also liable to vary according to the honesty of a Tackman, or Under-Factor. The weighing instruments of this period, as has been said, were quite unreliable. Both the pundlar and bismar were so crudely made that the basic principle on which they worked was distorted to the extent of always introducing an inaccuracy of 'one-seventh' which invariably operated to the crofter's disadvantage.

Viewed in retrospect from the present, the 1970s, it may now be seen that this era of poor farming methods and low prices might have continued even longer if the Napoleonic Wars had not brought about scarcities which resulted in a demand for more home-grown food. Rather ironically it was also the work of the Anti-Corn Law League which indirectly brought about the long overdue improvements in Orcadian farming. Reformers like Richard Cobden, John Bright and their Free-Trade followers successfully campaigned for the repeal of the Corn Laws and eventually opened our ports to duty-free imports of all sorts. Orkney's main industry of kelp-making soon became a victim of the competition of duty-free barilla imported from Spain.

The labour-force of over 3,000 people was no longer required and quickly dwindled to about one-tenth of that number, while the annual value of kelp exported fell from around £15,000 to less than £2,000. Some of the less prudent lairds were forced to sell their estates, and most of the kelp workers were faced with the choice of emigration or near-starvation.

As North Ronaldsay produced nearly a tenth of all the kelp made in Orkney the economy of the island suffered a severe setback which might have been even worse if this threatening situation had not been foreseen and partially avoided by such remedial schemes as Land Squaring and improvements to the wall of the Beach Sheep-run, but the story of these various agricultural implements must wait until the next chapter.

9

Developing Agriculture

*. . .land squaring, crop rotation, and the Scottish
Land Court fixes fair rents . . .*

"In North Ronaldsay the division of the land into
squared farms and the confining of the native sheep to
the shore lands took place in 1832, but it was not until
much later that the run-rig lands on most of the
mainland of Orkney were consolidated into separate
farms." Taking the isolated position of this northmost
island of Orkney into consideration, the reader may be
inclined to ask why these improved methods were
introduced at the fringe before they had been tried at
the centre or Mainland of Orkney.

"Scottish Farming" by J. A. Symon, from which the
opening statement was extracted, does not attempt to
give the answer. Neither does local memory retain a
satisfactory explanation, but it is fairly safe to assume
that overcrowding and threatened starvation due to a
prolonged slump in the kelp industry set the right
conditions. But this by itself might still have been
insufficient without the presence of an able and shrewd
Laird, and an equally enterprising Factor.

Mr Traill, who owned the island, had considerable
administrative experience, gained while in India. His
factor, or land-grieve, who carried out his policy in the
management of the North Ronaldsay estate, is still
remembered as a strong character, 'a mesterfu' man,'
whose decisions, although hard, were usually proved to
be right by subsequent events. For, however much the
innovations were resented, their wisdom began to be
realised once the crop rotation and other improved
methods of cultivation began to bring better yields of
grain and straw. The pool of manpower which had
become available through the fall in demand for kelp

also provided the extra labour required for improving
the enclosure-dykes, and for the draining of what had
hitherto been water-logged fields. With more grain and
fodder thus available, the cattle and horses also
improved with better feeding. More stock could be
carried after the native sheep had been confined to
their beach sheep-run and become accustomed to
depend mostly on the plentiful supply of seaweed for
sustenance, instead of wandering anywhere at will
until seed time.

With the end of the run-rig system, the individual
crofter now had most of his land grouped around his
home, and no longer needed to waste time going from
one field to another which might be situated more than
half-a-mile away. Larger and better shaped fields
facilitated the employment of more up-to-date
implements, and the old-fashioned wooden ploughs
were gradually replaced by iron ones of the two-horse
type, originally made by Small of Edinburgh. Horse-
drawn, iron-toothed harrows, scufflers, rollers, sowing
machines, reapers and horse-powered threshing
machines also found their way to North Ronaldsay
during the second half of the nineteenth century.

Every advance in agricultural implements, all
successful cropping experiments, and all worthwhile
efforts to improve the quality of livestock which had
been tried out by the factor, Robert Scarth of "Scar" in
Sanday, were always available to his more enterprising
tenants. Being an active man himself, he had no time
for the apathetic and lazy crofters. Like the
Agricultural Committees of the two World Wars of
1914-18 and 1939-45, who were empowered to take over
badly farmed lands, Robert Scarth had few qualms
about warning out any tenant who neglected the land,
or was suspected of resisting the improved methods of
cultivation.

The general increases in croft rents which were
imposed at the time of the land-squaring were
universally unpopular. Although they were spread over
a period of years, with certain allowances granted for
such improvements as draining and dyking, only a few
of the more enterprising people on the larger crofts

managed to increase their earnings sufficiently to meet their new rents and have some over. For most of the others it was very hard going to make ends meet.

It should, however, be pointed out that this state of affairs was common to many of the Crofter Counties in Northern Scotland, where it eventually became so much of a problem that the Government of the time decided that something must be done about it. A Commission of Enquiry was set up and established the case for remedial action in the form of an Act of Parliament, designed to overcome this depression. Although this measure was passed under the name of the Crofters Holdings (Scotland) Act in 1886, a Crofters Commission appointed to go around all the aggrieved tenants reached North Ronaldsay only in 1893, when many, or most, of the tenants had gone into arrears since their application to the Crofters Commission.

By this time the total arrears due to John Traill or his predecessors was £1,244 :11: 6d., four times as much as the annual amount to be fixed by statute.

The Crofters Commission and Land Court went to the island in 1893 for the purpose of fixing fair rents and dealing with the matter of arrears. The cases were heard by Commissioner Hossack, who had with him Messrs Mundell and Ferrier as Assessors. The hearing took place on 17th June in the U.F. Church and dealt with 53 applicants.

Reference to this visit is made in the Commission's Report for the year 1893 and they describe it as follows:—

"In North Ronaldsay, Orkney, which we reached by special charter of a steamer, we were favoured by unusually fine weather, and the cases were disposed of with the utmost dispatch. It may be mentioned that the common pasture there is of a different kind from that of any other district in the crofting area. The island is surrounded by a wall or dyke 6 feet high, and on the shore side of the dyke, sheep to the number of about 2,000 are grazed. This shore pasture is very poor and scanty, the extent being only 271 acres, and the sheep feed principally on the tangle and other seaweed growing on the rocks. At lambing time, the ewes and weakly sheep are transferred to a piece of green pasture within the dykes, and kept there until they regain strength, when they are sent to the shore for the remainder of the year."

Other interesting details extracted from the proceedings of the court show that the old rent total of £439 of the above applicants, was reduced to a new, or fair rental of £301, giving a reduction of almost one-third. The total acreage of the 53 crofts being revalued amounted to 778 acres (664 arable and 114 outrun) with the original average rent per acre working out at about 11/ 4d. an acre. After the Land Court had surveyed the ground and considered the other factors involved, the average per acre was reduced to 7/6d. The small size of the island holdings is highlighted by the fact that the adjusted overall average rent came to £5 :13: 8d. The highest was Cruesbreck at £17, while the lowest were Trebb and South Gravity at £1 each.

The holdings of Bewan, Dennishill, Netherbreck, Veracott, Antabreck, Scotsha', Milldam, Roadside, Hooking, Cavan, South Ness and Kirbest did not apply for a revaluation. Those with rent over £30, or those who for other reasons were outside the scope of the Crofters Act were Holland, Howar, Millhouse (Mills) and Sugarhouse.

Of the aforementioned arrears (£1,244 :11: 6d.), £980 was cancelled, leaving only £264 :11: 6d. to be paid by instalments, in some cases spread over three years. The value of new buildings, or of other improvements made after the Crofters Act became law, accrued to the crofter, who on giving up his holding could claim compensation. This helped to encourage new enterprise, for such improvements had previously gone unrewarded when a tenant was warned out, or had for any reason to leave his croft. Under such conditions the Laird invariably raised the rent for the next tenant, thereby benefiting from another man's labours.

The Crofters Act was further amended by an Order of 1911, which specified the conditions of the Holding and of the buildings, and other improvements, so as to clear up any ambiguities regarding the right procedure for claiming compensation. This resulted in a further batch of applications from North Ronaldsay crofters, who were of opinion that they either had to apply in order to qualify for this additional compensatory benefit, or that their fair rent, fixed in 1893, compared unfavourably with that of a neighbour's which was dealt with on the same occasion. These were lodged on different dates between March, 1912 and September, 1913, but the intervention of the first World war delayed this second visit by Commissioners of the Land Court until the Summer of 1920.

During this interval, the 1914-18 war had brought large concentrations of Naval Power to Scapa Flow and thus provided a ready market for all sorts of farm produce. Most crofters were better off than the original applicants for revaluation and also more prosperous than they had been at the time when their applications had been made. This improvement was therefore reflected in the verdicts of the 1920 court.

Of the four new applicants whose crofts had not been evaluated by the earlier court, two got a 20 to 25 per cent reduction, while the other two came away from the hearing with their rent exactly the same as they had been paying before.

One of the successful applicants, William Swanney, Veracott, had the reputation of being a local wit, and this was demonstrated during his cross-examination by the solicitor representing the Laird's interests. This agent disputed Willie's contention that there had never been any reduction in the rent of Veracott although ground had been taken from the croft to enlarge a neighbouring one.

"On checking over the old rent books, I have found definite proof that such an adjustment was made at the time when the land was squared," said the solicitor. "How do you account for this entry?" Back like a flash came Willie's retort: "Pen and paper refuse nothing!"

None of the other applicants, of whom there was a considerable number, received any rent adjustment, "no alteration" being the court's verdict for them all. So taken all round, this second visit did less to encourage better crofting than can perhaps be credited to the

earlier hearing. It should however be pointed out that
the intervening 27 years had already improved crofting
conditions. Advancements of farming methods, better
prices for produce, government grants for an island pier
and for new roads, had removed many of the hardships
that had to be considered by the 1893 court.

The improvements of this quarter-century are,
however, so intimately connected with the island's
agricultural development as to merit a more detailed
treatment. One of the ways in which this may be done
is by brief comparison of the prices and conditions at
the beginning and end of this period. The set-up of 1893
with which the first Land Court had to deal was much
the same as that which had been established at the
time of the land-squaring in 1832. These were,
fortunately, recorded by the Rev. Adam White, minister
of North Ronaldsay, and published in the New
Statistical Account of Scotland, Volume 15, (1845),
while the 1920 data is readily obtained from either an
almanac or local newspaper of that period.

A rough idea of the improved methods of land
cultivation may be gathered from the increased area
used for turnips and sowed grasses. Both of these are
essential to a proper rotation of grain crops, and for the
winter feeding of livestock. In 1832, and likewise in
1893, none of the smaller crofts grew any turnips, or
sowed any grasses, whereas by 1920 a croft of about 12
acres would have about ½ to 2 acres of turnips and a
similar or larger area laid down to rye grass and clover.
This better husbandry was also very marked in the
condition, albeit not in the number, of the well-fed
livestock. Improved breeds of cattle had also resulted in
larger animals, some of which might weigh four times
as much as the half-starved specimens of the 'run rig'
days. Most prices and wages had also risen between 3
and 4 times between 1832 and 1920.

Fishing on the other hand had declined during this
period. Only lobsters were fished by 1920, and the price
had increased from 3d. in 1832 to around 1/-, but the
numbers available were limited. From a strictly
agricultural point of view, this may have been an
advantage, for very few crofters can be good farmers

and good fishermen at the same time. The housing and living conditions of both people and animals had also improved slowly during this time, but the prospects were insufficiently attractive to retain many of the young men who came back from the first World war. By 1921, most of them had said good-bye to crofting and emigrated to America or elsewhere, thus starting a downward trend in island population, which has never been stopped let alone reversed.

The next half-century, 1920 to 1970, has witnessed a complete revolution of both agricultural methods and prospects. Mechanisation has been adopted, and tractors, with other powered-implements, have more than made up for the loss of island manpower. Depopulation has also indirectly increased the size of most of the present-day crofts. About 30 former holdings are either unoccupied or uncultivated by their tenants, who are mostly Old Age Pensioners beyond the age of heavy out-door work. As a result of this, nearly 322 acres (260 acres 1 rood 26 poles arable, and 61 acres 1 rood 36 poles out-run) have been apportioned amongst the other active crofters who have undertaken to be responsible for cultivating or grazing this land.

As these extra acres are scattered, and often at a considerable distance from the crofters who obtained them it would seem that the time is ripe for another land-squaring, a re-grouping of all the land on a more logical and convenient plan designed for what one of the islanders describes as only a 'skeleton crew.'

Be that as it may, one aspect of North Ronaldsay farming has remained almost unaltered for well over a century. The native sheep, and what the Rev. Adam White calls their 'shore lair' are still much the same as when he saw them. They are, however, more numerous than they were at the second quarter of the nineteenth century. With little more than a quarter of the human population of that time, less demands on both mutton and wool are made and the sheep are left to multiply.

Chief among the factors which have helped to transform a backward group of islands into one of the most progressive and well farmed counties of Scotland are the two World wars. Both occasions brought huge numbers of sailors and soldiers to Scapa Flow and to surrounding islands, thereby ensuring a ready market for all sorts of farm produce, especially for eggs, bacon and beef. With this seller's market for over ten years, money began to flow more freely. This in its turn bought better implements, machinery and stock, giving the crofters a new pride in their work.

Accompanying these war-time developments, other encouragements to grow more were offered in the form of various grants and subsidies. Such enterprises as breaking in new land, growing more grain or potatoes, producing more eggs, bacon, milk and beef have all in their turn brought the farmers a bonus. Expert advice has also become readily available from the Board of Agriculture, through the North of Scotland College of Agriculture on soil analysis, suitable artificial fertilisers, seed-testing, profitable grass and clover mixtures, animal breeding, stock improvement, and on animal health and diseases. A price has, however, had to be paid for these government aids which have thus been brought within the reach of all agriculture. The farmer has gradually been turned into a 'filler-up-of-forms' and must also conform to government regulations, which have a habit of multiplying faster than profits! In short, crofter and farmer have been subjected to a 'back door nationalisation,' which began early in the 1914-18 war and has continued ever since.

10

Island Fish and Fishing

*. . . lobsters, in-shore fishing, deep-sea, and
herring fishing . . .*

" The surrounding sea is so full of fish that a North
Ronaldsay crofter-fisherman does not even need a boat
in order to go fishing. He can go to one of the Fishing
Crags, and catch sufficient to keep him and his family
supplied with fish for weeks on end."

This statement, which may be a slight exaggeration,
was made by one of the laird's representatives during a
session of the Crofters Commission in which the fifty-
three crofters mentioned before were applying for a
revision of their rents.

Although it perhaps overstates the ease with which
fish may be obtained and creates an impression that
neither effort nor skill is required to land even large
quantities, it still has an element of truth. Without the
harvest of the sea it is doubtful if the island would have
attracted a human population as early as it did, or have
had so many parts of the shore named as Fishing Crags.

So, it may not be inappropriate to introduce this
subject of " Island Fish and Fishing" by listing some of
the Fishing Crags, and naming several kinds of fish that
are found in these waters. Not all of those mentioned
can be caught at the crags. Some require a boat and
suitable fishing tackle.

The rocky west side of North Ronaldsay provides
numerous ledges which can be used as fishing crags
when the tide is suitable, and the north side beaches
must have been even more popular in early times with
the suggestive Old Norse names of Suliber and Wheeber
and Skate Holter. Again, yet another indication of the
abundance of fish can be gauged from the large numbers

of British and foreign trawlers that used to operate round about. A look round Aberdeen Fish Market would have been interesting to see the great variety of fish that was caught in these waters at even the beginning of the century.

One would have to wait a long time nowadays before any of the local boats would bring ashore anything except lobsters and partans, with perhaps an occasional catch of cuithes, mackerel or haddock.

Things were very different when the island carried a population of between four and five hundred people. The harvest of the sea was essential, and fully utilised when there were so many mouths to feed. Whatever was surplus to immediate requirements was then salted and air dried for the Winter season, when the weather often prevented the small boats from going out.

During that time say, around the last three quarters of the nineteenth century and the early part of the present century, every island boat noust was full of skiffs and yawls. Larger herring boats also lay moored off Bridesness and Rue, at the south and north ends of Linklet Bay, ready to set out for the herring grounds on a Monday morning and return on Saturday.

As many as two dozen different kinds of fish might be encountered among the catches made by line, net, creels and fishing rods. Although it would use up too much space to describe each of them in detail, a list of names will help to show how varied they were.

Arranged alphabetically these included Bearded Rocklings, Cod, Cuithes and Cuithen (both stages in the growth of Coal Fish), Dog Fish, Eels (Conger and Sand), Flounders, Haddock, Halibut, Herring, Ling, Lobsters, Lythe, Mackerel, Partans (Large Crabs), Porpoises, Saithe (fully grown Coal Fish), Sharks, Sillocks (young Coal Fish), Skate, Turbot and Torsk. Of these the Coal Fish, or Saithe at its various stages of growth, was probably the most plentiful in North Ronaldsay waters. Lobsters and Partans, too have always been caught. Cod, Haddock, Ling, Lythe, Flounder, and Turbot are all well known, but intensive trawling seems to have forced some of them to abandon the shoals where they were formerly found. Herring and Mackerel have also, generally speaking, moved further off shore.

Local inshore fishermen have always reckoned that the West Firth was good for Saithe fishing. The Reef Dyke area was claimed to be best for Cuthen and Lythe, while Dennis Roost was likely to yield a catch of Cod, Ling and Turbot. A system of cross-bearings from various landmarks provided the key to the positions of these fishing grounds. The South East Shoal was found by having Fitty Hill (a hill in Westray, 557 feet high) in line with Burrian Castle, if at the same time the lighthouse was seen over the beacon. The North West Shoal was fixed by having Dennis Head lighthouse over the Green Skerry and the Old Kirk in line with the Craw Stane of Doo. Other fishing grounds were marked by having the Wart o' Versabreck, the knoll on which the lighthouse stands, aligned with Finno Croo. Another ground required the alignment of Breck on Trinley. In both these cases, the usual cross-bearings were left out. This might mean that the fishing grounds extended for some distance along these alignments, or that the best spots remained the secret of those who had gained the knowledge in the hard school of experience.

During this century, the effect of trawling has been to denude these traditional fishing grounds, and the occasions when worthwhile catches of cod and haddock have been landed by the island's inshore fishermen have been few. Exceptions to this downward trend did, however, happen in 1913, and again in 1919-20, but the reason for such isolated instances seems to be connected with a curtailment of trawling activities.

The summer of 1913 brought a long spell of very settled weather, which encouraged fishermen to visit all their former off-shore haunts. Cod were found to be plentiful at the North West Shoal, due perhaps to the absence of the Aberdeen and Granton trawler fleets, who were also using the prolonged spell of good weather to search for new fishing grounds to the northward. The 1919-20 occasion might also be explained as a direct result of the ceasation of trawling during the First World War. Then it was Haddock which again became plentiful on the inshore fishing grounds, off the west side of the island.

Something must now be said about the island's fishermen, to preserve the memory of the generations of crofter-fishermen, most of whom would sooner hold the tiller of a boat than the stilts of a plough. They all knew that they had only to 'sink' the lighthouse until only the lantern 'sat' on the horizon in a position midway between Fitty Hill and Foula, and run out fifty fathoms of hand line before it reached the seabed to experience a deep satisfaction. This recapture of the Viking seafaring spirit was independent of what might be caught.

Such seagoing also provided an opportunity to exchange bits of information with Dutchmen and Frenchmen, who could help them to forget for the time being the cramped living quarters on the island boats in the haze of tobacco smoke and alcoholic fumes that might result from a deal which brought some contraband shag and brandy. What was, perhaps, more important was the Frenchman's ability and willingness to consult his charts and give them an accurate course back to land if Dennis Head lighthouse, Fitty Hill and Foula had become blotted out by a sea fog.

This international fraternisation was probably at its height during the second half of the nineteenth century, before the universal use of steam tended to drive the sail boats from the sea, and before war came along to finish it off completely. It is for this period, just over three-quarters of a century ago that some record of North Ronaldsay's fishermen and boats is to be obtained.

Although almost every croft had its own 'cuithe boat' the actual number of skiffs and yawls which could venture to go to the outer fishing grounds, never rose above a score. All, or nearly all of them were of the open, undecked type well into the nineteenth century, but as the century advanced they gradually became larger and fewer in number. This development may be accounted for by the fact that fishing was all the time becoming more competitive and fish had to be sought further away from the land.

By the latter part of the century the island had somehow managed to accumulate a fleet of about a dozen or so decked boats, each with a crew of six men, instead of the three needed by the yawls. These 'muckle' boats were re-launched from their Winter quarters round about the end of April, and used for both cod and herring fishing until autumnal gales made it necessary to give them the protection of a land berth until next voar.

The most complete list of these former boats which can now be obtained only from retentive memories or research comprises the following sixteen names:— "Bull," "Caledonia," "Favourite," "Brothers," "Willie," "Hector," "Teaser," "Fiery Cross," "Needle Gun," "Star," "Maggie," "Granite City," "Emerald," "Lebanon," "Serene," "Foam."

The last survivors from this fleet were the "Foam" skippered by William Tulloch, Lochend: the "Serene" by Hugh Swanney, Nether Linnay and the "Lebanon" by John Tulloch, North Ness. These continued to fish until somewhere between 1905 and 1910, and remained shored-up in their winter quarters for a few further years.

The local fishermen who followed the herring can be divided into four categories: those who manned the island's own boats; those who went as hired hands on boats that belonged to, or operated from Burray, Holm, Kirkwall and Stronsay; those who hired themselves to the Moray Firth or East Coast ports; and the final group who went to the English late fishing at Scarborough, Yarmouth and Lowestoft.

Although the seasonal Monday-to-Saturday herring fishing by local boats was on the wane by the end of last century, a few hired hands from the island continued as members of the crews of Stronsay-based boats right up to the outbreak of the 1914 war. Three of those in this category, who were consistently lucky, were Jamie of Holm, Johnnie of Sangar and Tammie of Ancum. The average earnings of a hired hand was around thirty pounds for the three-months season, which started in May and lasted till about the end of August. This could, of course, he followed by a spell at the late herring season in East Anglia. Johnnie of Newbigging and John of Scottigar were the last two herring fishermen from North Ronaldsay to take part in this, and both

invariably returned well satisfied with their treatment,
and full of praise for the 'brotherhood of the sea' which
is deeply rooted in the fishing communities there. This
deeply ingrained sense of falr-play of the English
seamen was likewise shown when an English drifter,
making for the outer fishing grounds, saw one of the
North Ronaldsay boats becalmed and without any
prospect of sharing in the heavy catches of herring
reported from there. Realising this, the English skipper
threw the "Foam" a tow rope and took her all the way to
where the fish were being found.

The fleet of herring boats belonging to the island
were, on the whole, smaller and less well fitted-out than
most of those with which they had to compete. Again,
although they were always well handled in an
emergency, it is doubtful whether a set of men, always
certain of some return from their crofts, could ever be as
keen as those who depended entirely on the sea for a
livelihood. Against the hired man's average earnings of
£30, the man who owned a share and sailed with a local
boat was well satisfied with a return of £15 to £20 at the
end of the three months' season.

These island herring boats were also sometimes used
for deep-water cod fishing, and this might add another
£8 to £12 to the pay of each of the crew. Low earnings
did not, however, allow the building up of any reserve
for the purchase of larger boats which were coming into
general use at the beginning of this century. Two other
factors detrimental to the continuance of this home-
based herring fleet were the absence of a harbour and
the rapid increase in steam drifters which had invaded
the local fishing grounds

Although most of the sixteen boats listed earlier in
this chapter had been broken-up for firewood long before
the 1914 war, the fishing yarns connected with some of
them have lingered on. It is not surprising that two of
these are about the "Serene," as she happened to have
Willie, that superb teller of island tales, as one of the
crew.

"Oot o' da three Swanneys and three Cutts that
made ap wur crew, nane o' wus had a fraction o' da skill
o' Cottie. Withoo ten his left-haunded steering dat

coorse morning, nane o' wus wud be here t' tell da tale.

"Da wurld wus blawing ap, ond da ald baut listing well ower afore it, when Cottie took a loik at da sky and pulled oot da ald clay pipe he wus aye sucking away at. Withooten ony loss o' time, he then turned t' Hughie, ond advised da taking o' double reefs, while it wus still possible. He had barely got da words oot o' his mooth before it wus blowing a real snorter.

"By noo, we a' realised da danger, ond also kenned that oor best chance o' survival wus t' get Cottie t' da helm, whar' he'd spill da wund if ony mortal could do that. But Cottie wus never a mon t' shaw-aff, ond his namesake frae Milldom had t' coax him wi'n ell o' Three X Bogie Roll for da ald clay pipe afore he'd consent. Even then da danger o' changing ower at da steering wheel wud have been considerable wi' twa right-haunded men, but Cottie's left haund slipped in frae da idder side, ond ance he wus grasping da haundgrips, we a' felt safer.

"This apsurge o' confidence caused ane o' wus t' say that it might be a good idea t' carry oot t' sail reefing, but Cottie, noo fully in charge o' t' situation, wus having nane o' that. Back like a shot cam' his decision. 'The time for reefing is by and gone. You'll a' be stepping ashore in Whitehall Village. or through t' gate to that ither place, afore anither twa oors is ap.' Ond he wus as guid as his word, for we wur a' pooling wur pennies t' buy a much needed ro'nd o' drinks inside da twa hoors."

The other instance in which this same John Cutt or Cottie figured concerned a feat of rope splicing, which was so perfect that the repair became something of a show piece, and grew into a local legend. The other fishermen on the Stronsay station were so impressed with the handiwork of this man, who had never received any formal instruction in splicing, that the story of Cottie's left-handed magical adroitness more than equalling that of any right-handed fisherman to be found at that time spread all round the station.

I must finish off this section on fishing by also mentioning what another of his contemporaries did for the island's lobster fishing.

Hughie of Sholtisquoy and Johnnie of Longar were

boys of thirteen years, when with Hughie's slightly older
brother of fifteen, the trio began their apprenticeship in
'the hunting of the lobster.' As the years went by, all
three, working together, became skilful in their task.
When the older of the Muir brothers eventually left the
island, Hughie and Johnnie also went their separate
ways. Both got new boats and linked up with other
partners. In friendly competition, each, fully
appreciating the other's knowledge and experience, at
first strove to improve on his rival's record by taking
increasing risks.

Always on the lookout for any other way which might
help him to get a few more lobsters than Johnnie,
Hughie one day saw a Norwegian craft that carried the
sort of large, shallow-draught 'praam' about which he
had always dreamed. Admiring it longingly with a
scheme in his mind, he asked and got permission for a
close-up examination, so that he might jot down some
rough measurements and a sketch.

Armed with this tentative plan, Hughie now
approached the island joiner, who already had some
experience in boatbuilding. Together, they soon steamed
and shaped boards into a graceful craft, a new type of
praam designed for the shallow sloping beaches of the
island. Although it had twice or thrice the creel-carrying
capacity of the flatties which were still in use, the new
praam had more buoyancy and greatly improved
seaworthiness. It was also very free from drag, and
consequently far lighter to row than any skiff or yawl.

Hughie's rival Johnnie was said to have spent a
whole evening assessing this new boat while she was
still on the stocks, and came away ungrudgingly
conceding full points. Soon he, too, was leaving his skiff
to spend most of the season on dry land, and continuing
the friendly rivalry with a big praam as well, fashioned
on the same lines as Hughie's.

How right they both were is proved by the fact that
Hughie's original praam, built about 1919 or 1920, is
still maintaining its early reputation, but she is now
being propelled by twin outboard engines instead of the
oars and sail of former times.

11

The North Ronaldsay Sheep

. . . their origin, their unusual sheeprun, management regulations, ear-markings, and their former as well as present importance to the island's economy . . .

The small, short-tailed sheep, which are now rarely found outside the island of North Ronaldsay, were up to a century and a half ago common to most of the Orkney and Shetland isles. Whether they were brought in by colonising Norsemen or are indigenous, the descendants of a North European breed of primitive sheep that became marooned on the uplands when a major land-subsidence allowed the North Sea to flood the valleys and make the hills into off-shore islands, has never been decided. The answer to this riddle is in any case relatively unimportant. Nobody, for instance, ever bothers to think how the island's earth-worms managed to cross the Firth!

What is of considerable interest is the way in which these 'native' sheep, which are thought to be closely related to the prehistoric Palustris, have become almost extinct apart from North Ronaldsay. Their disappearance elsewhere in Orkney has been caused by cross-breeding with larger types such as Merinos and Cheviots to improve the body-size and wool-yield.

Similar attempts have been tried in North Ronaldsay, but no long-term improvement ever resulted from these experiments. No cross-breeding with imported breeds seems to produce sheep capable of withstanding the hard conditions under which this flock of seaweed-eaters are kept. They are confined to a narrow strip of beach and foreshore where they feed on seaweed, as there is scarcely any grazing pasture.

The only relaxation of this policy of thus confining the sheep is at lambing time. The breeding ewes and their lambs are taken inside the sheep-dyke from about the beginning of May until August, during which time they are allowed to graze with the other domestic animals. The whole flock is at all other times kept on the seaward side of a six-feet high dyke which surrounds the island and measures between twelve and thirteen miles.

Regulations covering the authorised allocation, management of the flock, and the maintenance of the sheep-dyke were worked out and agreed between the laird and crofters in 1839, or shortly after the time of the land-squaring. These regulations of 1839 were revised and brought up to date in 1873 and 1902, and recently, although the agreed alterations have not yet been made public. The 1902 regulations were a code of at least seventeen rules, some of which are so basic that they will always be applicable to a common-flock of this sort.

The version of the regulations presented to the Crofters Commission in 1893 was as follows:—

(1) There are 71 crofts or farms on the island of North Ronaldsay. Crofters or others are allowed to keep from 10 to 60 sheep each according to the size of their holding. Six non-tenants are allowed to have a total of 65 sheep. It is hardly conceivable that such a large flock as 2,250 sheep can be maintained on seaweed and confined to the island beaches, living on the outside of a surrounding dyke (12 to 13 miles long) which partitions their sheeprun from the cultivated part of the island.

(2) Each tenant shall on or before the first day of February record his sheep-mark in the sheep book.

(3) Hoggs found without marks and not recorded as above shall be forfeited.

(4) The tenants shall be bound, whenever called upon by any of the elected Sheepmen, to repair and maintain the whole island-surrounding dyke in proportion to their allocation of sheep.

(5) No native sheep shall be allowed inside the dyke, except ewes during the lambing season.

(6) A man from each house shall attend at each 'pound' on the publicly appointed 'pounding days' and no tenant shall be permitted to 'roo' his sheep anywhere except in the said 'pounds.'

(7) No sheep shall be killed in the island without first being shown to one of the Sheepmen.

(8) Two Sheepmen from each five Toonships shall be elected in order to carry out and enforce the Sheep Regulations.

(9) New Sheepmen are to be sworn-in before a Magistrate, or Justice of Peace. The keeper of the Sheep Register shall for his services be allowed to keep 15 sheep over and above any other allocation he may have, and each Sheepman is likewise allowed an extra 10 above the normal allocation.

(10) About Twenty Ear-Marks are in use and by means of the various combinations (such as either marking the right ear, or the left ear; putting the mark on the front edge, or back edge of the ear) this number of basic marks was found to be ample. Some of the names given to these marks were: Axe and Hole: Shear: Crook: Rip: Stair Axes: Bits: Thumb Bit: Hemlins: Stoo and Bits: Stooed and Hemlin: Stooed and Rips: Piece Off: Scart and Hole: Two Bips: Hemlin and Bit.

The lambs are marked when they are still young, and little or no bleeding results and there are no signs of pain. The wound generally heals in a few days after the marking takes place.

Another interesting document relating to the North Ronaldsay Sheep takes the form of a Schedule presented to the Crofters Commission when they visited the island for the purpose of fixing fair rents in the summer of 1893.

ISLAND OF NORTH RONALDSAY – PASTURE RIGHTS

The common or shore pasture of the Island of North Ronaldsay, the property of John Traill of Woodwick, extending to 271 acres or thereby, is shared in by the whole crofters and others of the various holdings enumerated in the sub-joined Schedule (which was lodged at the hearing of the Applications) in the proportions shown therein by the number of sheep stated opposite the name of each person. Those marked by an (*) were not dealt with by the Commission. The following is the Schedule referred to:—

STATEMENT showing the Number of Sheep which Tenants on Estate of North Ronaldsay, the Property of John Traill of Woodwick, are entitled to keep on the Shore Pastures outside the Dykes.

Holdings of £30 and under.

Name of Holding	Name of Occupier	No. of Sheep
• Bewan	Widow Jean Thomson	5
Rue	John Tulloch	25
Vincoin	William Swanney	25
• Dennishill	John Thomson	25
Scottigar	Sibella Tulloch	25
Grind	William Thomson	25
Sholtisquoy	Peter Muir	25
Westhouse	William Scott	25
Senness	Widow Mary Cutt	25
Sandback	John Tulloch	25
Quoybanks	John Thomson	25
Conglabist	Thomas Thomson	25
Lochend	John Tulloch	25
Garsow No. 1	Widow Jessie Tulloch	25
Garsow No. 2	Thomas Tulloch	25
Midhouse	Hugh Muir	5
Niven	Thomas Muir	5
Senness (b)	Thomas Tulloch, Merchant	5
• Netherbreck	Mrs Margaret Cutt	6
Parkhouse	Mrs Mary Cutt	5
Westness	Mrs Jessie Tulloch	60
Nether Linna	John Swanney	50
Upper Linnay	John Muir	50
Brigg	James Muir	21
Burray	John Muir	21
Upper Cott	William Swanney	40
Longar	William Tulloch	42
Ancum	Charles Tulloch	40

Name of Holding	Name of Occupier	No. of Sheep
North Manse	John Scott	30
• Veracott	William Swanney	24
• Antabreck	Donald Thomson	40
Trebb	John Kelday	10
Purtabreck	Thomas Tulloch	40
Sangar	John Swanney	25
North Gravity	John Swanney	20
South Gravity	Mary Thomson	6
Greenspot	William Kelday and Peter Kelday	21
Waterhouse	William Muir	20
Phisligar	Alexander Tulloch	27
• Scotsha'	Thomas Muir	20
Barrenha'	Mrs Ann Tulloch	6
• Milldam	Peter Cutt	12
Cauldhame	John Cutt	24
• Roadside	Mrs Mary Scott	6
Holm	Mrs Mary Swanney	20
• Hooking	Thomas Tulloch	60
Peckhole	John Thomson	60
Howatoft	Thomas Thomson	30
Cursitter	Mrs Sarah Tulloch	12
• Cavan	Stewart Swanney	8
Garbo	Mrs Mary Cutt	18
Gateside	Thomas and Neil Tulloch	20
North and West		or 10 each
Newbigging	William Swanney	45
Nessmuir	Samuel Swanney	15
Claypows	William Swanney	30
North Ness	Thomas Tulloch	20
• South Ness	Martin Tulloch	24
Stenabreck	John Cutt	12
Bridesness	James Cutt	12
Viggay	William Swanney	15
Greenwall	Hugh Tulloch	50
Greenwall (2)	Mrs Mary Tulloch	10
Breckan	Robert Cutt	10
Cruesbreck	William Tulloch	70
• Kirbest	John Tulloch	70

—————
1647

List of Holdings over £30 rent, and others who are not Crofters but entitled to have Sheep outside Dyke.

Name of Holding	Name of Occupier	No. of Sheep
• Holland	James Angus	300
• Howar	Mrs Seatter	118
• (Mills)		
Millhouse	John Thomson	80
• Sugarhouse	Sibella Tulloch	6
	Total	**2151**

The above was revised in 1902, making 60 sheep the highest number for any tenant, and 10 sheep the lowest number for any sheep owner.

Distribution of Island Names (Tenants) in 1893:— Cutts 9, Keldays 3, Muirs 8, Scotts 3, Seatters 1, Swanneys 12, Thomsons 9, Tullochs 24.

Such comprehensive regulations highlight the economic importance of these sheep to the island community. The reader may be tempted to ask: "How long did it take to turn a grass-eating animal into one which can thrive on a diet which is almost confined to seaweed?"

While this evolutionary development has undoubtedly gone on for a very, very long time, perhaps thousands of years, it is only since the land-squaring of 1832 that the shore sheep-run has become an almost all the-year-round home for the North Ronaldsay sheep.

The abundance and variety of seaweed which grows on the shallow, tidal beaches of the island was probably the prime factor in the existence of this unique flock, but there are also other ancillary ones.

The urgency of the problem of raising more food was also intensified by a falling demand on seaweed for kelp, following the close of the Napoleonic Wars. The wasteful run-rig system, with its complete lack of enclosed fields, could not be tolerated, and neither could the native sheep be allowed to roam about as they pleased.

The introduction of land-squaring resulted in fewer

but larger crofts where the fields could be enclosed by dykes or fences. It also called for a better rotation of crops, with the growing of rye-grass and turnips for the winter feeding of the cattle. The search for other ways of making more use of the island's natural resources also brought up the idea that the native sheep, already supplementing their diet with seaweed, might be conditioned to live entirely on what they could find on the beaches and foreshores. The surplus labour released by the post-Napoleonic slump in kelp was, therefore, set to work to heighten and close the gaps in the encircling wall, most of which had already been built a long time earlier.

As has already been stated, the work was completed and the dyke made 'sheep-tight' by 1832. From that time onwards North Ronaldsay's flock has been subjected to a rough-and-ready experiment that has successfully turned a grass-eating animal into one which lives almost entirely on a diet of seaweed. While it would be foolish to claim that 139 years have brought about all this change, for evolution is a far slower process than that, yet it would be equally shortsighted not to recognise that local environment, guided by human planning, can either aid or retard the evolutionary progress. Without the abundance of seaweed, and the former over-population of the island, it is doubtful whether the world would have this rare breed of sheep, or their equally unique sheeprun.

Any attempt to describe the special instincts of a flock of sheep which might be said to have been almost forced to live in the ebb must emphasise that they have on the whole survived and thrived beyond expectation, despite their difficult surroundings. Put another way, this natural 'survival of the fittest' has produced an animal which knows the ebb and flow of the sea as accurately as any Admiralty Tide Table!

Once the tide begins to ebb and leave a row of stranded seaweed at the high-water mark, the sound of the retreating wavelets acts as if it were a sheep's alarm clock. Their spell of sleep, rest, and cud-chewing, which has lasted since about half-flood-tide, is over. Intermittent foraging then goes on until the next half-

flood-tide signals the time for further rest and sleep.
During the feeding time, most of the flock will follow
the falling tideline, trying to outdo one another in being
the first to reach the crisp blades of ware as they rise
above the water. Some of the fitter and stronger
specimens may even swim to an outflow in order to
have a better choice of seaweed. To establish their
claim this small herd will then combine to 'doose'or
butt-off any other sheep who try to dispute their
territory.

This urge for adventure and hazard does, however,
take a toll of these swimming sheep. The younger and
less experienced ones are sometimes tempted to stay
too long on their outflow at such danger points as the
Lurands of the Sound. There, owing to the
comparatively narrow channel between the Island and
Seal Skerry, the rising flood quickly becomes an east-
going millrace. Any sheep which lingers even a few
minutes too long is almost certain to be dragged out to
sea and drowned.

Feeding during the winter months takes on a
slightly different pattern, for the storms and rough seas
of that season break off and drive ashore enough
seaweed to make any foraging of the low ebb unneces-
sary. The condition of the flock is at its best in
December and January, and those sheep which are to
be slaughtered for mutton are usually selected at this
time.

In accordance with regulations, this selection of
animals for slaughter required that all the sheep in a
'clowgang' or particular section of the beach sheeprun
had to be 'punded.' There were five main pens, or
'punds,' and one of the island's oldest men remembers a
time when as many as 120 well-fattened sheep were
collected from the Dennis Ness 'pund' during the
fortnight covering the Christmas-New Year period.

Owing to the drastic depopulation of the island,
which has reduced a population of over four hundred
people at the beginning of the century to less than one
hundred and thirty today, there is no scarcity of mutton
now. The shortage of labour has, however, brought
other problems in the management of the sheep.

Maintenance of the surrounding sheep dyke and 'punding' for dipping, clipping and numbering have all been reduced to a minimum by sheer lack of manpower.

Other environmental factors that have changed since the Regulations were revised in 1902 are that the sheep have less supervision and more seaweed than was formerly the case. The increase in seaweed is due to a change in agricultural methods. The large quantities which were formerly carted on to the land as manure have been replaced by artificial fertilisers bought under government-aided schemes. As a result of this, over two or three thousand tons of extra seaweed is left for the sheep. Another development which has arisen as the result of less handling and fewer people visiting the beaches is the increasing wildness of the breed.

The actual animal itself is sure-footed, having the appearance of a cross between a sheep and a goat. It is Long-limbed in proportion to its body size and the best fed wethers seldom exceed 36 to 42 lbs. in carcase or dead-weight. Wool yield is small: the average fleece weighs about 2 or 3 lbs, the main shades being grey, white, and black. The percentage distribution of these colours, also reckoned on a year's clip bought by the Wool Marketing Board, shows 53 per cent. grey, 40 per cent. white, and 7 per cent. black.

Both the black and grey fleeces contain a considerable proportion of black hairs among the wool. This tendency is more pronounced in the rams than in the ewes. Some former statist;ics on colour distribution, collected in Sanday around 1730, showed a higher ratio of white sheep at that time. This may, perhaps, be interpreted as showing a slow deterioration in the wool content, possibly due to the abandonment of any effort in selection and breeding for wool nowadays.

The 'punding'or penning of the sheep was formerly done six times every year. The first, called the 'scoring punding,' took place in February when the sheep were numbered in accordance with the sheep regulations. The second and third 'pundings' were for 'rooing' or clipping. The earlier of these took place about midsummer and the other about a fortnight later.

Sheep dipping made another 'punding' necessary before the start of harvest work. The selection of suitable animals for slaughter accounted for the fifth and sixth 'pundings' of the year. These were carried out just before Christmas and the New Year and Dennis Ness, being considered the most important 'pund' of the island, was always 'punded' on Christmas Eve and New Year's Eve. All 'punding' dates and times had to be fixed so as to coincide with spring tides and high water.

The twelve mile long sheep dyke with its nine 'punds' (five main and four supplementary ones) seldom fails to attract the attention of visitors. Both the age and quality of masonry of the dyke varies greatly. Some of it is very old, while other parts like the section known as the 'moonlight dyke' and some of the outer field-dykes at Dennis Ness and Twinyas are of more recent construction. Built with the sort of stones that lie to hand, it ranges from round sea-polished ones to great boulders that required the combined effort of as many as a dozen men to lift into position.

On the whole it seems to be reasonably well suited to the ground on which it is built. A sandy foundation is matched with a lightly-constructed wall with numerous window-like openings to prevent wind pressure building up and flattening it. On the other hand, sections which have to act as a rampart for houses located near the highwater mark are generally substantially constructed, and may even be dove-tailed into the rock. Another intriguing aspect is the manner in which the dyke thrusts seawards, or bends back leaving a fairly wide margin. This can to some extent be taken as an indication of the degree of land-hunger exhibited by the various crofters concerned. The annexation of common-l!and was, however, disallowed by the Crofter's Act.

Present day conditions have affected people and sheep differently. The dramatic reduction in human population, from 546 in 1881 to a little over a hundred, seems to have had an opposite effect on the sheep.

Very few sheep are used as food nowadays like formerly, and the price of wool is also too low to justify much time being taken away from the more remunerative pursuits of lobster-fishing and beef raising.

With insufficient manpower to maintain the round-the-island dyke in good order, or even keep it sheep-tight, there is already difficulty in preventing the sheep from damaging the growing crops, and in the event of any major dyke damage caused by storm, the animals would be free to stray all over the island as they did before the land squaring. Would such an emergency for the islanders make headlines for the National Press and, perhaps, produce assistance from outside?

Yet, as one of the islanders said, "Lobsters are showing signs of being over-fished; the poultry industry, formerly so profitable, has also fallen on lean times. Crops are always chancy, and Britain's entry into the European Common Market could reduce farming subsidies almost overnight. So everything considered, it would be an evil day if any disaster were to overtake that special breed of North Ronaldsay's native sheep."

It was always believed that the North Ronaldsay or Orkney native sheep are Siberian in origin, though in all probability they had been imported long before the Vikings colonised the islands. This belief has been strengthened recently, when the rare breeds of Asian arkhan sheep have had one of the 50 nature reserves in the Taldy-Kurgan regions in Kazakhstan reserved for them. In pictures they seem almost identical with the present-day North Ronaldsay native sheep.

12

Kelp Making

. . . after 200 years of ups and downs in both demand and price, the tangles—Laminaria— are no longer burned to make kelp, but used as the raw material in a new industry which has come to take its place . . .

Before 1722, North Ronaldsay's profusion of seaweed was being only partially utilised. The self-supporting economy of the island had at that time found just three ways in which this asset could be used. Some of the seaweed was then being dried for domestic fuel. A larger amount provided manure for the cultivated crops, and the island's flock of seaweed-eating sheep also ate as much as they could.

With all these demands fully met, about half of the seaweed was still being wasted. So the introduction of kelp-making to Orkney by James Fea of Stronsay in 1722 soon suggested a way by which one of his relatives by marriage, Mr James Traill, who was then practising as an Edinburgh lawyer, might get in at the beginning of what was likely to be a profitable venture. Anyhow, by 1727 Mr Traill had persuaded Archibald Nisbet to sell his North Ronaldsay estate for £2,222 which probably represents a price of £1 per acre, for the island has an area of just under four square miles.

This new acquisition, with as much as twelve miles of beaches and foreshore, could hardly fail to give a considerable output of kelp once Mr Traill got the industry organised. Like the other Orkney lairds, he was fully aware of a landlord's legal rights and lost no time in allocating the tangle beaches among his crofters, who were expected to make kelp production a condition of their tenancy.

All decisions regarding the management and

marketing were also prerogatives of the laird, but the day by day problems arising from the actual kelp-making were left to the factor and kelp-grieve to settle as they felt inclined, provided that they always encouraged the output from the estate.

As the tangles and ware came in at certain parts of the shore only, these ware nousts and kelp beaches had to be fairly divided among all the crofters and cottars. The way in which shares were apportioned fairly deserves to be mentioned as an example of democracy in action. When all the tenants, to which a particular ware beach had been allocated, gathered to commence the day's work, they first of all divided themselves into two equal groups. Then drawing lots, they decided which group was to make the divisions. A rough-and-ready survey of the ware would then be made by pacing the area and estimating its depth. The required number of shares was then laid out and marked off by pushing in upright pieces of tangle to mark the boundaries. After that it was the turn of the other group to pick their individual shares, and those who had carried out the division could hardly grumble if they happened to be left with inferior lots! The long-term fairness of the system was safeguarded by a change-over of the groups each working day.

Tangle beaches were divided on a permanent yearly basis. Each household was given six to seven yards of beach-head. These divisions were marked off by 'trips' or boundary marks, made by placing two or three stones on top of one another. When necessary further 'trips'could then be used to project these narrow strips of ownership right down the beach to the tide-mark where the tangles were stranded.

The tangles had then to be individually pulled out of the heaped mass of seaweed and 'tailed,' i.e. their fronds removed. The stalks, four or five feet long, had to be carried up above high-water mark. Under ideal conditions they might be carted up to the 'steeths' or stone platforms on which they were 'stacked' in order to dry out for being burned to kelp when the spring and summer came round. When the beach was steep, or otherwise unsuitable for a horse-drawn cart, the tangles had to be carried on a hand-barrow or thrown singly towards the upper end of the beach, to be piled above high-water mark.

In years when seaweed was particularly plentiful the sheep dyke was often used as a ready-made 'steeth.' Crowned by layer upon layer of unshrunk tangles, it became built up to nearly twice its normal height. Later, the drying, 'wuzling'action of a Voar wind reduced this elevated pile to a fraction of its original bulk.

During those good kelp seasons between 200 and 300 tons were produced, and the average output was probably about 150 tons a year for the whole two hundred years that it was made. Like the Stewart's inheritance of the Scottish Crown, North Ronaldsay's kelp industry might have been said to have come with a Traill and gone with a Traill, for the last shipment took place in the early 1930s, a few years after the death of the late William Traill in 1924.

The market price of kelp had fluctuated widely during those two centuries. The Napoleonic wars saw it rocket to £20 a ton, and it was reputed to have reached a peak price of £80 per ton at the height of the 1914-18 war. Such freak prices were, however, short lived. The price being received by the Orkney lairds at the time when the Crofters Commission visited the islands towards the end of the nineteenth century was around £5 per ton.

This price was confirmed by Mr Robert Paterson, Chemical Works, Falkirk, who in replying to a request from the Crofters Commission, stated that he had bought from 1,000 to 1,500 tons of Orkney kelp at that price in 1877-78. The same court also found that freight, insurance, harbour-dues and other expenses worked out at from 8/- to 10/- a ton. In the breakdown of the returns of a particular cargo) to show the exact distribution of kelp money between the laird and his kelp workers, the result was as follows:—

120 tons of kelp were sold for £614 nett. Of this, the kelp workers got £319, leaving £219:18:6d for the landlord after shipping and other expenses had been met. In a percentage form the kelp workers got 52%,

the landlord 36%, and the other 12% was absorbed in shipping and other expenses.

While in the early days of kelp making prices were governed by the law of supply and demand, later on price fluctuations were also caused by changes in the kind of kelp required by manufacturers as a source of certain chemicals. At first the crude alkaline ash was mostly used in the manufacture of soap and caustic soda. Glass-making called at one time for a special kelp made from 'tang,' which had to be cut from the rocks at low tide, and then carried up the ebb above high tide mark and dried in the sun, before being burned.

Iodine was discovered by B. Courtois in 1811 when he was experimenting with kelp-brine during the manufacture of saltpetre. From then onwards iodine and potassium became the chemical elements mainly sought after, and the extent to which these were present influenced the value of all consignments of kelp sent to the market.

As it took from forty to fifty cart-loads of wet seaweed to produce one ton of kelp, it is no exaggeration to say 'it needed a large mixture of drudgery as well as tangles to fill a small bottle of iodine.' A ton of kelp yielded only about 8 lbs. of iodine compound, so other and more convenient sources of supply were always being sought. Extracts from nitrates imported from Chile, and of a by-product from the Californian oil wells, gradually replaced kelp as a source of iodine, so the industry became unprofitable after the end of the 1914-18 war.

Looking back, one has to admit that kelp making was not all unrelieved toil. There were hours of delight as well as weeks and months of drudgery: brief spells when the spring or summer day set aside for burning the tangles brought a blue sky and sparkling sea to wipe away the memory of the cold wet task of collecting the fuel that would keep hungry fires going all day long.

Each of the kelp beaches might have as many as a dozen pits burning at the same time. A pit consisted of a circular hollow with a diameter of five feet and a depth of twelve inches, because experience had shown that, filled with burned ash, one of such dimensions would yield a cart-load of kelp, weighing about half-a-ton or more. It also accommodated all the seaweed that could be conveniently burned in a day.

Although the pits were always sited at, more or less, the same places, they still required to be dug afresh and have their rims relined with new stones each year, owing to damage done by the storms of the previous winter. With the pit ready, a slight breeze blowing straight out to sea was needed to make the ideal 'burning day.' If the weather happened to be almost calm the rate of burning became too slow, and any slight air current had to be caught and directed into the burning seaweed by means of a baffle, a process which was given the local name of 'skyling.'

An alteration to the position of this simple device, which was often improvised by hanging empty sacks on a hand-barrow propped up on edge, could also be used for guiding the flame to any slow-burning part of the pit throughout the whole day. The pit fire had to be started with dry straw, or some other fire-lighting material, and then fed with very dry seaweed until there was a spread of flame to the whole circular furnace. By that time most of the day's fuel would also have been brought within easy reach of the pit attendant, and the tempo of work slowed down to throwing a bundle of tangles whenever the flames burned through to the surface.

Once the flames had a thorough hold, the stoking became less critical. The tangles could then be safely piled much higher, leaving the pit attendants time for strolling over to their neighbours at the next pit for a yarn.

Normally, both men and women shared in the work of kelp burning, relieving each other as required. A spell of settled weather could, however, upset this arrangement. Most of the menfolk would desert the kelp-beach to go haddock fishing. The women-folk, helped by old men and boys, would then take over the tangle burning. Under these conditions, the day's food might be brought to the beach, and the older children enrolled for such minor tasks as they were able to do.

Between their errands the juveniles would always have ample time for playing along the shore, and wading in the sea. The turning over of flat stones in the ebb would always send all sorts of crabs scrambling in search of a new hiding place. The squirming eels would also evade all attempts to catch them, and there would always be flocks of Arctic terns and other sorts of seabirds to watch.

Away out to sea the lobster praams and brown-sailed skiffs or yawls would shuttle past to etch variety into the scene. An occasional passenger liner, and a sprinkling of tramps and trawlers, might also come up over the horizon to add still more memories to those perfect days on the beach.

When called back from these childhood pleasures, the older boys might be asked to take temporary charge of the pit while a sort of picnic meal was being laid out. They had instructions to watch for any spurt of flame and immediately cover it with a bundle of tangles, and these half-hours spent in acting like grown-ups made a welcome break in their enjoyment. The responsibility given them of watching also helped to pass on the practical skills to a rising generation of kelp makers.

By repeating the routine of adding more tangles every time the flames burned through to the surface, all the seaweed would eventually be burned. The molten ash would then almost fill the pit, and hard knots of tangle, or any other imperfectly burned bits, had to be shovelled over and well raked in so as to give an even texture to the finished product.

Two special tools, fashioned by the island blacksmith, were needed for this part in preparing the kelp. The rake and the shovel were both designed to protect the pit attendants from the heat. This was done by giving each a handle of about eight feet long. To withstand the heat, the main part was made of iron, into the split upper end of which the wooden part was fixed. The blade of the shovel was smaller than a normal one and measured only about eight inches by five inches. The rake was also specially designed for its particular purpose by having the working-end bent at a right-angle to the handle.

The six-inch head of the rake allowed a deep-stirring of the white-hot ashes, and this agitation was sometimes increased by simultaneous raking from opposite sides of the pit. The finished kelp would then be smoothed down and sprinkled with water so that he fuzed mass would crack into pieces of convenient size for handling. Without this being-done it would cool into a solid circular slab, and need to be prised up with a crowbar and broken into lumps by a heavy hammer before it could be carted to the storage depot or shipment to the kelp market at Falkirk, or Newcastle upon Tyne.

Every load of kelp had, however, to be weighed and recorded before it could be added to the storage pile. The heavy, grey lumps, with sharp edges and a coarse texture like lava, was hard on hands and clothes as well as on the tempers of those who had to handle them. This sometimes led to a wordy-warfare between the queuing carters and the kelp-grieve.

On one of these occasions, two Easting men who had to cart their kelp from the north to the south end of the island, a distance of nearly five miles, were unfairly upbraided for failing to stow their kelp properly. The upshot of this unjust accusation wasn't the customary observation, "I'll see you in h— before I shovel up kelp belonging to other people," but the terse retort, "I'll see you as matlos on the Auld Kirk windows afore you'll get me doing that." The meaning was, of course, well understood, because dead fish and other carcases always produced swarms of flies!

Yet, in spite of the laborious work and the drastic shrinkage losses in kelp making, the industry brought money to the crofters and also helped to change the barter system. Island rents, formerly paid in grain, or other farm produce, which could often be ill-spared, no longer constituted a threat to next year's seed-corn. If the crofter's family was large and hard working, the kelp would bring enough to settle this yearly exaction, and leave a little over for other purposes.

As long as the demand was good and kelp prices remained reasonably firm, the changeover to a cash economy suited both the laird and the crofters. It also tended to cause a steady build-up of population, eventually so pronounced that any serious set-back to the industry could have brought hunger to the whole community. Many of the small crofts were supporting two brothers with their wives and families, and in one extreme instance a holding of only twenty-seven acres housed and fed three separate families, totalling twenty-four people.

The island laird, Dr. Traill, who also held an important administrative medical post in India, had the business-like acumen which could hardly fail to doubt the long-term wisdom of this development. Against the background of the 'hungry forties' and the 'Irish potato famine,' he eventually decided that a bargain with the laird of Eday to take some of the surplus kelp workers might work out well for all the parties concerned.

After certain negotiations, the landlord of Eday accepted 32 North Ronaldsay people for settlement on the west side of his estate. This transfer took place in 1851, but he may not have been altogether altruistic, for the soil was poor and for the most part uncultivated. It was, however, close to a considerable stretch of mossy banks from which peats might be cut for domestic fuel and for marketing.

Like kelp making, the peat industry also needed a large labour force. It, too, was owned and managed by the local laird, who found it a more lucrative source of income than the actual rents from his estate. Eday peats were at that time in constant demand, as they were used by the whisky distillers of Orkney and other counties of Scotland. So, encouraged by this steady market, which provided constant work, the new community took root. In forty years it had established itself sufficiently to absorb another 13 settlers from North Ronaldsay.

In the latter island, kelp-making continued to absorb so much 'manpower' and 'woman-power' that other enterprises were to a large extent neglected. Neither agriculture nor fishing got the attention and planning which might have made either of them a better proposition than 'tangle gathering.' Other influences and events which were happening far away from the kelp beaches of North Ronaldsay were, however, destined to bring about a change.

New sources of iodine and potassium were being found, and Japan had begun to supply kelp at a cut price that made it difficult for the original suppliers in Brittany, Ireland and the Scottish Islands to hold their share of the market. It was only during the 1914-18 war, and for a short time afterwards, that it again became profitable. By the late twenties, this demand began to dry up, with the result that the two-hundred-year-old industry died, and new ways of making a living had to be found.

This loss proved to be more apparent than real, for the substitution of egg production soon brought not only more, but also more easily-won money than the kelp had ever done. Hardly anyone lamented the passing of what had for so long been 'a way of life.'

But this did not, however, remain the case for long. The 'windrows' of tangles driven ashore by the winter storms were once again to prove their value in a world which had discovered the way to new transformations. With the second world war finished, and peace-time industries re-establishing themselves, tangles once again became a source of some of the chemical elements which in their various combinations help to produce some of the clothing and food required for an ever-increasing world population.

When at this time Alginate Industries started to buy air-dried tangles from North Ronaldsay, interest in seaweed gathering soon re-asserted itself to such an extent that the market became overstocked. In the early 1950s tangle buying from the island had to be suspended for about four years.

Tangles were once again shipped from the island when the demand revived. Alginate Industries bought 150 tons from North Ronaldsay in 1956; 275 tons in both 1957 and 1958; and made a peak purchase of 508 tons in 1959. Since then the yearly shipment has varied between 100 tons and 250 tons. This fall in tonnage is entirely due to depopulation; but the introduction of mechanical aids, and the abandonment of the old system of "parting" the beaches among the crofters of adjacent toonships, so that the island's available manpower can now gather tangles wherever they can be found, have helped to arrest the downward trend. The average annual shipment seems to have stabilized itself at 175 tons.

The price per ton of air-dried tangles has risen from an initial £3:15:0d to £6 in 1956; £8 in 1957; and by degrees to £12 in 1968, £14 in 1969, and £16 in 1970 onwards. Alginate Industries is prepared to help keen tangle gatherers with loans towards the purchasing of tractors, winches and other aids capable of boosting output.

With so many incentives, it is not surprising that all this mechanical equipment more than compensated for the drastic reduction in manpower. It is also interesting to find that at least one of these tractors, with such refinements as an electrically-heated driver's cabin, was made in Czechoslovakia.

It would now seem that the temporary halt in the collection of seaweed during the thirties and forties was only a pause for taking stock, and for finding easier, better and more profitable ways of gathering this harvest from the sea.

13

Island Shipwrecks

*. . . were so frequent that they became a factor in
shaping the island way of life . . .*

Lying close to an important shipping lane, North
Ronaldsay's physical features and lack of height tend to
make it a trap for passing vessels. The low, flat island
might almost be said to hide itself behind a curtain of
spray in winter, and to merge with the banks of fog
that roll in from the sea in summer. These dangers are
intensified by four off-shore shoals: the Altars of Linay
on the north-west corner, the Seal Skerry on the north-
east, the Reefdyke on the southeast, and Twinyas Point
on the south-west. And, as if all these dangers should
prove insufficient, the arrangement of land and sea is
such as to cause a very strong tidal stream to build up
all round this most northerly island of Orkney.

Shipping losses were naturally higher in former
times when there were no aids to navigation, but it has
taken a powerful fog signal and radio beacon, as well as
a tall lighthouse, to make these waters comparatively
safe for the ships that follow this route.

Before 1787, the whole Scottish east coast north of
the Isle of May was still unlit, and although Thomas
Smith and Robert Stevenson completed building the
light at Kinnaird's Head that year, and at North
Ronaldsay two years later, the latter lighthouse did not
prove to be much of a success. Its fixed white light with
an elevation of about seventy feet above sea level could
be mistaken for the mast-head light of another ship,
and it was superseded by a revolving light on the Start
Point of Sanday in 1809.

Many wrecks took place on North Ronaldsay before
the coming of the lighthouse, and in the period between
1809 and 1854, when the present one was lit, there

were many more. Accurate information on all these strandings is, however, difficult to collect, for a systematic record in the form of a 'Wreck' Book kept by the various light-keepers was started only in 1872: eighteen years after the present lighthouse was built, and eighty-three years after the island's first one came into commission.

The details of shipping casualties before that date, and they are numerous, can only be found by patient research. Tradition can generally provide a starting point, but one soon discovers that there is no government department responsible for keeping a record of such information. The back-files of local and shipping newspapers are perhaps the best two sources, provided the searcher has plenty of spare time. Here again though, a difficulty presents itself in the absence of any newspaper index.

Other sources, such as the Hydrographic Department of the Admiralty, the Board of Trade, Lloyd's Register of Shipping, Trinity House, Northern Lighthouse Board, Imperial War Museum, National Maritime Museum, the Shipping Editor, Corporation of Lloyds, and the Registrar of Shipping and Seamen may all help when they are given the exact name of the ship and the date of the disaster. One or both of these requirements are often missing; when, for instance, the handed-down memory may provide only a vague hint like: "The Biscuit and Butter Ship was wrecked somewhere near the old lighthouse when Peter of Cursiter was a growing boy, for one of the shipwrecked crew ripped open a sack of biscuits in order to give some to Peter and the other hungry boys who were playing around at the time. This kindness was, it is said, frowned on by old Charlie o' Howar, who held the post of Receiver of Wrecks at that time." Such a scrap of news has, it will be noticed, failed to preserve the name of the ship and only gives an approximate time for the stranding.

While diligent probing might show that old Peter could have been between six and twelve years of age in c. 1844-50, the absence of the ship's name would most probably make the search fee prohibitive. So a list of the shipping losses that have taken place on North Ronaldsay, or on the off-shore shoals, must be classified in some way other than by strict chronological order.

There are many ways in which different types of shipwreck might be distinguished, and some of the main categories may be listed: Wrecks which have resulted in heavy loss of life; ships which have been reputed to carry valuable cargoes; shipwrecks which have had in one way or another a direct effect on the island way of life; abandoned ships which have been found and towed ashore by the islanders; vessels which have gone aground on the island, or on some off-shore shoal, and which have been refloated.

There is a total of at least 60 or more known shipwrecks which come under one or other of these categories, and the Swedish East Indiaman "Svecia" must head the list. This comparatively new ship went ashore on the Reefdyke in 1740, and sank with the loss of 91 lives and a valuable cargo worth £250,000.

Due to the efforts of Mr Bruce of Sumburgh at the beginning of the present century, Swedish records of this loss became available and were published in Old Lore Miscellany (collected and edited by A. W. Johnston and Amy Johnston 1907 onwards). This item runs as follows: "Orkney Shipwrecks—In Miscellany Vol. 1, page 205, Mr John Smith makes inquiries regarding a wreck at North Ronaldsay in 1740. This was the 'Svecia,' not the 'Suetia' as given in Vol. 3, page 135." Recently, I had some correspondence with the Keeper of the State Archives of Sweden regarding certain Indiamen lost at Shetland, and he further supplied me with the following information, which may be of interest to Orkney friends. The particulars may also be regarded as absolutely reliable.

"The 'Svecia' was owned by the Swedish East India Company, and was built at Gothenburgh. She carried a crew of 100 men, was armed with 30 guns, and had a carrying capacity of 280 Swedish Lasts (560 tons). The 'Svecia' was commanded by Captain Johan Lorentz Rattenborg, and was lost on the homeward voyage from Bengal on 18th November, 1740. She belonged to the port of Gothenburgh, and her first voyage was in 1735, when she went to Bengal. She returned safely to Sweden, and in January 1739 set out on her second voyage to Bengal. It was on the homeward passage of this second voyage that she was wrecked. The carpenter and twelve seamen were saved, and only a small part of her cargo was salvaged. In a letter dated January, 1741 from The Directors of the Swedish East India Company to the Swedish Government, the 'Svecia' is stated to have been wrecked at 'North Ronaldsay' and the Directors solicited that the Secretary of the Swedish Legation in England be asked to try and obtain orders to the Admiral of the Orkney Isles, for 'My Lord Mordon (sic) to assist the Commissioners of the Company with regard to the saved crew and baggage.' "—R. Stuart Bruce.

It has to be added that there is still a lingering island memory, a tradition which, as it seems to fit in with and perhaps strengthen belief in this official version, may be given. It claims that the ship with cargo was jointly owned by twelve wealthy merchants of Gothenburg. These merchants were either on board or represented by close relatives. It is further claimed that these passengers, or Supercargo, hurried below decks in order to save some of their more valuable belongings when they realised that the ship might become a total loss. On getting back to deck, they were horrified to see that the only seaworthy boat had already cast off and was making for land. A hastily constructed raft was, it is said, used to carry all the remaining ship's company to land, but that caught in the ebb-tide and broke up off the Kirk Taing, drowning all on board.

Further research [the outcome of which only became available after this chapter had been compiled] does not agree with this version of what befell the luckless ship's company. The almost daily reports sent from the scene of the disaster to the Vice Admiral of Orkney at that time are still in existence. This correspondence, contained in the Private Morton Papers, and now lodged in the Scottish Record Office, shows that the 13 survivors reached the land on a large piece of the ship's quarterdeck, while the main contingent of those who

perished were making for land on a large raft. This raft
seems to have had a mast and sail as well as having
three punts attached. Unfortunately, this contrivance
sailed into a tide-rip and broke up, drowning all aboard.
The same fate overtook those crewmen who decided to
stick to the ship when she quickly broke apart and sank
to what was described as 'lying at depth of three
fathoms below the surface.'

It is also stated that a regular beach patrol was set
up during the hours of darkness in order to collect the
drowned seamen awaiting identification and burial.
Other islanders were engaged to salvage any cargo
washed ashore.

A list of the ship's Company, supplied by the
Swedish East India Company, shows that the ship was
commanded by Lanziel Agell when she struck the
Reefdyke, both Captain Rattenborg and the First
Officer having died in India. The ship's manifest shows
a valuable cargo, mainly of silks and cottons, but also
including 2,000 maunds of Red Wood (Dye Wood) and
4,000 maunds of Saltpetre. Of the 18,969 handkerchiefs
which were salvaged, it is interesting to note that one is
still preserved. This unhemmed example measures
about 10 inches by 10 inches and carries an in-woven
design. Although now well over two centuries old and
showing slight iodine stains from its contact with
seaweed, it is still strong and stands handling.

In Orkney literature James Fea, a Naval Officer and
a descendant of the Fea of Clestrain who captured the
pirate Gow, writing in his book titled "The Present
State of Orkney and Shetland," mentions the wreck of
the "Svecia," giving the value of her cargo as £500,000.
In this item, which is really a plea for better lighting on
the Orkney coast, a subject also taken up by the Rev.
William Clouston when writing on North Ronaldsay
and Sanday in "The Old Statistical Account," Mr Fea
calls attention to another valuable Indiaman lost on
North Ronaldsay in 1744, only four years after the
wreck of the "Svecia." He says that the "Crown Prince
of Denmark" had thirty chests of treasure aboard, but
that these were saved.

Memories to hand of this disaster are in agreement

that it probably happened on the north-west corner of the island at Sava Geo, but there is some confusion about the name of this vessel, some people thinking that this wreck may have been the "Crown Herod." The real facts seem to have been obscured by time and by lack of local records, but there are still some believers in the "Herod" version who go so far as to say that there used to be a ballad describing how some members of this stranded crew jumped overboard, mistaking the white foam within the geo for firm sand.

This "Crown Prince"—"Crown Herod" legend has now, to a large extent, been cleared up as the result of inquiries at the source. The Curator of Danish Archives and other Danes have been most helpful in this search, and it can now be stated authoritatively that the "Kronprinsen" commanded by Captain Rolf Kjaerulf, carrying a complement of 160 men and armed with 24 carriage guns, grounded on North Ronaldsay on 21/1/1745 (New Style Calendar). She also carried in silver money some 300,000 Rigs dollars (worth about £43,000 Stg. or £516,000 Scots). Such a large amount of money is stated to have been for the purchase of a return cargo from China, to which she was then bound. This was necessary because Denmark was at that time a non manufacturing country. In livestock the "Kronprinsen" had on board 4 bulls, 287 cows, 24 each pigs and sheep, 79 geese, 60 ducks, and 30 turkeys.

There was no loss of life, but the stranded crew managed to land only after considerable difficulty, the Mate Hjort being the hero of the operation. All the money and most of the valuable parts of the ship were salvaged and stored on North Ronaldsay until they could be transported back to Denmark. This took nine months, during which period the Dannebrog was flown on North Ronaldsay and a half-battery of guns salvaged from the wreck stood around Captain Kjaerulf's headquarters.

The rescue operation brought four Danish ships to the island before the last of the men and money were safely back in Copenhagen.

Local names for beach features associated with the wreck are "Crewgather"—where Kjaerulf mustered his men to hear a reading of the ship's Articles, after there had been signs of an incipient mutiny by some malcontents in the camp. The "Geo of Denmark" is probably the place from which the salvaged goods were boated out to the waiting Danish ships at anchor in Linklet Bay.

The Archives of Denmark were, however, unable to trace a vessel called "Crown Herod."

Another Danish ship, captained by Brast and given as 450 tons burden, with a cargo described as sundries and valued at £12,000, also went ashore on North Ronaldsay during the stormy winter of 1782. Although the crew were saved, this wreck was indirectly responsible for the loss of 14 lives. The unfortunate accident is described in a letter from John Traill of Westness, Rousay, to his relative Charles Stewart. This correspondence has also been included and published by Viking Society Publications, London, in "Old Lore Miscellany."

"Kirkwall—24th January, 1783.—The Winter has been very severe in this place, more so than has been remembered by any living. Several ships have been wrecked on our coasts, among them one in North Ronaldsay, Danish property, 550 (?) tuns burthen, loaded with provisions etc., for some of their Colonies.

"There went a boat from Kirkwall with Custom House Officers, and Inspectors etc., to the number of 14 persons. They set out from Kirkwall on 28th December, 1782, but a violent storm breaking out before they could reach the island drove them out to sea and they have not been heard of since, which makes them almost despaired of as it was thought scarce possible that they could live in the open sea. There were nine of the fourteen married, who amongst them leave eighteen children and two of their wives are with child. Mr Thomas Baikie of Burness, brother of Mungo Baikie, whom you know, was one of the officers much regretted, and that worthy gentleman, Mr George Craigie, who went on his own accord as it was requisite that Westness should send some person to prevent imbezzlements by his Tenants. I cannot express what Westness and Lady Westness feels on his account . . ."

The next instance of a wreck accompanied by the loss of life is the Bristol ship "Kit of Bristol" in which the Mate was drowned and was buried in North Ronaldsay churchyard. Details of this mishap are scanty, but as the ship was carrying a cargo of meal, and, in view of the island custom of sometimes naming a beach geo by the nature of the cargo of a vessel wrecked on the spot, it is a fairly safe guess that the "Kit of Bristol"came to grief in Meal Geo, on the south side of Bridesness.

Another shipwreck which resulted in some loss of life was that of the "Prince." She was driven ashore near Versa Geo with a cargo of Archangel tar, of which it is said that traces can still be seen in the cracks and crevices there. This may, however, have no connection with the wreck, as in the geological formation of some Orkney rocks slight traces of tar ooze out of the seams. What is, perhaps, more convincing evidence of the loss of life from this and other shipwrecks at the north-east end of the island is a number of crudely-made graves along this part of the beach.

The winter of 1847 or thereabouts brought another shipwreck that resulted in the loss not only of a new ship, but also of a considerable number of lives aboard her. Carrying a spread of canvas, the large barque "Lena" was taking full advantage of the strong southeaster, when a slight error in course caused her to run ashore at the East Banks (near the Skerries of Senness) instead of clearing the island. As the stranding took place during darkness, and at a time when there was no lighthouse on the island, the chances of such an accident happening must have been very high, so there can be very little doubt that the subsequent inquiry into the loss would stress that a revolving light on the Start Point of Sanday could give only an indifferent guide for safety rounding Dennis Head and allowing plenty of seaway to such dangers as the Reefdyke and Seal Skerry.

There are many local stories about this catastrophe. Whenever the menfolk get round to yarn about shipwrecks, the miraculous survival of the "Lena's Captain" is sure to be mentioned. The story relates how a party of islanders who had gone to the shipwrecked sailors' assistance found a semi-conscious man thrown up by the sea. It was decided to carry him to a nearby house where the "Guidwife" was left to care for him as best she could while the men returned to the wreck to render any necessary assistance.

Such a situation certainly called for resourcefulness, but the Guidwife o' Sholtisquoy seems to have had this quality in good measure. She placed the half-drowned man in the still-warm bed she had just vacated, and then tried to raise his body temperature by giving him a drop of brandy. As there was still no sign of recovery, and fearing that she was losing her battle with death, she decided that she must revive the man with her own body heat. So, removing her outer clothing, she crept in beside the exhausted man and warmed him back to life.

On wakening up, the seafarer came to realise what had happened and that he owed his life to this woman's resourcefulness. Thanking her, he disclosed that he was the captain of the unfortunate ship which had been wrecked that morning, adding: "I shall never forget your kindness, and must send you some token of my appreciation once I get back to my home port."

The remainder of this tale confirms that the captain was as good as his word, and sent his benefactress a silk dress. This present, it seems, came through the local Receiver of Wreck, whose wife is alleged to have thought it far too good for a crofter's spouse. Substituting a cheap, printed cotton, she kept the silk dress for herself. In doing so, however, she collected an unenviable reputation which has long outlasted the silken gown.

Faced with a heavy claim for the loss of this ship and cargo, the underwriters would likely have lodged a strong plea for a lighthouse to be erected on North Ronaldsay.

Evidence of growing pressure for this may perhaps be deduced from the chart-making activity carried out by H.M.S. "Mastiff" in 1847-48. Her soundings were carefully studied and resulted in the building of the present lighthouse at Dennis Head in 1854. This light, generally described as one of the best on the British

coasts, was the work of Allan Stevenson, and the
contractor, Mr Kinghorn, is said to have made a profit
of £6,000 on the job.

Apart from local boating accidents, which will be
included later on in this chapter, there is no record of
any further loss of life in the immediate vicinity of
North Ronaldsay until the tragic foundering of the
sailing ship "Isle of Erin," with the loss of all hands, in
1908. This vessel was thrown on her beam-ends by a
sudden veer to windward in order to avoid running
ashore near the Start Point of Sanday. Damaged and
with shifted cargo, she then remained in distress as she
drifted past North Ronaldsay during the afternoon and
evening of Monday, 19th October, 1908. The plight of
those aboard could not be intimated to the Coastguard
or Lifeboat services, as there was no link by telegraph
with the Mainland of Orkney at that time.

The subsequent Board of Trade inquiry into the loss
advocated the establishment of a Post Office Wireless
Station on the island, and this recommendation was
carried out within a year or two, making North
Ronaldsay one of the first islands in Britain to have a
radio link with the telegraphic system.

In investigating the loss of life occasioned by local
boating accidents, in so far as these are remembered or
are recorded, we discover that nearly all of them have
been connected with transporting people and goods
rather than with fishing. As the island has no natural
haven, or safe anchorage, this is readily understood. In
these accidents, covering a period of over a century, a
total of eleven lives were lost. The first of these
disasters took place when a heavily-laden peat boat
bringing home fuel from Eday was caught in a tide-rip
at Twinyas Point and sank, drowning a Kelday, a
Swanney, and a Thomson. In another Eday accident
three North Ronaldsay men were drowned when their
small boat capsized as they were landing from a larger
craft. The names of those lost on this occasion were
Cutt, Swanney, and Tulloch. The next fatalities took
place in 1873 as the island's parliamentary voters were
returning after casting their votes at the polling booth
in Sanday. The voters had actually been brought back

to the Noust of Howar and were being landed in a small boat from the larger craft when the former was struck by a wave and capsized. All six occupants were thrown overboard, but one of them, John Tulloch of North Ness, managed to grasp an oar and he was rescued. The tide dragged him eastwards towards Stromness Point, where young Charlie o' Howar waded out at considerable danger to himself and managed to lay hold of the man and oar in the nick of time. James Rendall, a Westray man, who was skipper of the parent craft, and his other two companions in the small boat were drowned. Both of them were Tullochs from North Ronaldsay. The other two men, a Cutt and a Tulloch, had meantime reached the shore.

The Noust of Howar claimed another victim in 1895. In the late evening of a December day of that year a boat capsized as it came in to land after returning from Sanday. One of the men, Robert Cutt of Gerbo, failed to get ashore. He was a married man, and left a widow and three young sons, the eldest of whom was only 7 years.

The year 1914 brought another kind of accident connected with the sea which claimed the life of a promising young man, Bobby Tulloch, son of Tammie o' Breckan, the Post Boat man, who had gone as a hired hand for the herring season. The Stronsay boat on which he was serving was returning from the fishing ground when Bobby came into close contact with a suddenly tightening sheet. Thrown off his balance, and perhaps stunned by the blow, he went overboard and was drowned before the boat could turn round to pick him up.

Another category of wrecks that may be grouped together are those where, although there was no loss of life, the salvaged ship or cargo seems to have had an influence on the island economy and way of life. The "Royal Oak," which grounded at Bride's Eddy (Ethy) during dense fog on 15th August, 1882, provides a good example. This vessel became a total wreck, but the cargo of dressed timber was salvaged. It was bought by a Kirkwall wood merchant, who employed local labour and boats to discharge the wood and ship it to Kirkwall.

Not only did this bring some money to the islanders at a time when the kelp industry was at a low ebb, but also helped to make many of the houses more comfortable by providing cheap tongued-and-grooved boards for wooden floors and ceilings.

The "Skotfos," a Norwegian vessel of 767 tons, went ashore on the Seal Skerry on 15th January, 1915. This wreck was probably due to Dennis Head light being obscured in conformity with wartime regulations in force at the time. As the ship grounded shortly after high water, she was left almost high-and-dry with full ebb. This allowed the crew of 16 to land on the rocks and climb on to the higher part of the Skerry. They were then brought ashore in three island boats during the afternoon of the following day. The weather remaining comparatively calm for the next day or two, enabled Captain Jorgensen and some members of the crew to return to collect the ship's papers and other personal belongings that had been left behind when they first abandoned the vessel. Conditions deteriorated shortly after this visit, and the grinding of the iron hull on the rocks produced sparks which are thought to have ignited the combustible cargo of carbide, wood pulp and timber, turning the blazing wreck into an unauthorised lighthouse that defied the wartime security regulations.

The ship and charred remnants of the cargo were eventually purchased by a group of local fishermen, who on starting salvage operations found that most of the carbide had escaped destruction. It had been loaded in one, or two, hundredweight drums and a good proportion of these remained intact under a protective layer of burned debris.

Although most of the recovered materials were sold on the open market, sufficient carbide was bought by the local crofters to light every island home and steading for years to come. As one North Ronaldsay man put it: "The 'Skotfos' exorcised the last remaining ghosts and trows by lighting up all the dark corners where they used to bide!"

Another two Scandinavian timber ships, the Norwegian "Geizina"and the Swedish "Munin," might be said to have provided a bonus of low-priced wood for the island at just the right time for making henhouses and allowing the crofters to take advantage of a producer's egg market. Both of these vessels grounded during dense summer fogs: the "Geizina" in July, 1925 and the "Munin" in August, 1926. The "Geizina" ran aground on the north side of Dennis Head, near the Old Beacon, while the "Munin" struck the Reefdyke. Both ships refloated after jettisoning their deck cargoes. The drifting wood either floated ashore, or was picked up by local boats in order that it could be bought from the underwriters and used as stated. These two mishaps may have also increased the pressure for better navigational aids in these waters, and thereby hastened the arrival of a Fog Signal and Radio Beacon. Anyhow, additional safety aids were installed at Dennis Head Lighthouse a few years later.

Many other vessels, stranded on the island or on the off-shore shoals, seem to have been refloated. Occasionally this was accomplished by a rising tide and the vessel's own efforts. In other cases local people rendered valuable assistance in helping to get out kedge anchors. It might also happen that a passing trawler would help to tow the grounded vessel off. Most of these later cases resulted in a disputed salvage claim which had to be resolved in a court of law.

Some of the vessels which ran ashore and were later refloated were the "Brother Falken," "Cavae," "Loch Kildonan," "Howard," "Brinbilla," "Wulf," "Fray Montes," and "Slepner." A German trawler grounded near the Galt Rock in Linklet Bay. The name of this trawler, "Griff," seems to have been generally forgotten, although some of the island's older generation can remember that the crew of one local boat were awarded £10 for helping to place the kedge anchor by which the vessel managed to pull herself off the sandy bottom. Several German emigrant ships are also reputed to have been stranded and later refloated from the Reefdyke, or from Linklet Bay. On being surveyed for damage upon her arrival at New York one of these ships was still carrying a lump of North Ronaldsay rock wedged in her fore-foot.

Local tradition retains the story of another German emigrant ship, with a large proportion of female workers on their way to join their menfolk in the United States, as having been stranded near Hooking, but later refloated. This vessel is said to have been damaged when being kedged off, but to have continued with the voyage in a forlorn attempt to reach her destination. She appears to have gone missing, presumed lost with all on board. Although the name of this unfortunate ship has not been preserved, the approximate time of the tragedy was between 1847 and 1866, during the period that the Rev. John Keillor was Parish Minister.

In yet another category, at least two 'abandoned' ships were found and towed to the island. One of these, "Betsy," a brig, was found drifting off the northern part of the island and towed into Garsowick. The other, also a brig, named "Joel," had been ashore on the Reefdyke and lost her rudder before the crew left. They were presumably picked up by some passing craft. After being found she was salvaged and brought to land by John Muir, Burray, who had himself sailed to most of the world's ports and served on a variety of different rigs, ranging from coastal smacks to full-rigged ships.

Of the wrecks not yet mentioned, at least 23 happened before any Record of Wrecks was kept at the Lighthouse. This log was, however, commenced in 1872 and has been regularly entered up since then.

Brief details of previous island shipwrecks going back another 144 years, from 1728 to 1872, have, however, been collected from various sources such as the Scottish Record Office, Orkney books, newspaper files (especially "The Orcadian") and this help is gratefully acknowledged.

This list runs as follows:—

1728—English Whaler homeward bound with a full cargo of oil and skippered by Anderson, a Scotsman.
1732—"Zaandam of Zaandam," Master Gerabrud, and also the "Vrow Maria" of Amsterdam.

1734—"Den arend" of Zaandam, Holland.

1768—"Drottingham" of Stockholm, Master Lisberg.

1771—"Rose" from Dantzig, Master Wardlaw: and also the "Brothers"of Greenock.

1778—Dutch ship of 350 tons, Master Tromp.

1787—"Fanny," a 200 ton British ship, Master Wetheral, and an unnamed Danish ship of 500 tons, Master Dewes.

1788—Another unnamed German ship from Dantzig, Master Clingenberg.

1793—"Forunta," Norwegian ship, bound Barcelona, Master Andrewsen.

1814 (pre)—Ship carrying, a cargo of claret, mentioned in Stevenson's Memoirs.

1815—"Soltes" of Gothenburgh, Master Martinsen.

1818—Unnamed timber-drogher bound for Belfast from Norway.

1826—"Ida," "Wilhelmina Henrietta" and "Neptunus," three German ships stranded on the same day (see fuller description at the end of this list).

1830 (circa)—"Eva," ex-frigate, carrying bricks and tiles designated for a British port.

1830 (circa)—"London," an American ship of Newburgh N.Y. In this shipwreck the Captain's son was drowned and is buried in the North Ronaldsay Kirkyard.

1840 (circa)—"Kit of Bristol" at Meal Geo. Mate drowned and buried in North Ronaldsay Kirkyard.

1880 (circa)—"Brother Falken" and "Cavae," both Norwegian ships. Both refloated.

Regarding the convoy of three German ships on voyage from Dantzig to Liverpool, which all stranded close to each other on the night or early morning of the 11th March, 1826 between the Geo of Bewan and Dennistaing, the mishap must have taxed the island's ability to feed so many extra people, especially at the end of the winter, when supplies of both food and fuel would be low. {The sheltering of the 30 or more sailors would also have had to be shared, for there are definite indications that these officers and men stayed on the island for a considerable time in order to carry out the salvaging of material from the wrecks.

Strong evidence of this stay is afforded by the fact that the names of three Captains concerned are still remembered, while those of most ships' officers who have been wrecked since then are forgotten. It is understandable that time, helped by the distinctive North Ronaldsay dialect, has handed on its own version of these German names.

Schurer of the "Ida" has become Sho'er.
Thurlow of the "Welhelmina Henrietta" has
    become To'er.
Bradenahl of the "Neptunus" has become
    Broadnal.

Wrecks extracted from the aforementioned Lighthouse Log of Shipwrecks are:
1872 "Antonia"; 1875 "Arthur"; 1882 "Royal Oak"; 1886 "Garibaldi"; 1897 "Elgin"; 1898 "Jessie & Catherine"; 1905 "Swallow"; 1910 "Strathcona" and "Helios"; 1911 "Alice Doods"; 1912 "St Nicholas"; 1915 "Skotfos"; 1916 "Brindilla"; 1925 "Geizina"; 1926 "Munin"; 192(?) "Ludwick Saunders"; 1939 "Mim" and "Hansi"; 1942 "Lagnholm" (Swedish ship sunk 60 miles W.N.W. of island by gunfire from enemy submarine and crew landed in 2 boats); 1957 "Mistley."

As full details of all the above losses may easily be had by anyone sufficiently interested, it may be sufficient to close this 1872 to 1957 list with the names of some "Refloated" vessels that it has not been considered necessary to enter, but which are still remembered locally.

1905—"Griff."
1908—"Loch Kildonan" and "Howard."
1916 (circa)—"Wulf " (armed German Raider of 1914-
    1918 war).
1917—"Varing" (Swedish ship sunk by submarine in a
    position N.W. of the island. Crew landed in 2
    ship's boats).
1919—"Vedic" and "Frayes Montes" (both troopships
    bringing back soldiers from Murmansk).
1924—"Slepner" (Icelandic Packet) .

1936—"Bohemian Boy."

No stranding or other shipping casualty has occurred at the island since 1957.

As there is now Coastguard equipment, and a lookout is maintained during rough weather, it may not seem amiss to recall a rescue of former times when there were no such organised aids at hand. The rescue of the crew from the Aberdeen trawler "Swallow," which ran ashore on Tonguee (the west point of the Seal Skerry) during the hours of darkness on the night of 1st September 1905, has always been accepted as the perfect example of what may be accomplished by small undecked boats when every member of their crews is fully experienced, and intimately acquainted with tides and other local conditions. By taking advantage of the right state of tide, when the heavier breakers are temporarily pushed away from the rocks, both the crews of North End fishermen were able to dash in and snatch Skipper Caie and his crew from certain death. So critical was the timing of this rescue that the next flood-tide brought the break-up and disappearance of the trawler.

The following sequel to the wreck of the "Garibaldi"is interesting. The ship's white-painted figurehead of the Italian Patriot somehow found a place in the garden of the Kirkwall Receiver of Wrecks. There it gradually acquired the description of "The Ghost at the Bottom of our Garden." It was ultimately donated to the Nautical Museum and lodged in the "Cutty Sark," where it may still be seen.

14

The Lighthouses

*The present-day lighthouse of Dennis Head and
the former one, now an unlit beacon standing
near the high-water mark on Kirk Taing,
represent between them one hundred and eighty-
two years of lighthouse development culminating
in such refinements as a visibility-range of
eighteen miles, an up-to-date fog signal, and a
radio beacon.*

Many shipwrecks, both British and European, had
taken place at North Ronaldsay before their too
frequent occurrence forced the government to build a
lighthouse there. There can be little doubt that it was
the alarming stories of discontent and unrest leaking
out of France and eventually leading to the French
Revolution, that convinced our government of the
English Channel suddenly becoming a dangerous place
for British shipping.

A study of the conditions under which the Pentland
Firth, or the fifty mile wide channel between the
Orkneys and Shetlands, might become the nation's only
outlets to the Atlantic led to an alarming discovery. The
whole North-East and North-West coasts of Scotland
were still un-lit.

A hurried plan to build at least a few key-
lighthouses on these coasts resulted in an approach
being made to Thomas Smith, who carried on the
business of ship's chandler in Edinburgh. His
knowledge of ships' lanterns may have been considered
a useful qualification in one who was being asked to
light up the coastline, but an additional
recommendation could have been his close ties with an
already well-established firm of builders. At any event,
nothing was left to chance, for Mr Smith and his son-in-

law, Robert Stevenson, were sent to Cornwall and Devon on a tour of the lighthouses so that they might return with a practical insight into their construction.

It had by this time been decided that funds would be made available for four new lighthouses on the Scottish coast; two on the north-east coast and another two on the west. The two on the north-east side were located at the danger points of Kinnaird Head and North Ronaldsay. The siting on the northmost island of Orkney rather than at the entrance to the Pentland Firth may have been decided on because of the greater sea room for sailing ships to pass between Orkney and Shetland than was available in the shoal-studded Pentland Firth, where the strong tides would have been another obstacle.

The construction of Kinnaird Head lighthouse was immediately put in hand, and completed in 1787, whereupon Smith and Stevenson began to plan and make preparations for the second north-east coast one at North Ronaldsay. It was positioned close to the high-water mark at Kirk Taing (the north-east corner of Dennis Head). The tower was about 70 feet high and it was built of undressed stones obtained in the vicinity. The mortar, or lime, was also procured locally by burning sea shells collected in the island. It must be said that this combination has produced a very strong and substantial structure, which nearly two centuries of wind and weather have left absolutely sturdy and upright.

Although there is no full record of the ships lost while this Old Lighthouse was in commission, there can be little doubt that it was considered unsatisfactory after nearly twenty years' trial. In 1806 it was Sanday's turn for a lighthouse. With an unlit beacon at the Start Point of Sanday, the lantern from North Ronaldsay was transferred there, and the round stone ball (9 feet in circumference) which had hitherto marked, or identified, the Start Point beacon was shipped across to Dennis Head in order to fulfil its purpose in its new situation.

The improvements which were being introduced in lighthouse illumination at the beginning of the nineteenth century resulted in the Start Point being given a revolving type lantern before the end of 1809. While this refinement overcame the difficulty of distinguishing between a low-powered fixed light, like the former one at Dennis Head, and that of a ship's mast-head light, its benefits were confined to the vicinity of the eastern approaches to Sanday. Navigators proceeding northwards to pass North Ronaldsay soon came to realise that the island's off-shore shoals of the Reefdyke and Seal Skerry made necessary another lighthouse to be sited somewhere near its north-east point.

But funds were scarce and a further forty-eight years were allowed to pass before the government of the day granted the money for the Northern Lighthouse Board to send another Stevenson to plan and build this much needed one.

During the time that the island remained unlit, the old, ball-surmounted beacon could serve only as a daytime landmark when visibility was good. Some of the associated buildings did, however, come to be used in a way that the builders can hardly have had in mind. The living quarters of the former lightkeepers are said to have been brought into use as a temporary dwelling for one of the new crofts then being broken out from the uncultivated common ground at Dennis Head. This in an indirect way also helps to illustrate the ill-considered siting of this first lighthouse, for this family were twice forced to leave this dwelling hurriedly when storms with high tides flooded their home.

Despite the scanty records of this period, there is some evidence of at least nine ships having been wrecked on the beach or on the off-shore reefs between 1806 and September 1854 when the new Dennis Head lighthouse was brought into commission.

Lighthouse engineering had made considerable strides in these forty-eight years, giving Allan Stevenson immeasurably better resources than those which had been available to Mr Smith and his son-in-law Robert Stevenson when they first tried to light the island. The surrounding coastline had now been carefully surveyed by H.M.S. "Mastiff." With accurate charts and other essential data available, the new lighthouse was so located as to give the maximum warning of such dangers as the Reefdyke and the Seal Skerry, as well as the island itself. This was accomplished by building the tower on the knoll of Versa Breck and employing a powerful lantern placed at a height of 140 feet.

Looked at from a distance, this slightly tapering tower surmounted by a circular, railed platform leading to the lantern casing, makes an impressive contrast to the flat countryside with its low-set crofts. The lighthouse is built with red bricks, and marked by two white bands. From ground level upwards the sequence is red brick, white band, red brick, white band, red brick finishing with the lantern casing. The light itself consists of a white flash of about 1 second duration every 10 seconds, visible for 18 miles in clear weather.

Near the lighthouse there is also a flagpole which was formerly used to exchange signals with passing ships as well as for a time-flag, hoisted at exactly nine o'clock every Sunday morning. The latter signal provided the islanders with an opportunity to synchronize their clocks and watches, an operation which incidentally removed any excuse for being late for the kirk! When the advent of broadcasting also gave the correct time the custom was discontinued shortly after the First World War.

This "Nerv" Dennis Head lighthouse still has its masts, even if they are of a different kind. Aerial masts, buildings to house electrical generators, and air compressors break up the immediate foreground. A stand carrying rows of differently-pitched horns also adds variety to the scene. All this equipment is now considered necessary for the greater safety of life at sea. How they have gradually come into being is a different story which may now be told in greater detail.

Allan Stevenson, and his building contractor Mr Kinghorn, had every reason to be proud of their handiwork. Labour was plentiful and cheap in North Ronaldsay in the 1850s, allowing a well-built structure to be erected. The lighthouse is claimed to have cost around £30,000, out of which Mr Kinghorn was reputed

to have made a profit of £6,000; but he was not so lucky
with his next contract at Whalsay Skerries, where he
miscalculated the difficulties and lost most of the profit
from the North Ronaldsay job.

The lighthouse pier, making the Geo of Bewan, is
another example of the work carried out under the
Dennis Head contract. As the island had neither a pier
nor any natural haven where building materials could
be easily unloaded, the construction of a jetty had to
preclude the building of the lighthouse itself. This jetty
is, however, unlike the concrete structures of today. It
consists of very large slabs of stone set on edge and
bolted together to provide a landing stage where boats
can come alongside at most stages of the tide. Such
stores as coals, oil, and other necessities were landed
there and carted to the lighthouse, a distance of nearly
half-a-mile. Whatever its merits or demerits, this
particular style of pier construction has this to
commend it—its durability. Over a century of fierce
south-easterly gales has left it practically intact;
perhaps the most appropriate memorial to the Easting
Men, who quarried and placed these large stone slabs,
some of which weigh over a ton!

There is no doubt that the lighthouse was, and still
is, the only building in the island which can be said to
have lines and proportions which can really be
regarded as of good architectural design. It shows what
can be achieved by a skilful architect when he is
provided with adequate resources. A comparison of its
graceful proportions with the stiff lines of the former
tower shows just how far the Stevenson family had
progressed in lighthouse engineering in the period of
sixty-five years between 1789 and 1854.

North Ronaldsay men and boys who either took part
in, or watched the building being erected, must have
benefited from this practical demonstration of the
mechanics and construction, and of the handling of
heavy materials. Any youngster with a curious and
inquiring mind could not fail to absorb the principle of
cranes and derricks and come to appreciate that such
aids as long crowbars, and multi-fold tackle 'gave one
man the strength of ten.' Some of the tips picked up

there would in time be applied in raising and positioning the heavy flagstones since used in roofing the island houses, and also in hauling ashore the herring boats to safe winter quarters after the fishing season was finished.

The flashing white light which sweeps over and lights up the land as well as the sea has always given direction to those who go out visiting on a dark night in that it has helped them to avoid the pitfalls of ditches and dykes. There can be no doubt that this 'beam' has always been a grand morale-booster for us islanders as well as a welcome sight to the duty officer of many a passing ship.

It is understandable that the Lightkeepers would always be accepted as members of the community and have on their part often given unstinted aid in helping forward such projects as a community centre and other self-help objects. As those who served in last century, or the early part of this one, are now almost forgotten, it may not be inappropriate to mention two of them. The one was a Lightkeeper long before my own period as an 'occasional,' the other was serving during my time.

Records show that the very first Principal when the lighthouse was lit in 1854 was John Sinclair. It was nearly a century later that Principal Arthur Hughson, who hailed from the island of Unst, Shetland came to do his ten years' stretch there. Hughson not only had a pleasant personality, but was also an excellent organiser. This was fully recognised by his employers, the Northern Lighthouse Board, who selected him as Head for their, then, latest light at Strathy Point, Sutherlandshire. He was also allowed two outstanding Assistants to accompany him to his new station, and the official opening ceremony attracted many notable planners of the Lighthouse and Shipping world.

Almost every generation that has grown up in the island since 1854 has given its quota of young men as lightkeepers. The Northern Lighthouse Service has never had any difficulty in finding the occasional keepers required for covering such eventualities as holidays or illness of the regular staff at Dennis Head

Lighthouse. A number of local girls have married into the Service throughout the years.

Some record of the local men, who have spent most of their lives on the lonely rocks and other isolated places where the Scottish lighthouses are located, may be of general interest and therefore justified at this stage.

Of those still remembered, Thomas Tulloch of Rue left the island to become a lightkeeper some time after the middle of the nineteenth century. The next thirty years, or thereabouts, saw Martin Thomson, Peckhole, John Thomson, Bewan, and John Muir, Midhouse join the service. After another interval Robert Tulloch, Upper Linnay and Robert Thomson, Antabreck donned the 'blue uniform and brass buttons.' Then, shortly after World War One, John Scott, North Manse, and Charles Tulloch, Ancum, followed their example. This trek from a remote island to what was sometimes an even remoter lighthouse station continued again after World War Two, when two brothers, John W. Thomson and Thomas H. Thomson, both of Nether Linnay, followed suit.

Every one of these ten men seems to have had the right temperament for making good lightkeepers. Only the last-mentioned two are still serving. Of the others who are still alive, John Scott and Charlie Tulloch are now retired after having been Principal Lightkeepers on a variety of lighthouse stations. John Scott also made a very efficient secretary of the Union of Lightkeepers for a lengthy spell.

Of those who joined during the last century, John Muir of Midhouse had already served a full apprenticeship as a ship's carpenter, and had been employed on the Forth Railway Bridge throughout its entire construction. He had thus acquired a variety of skills and experiences which was to stand him in good stead during part of his life on a rock-station.

His record of twelve years' continuous service on Skerryvore is most unlikely ever to be broken. While in charge of that station, he planned and carried out a scheme that greatly improved the landing facilities.

The Lighthouse Board no doubt appreciated such

voluntary work by their employees, for the annual Parliamentary Grant to the Scottish lighthouses was far from generous if that of the "1871-72 Mercantile Marine Fund: Northern Lighthouses" is taken as an example:—

Maintenance of Lighthouses ....£	24,063	12	8
Buoys and Beacons	1,229	10	4
Steam & Sailing Vessels	7,284	10	8
Office & House Expenses	641	0	0
Salaries	2,870	19	5
Miscellaneous Expenses	1,415	6	4
Collection Charges	519	15	3
Superannuation of Officers & Clerks ...	1,781	19	3
TOTAL	£39,806	13	11

The same set of approved estimates showed that the grant to Trinity House for its English lighthouses in the year 1871-72 amounted to nearly six times as much as the sum allowed the Northern Lighthouses.

A parlimentary discussion on lighthouses in the year 1908 elicited the fact that the lighting of the French coast was superior to that of the United Kingdom. It provided undisputed proof that France had three times more lighthouses per mile of coast than Scotland.

With these glimpses of general lighthouse information, it would have been a miracle if the new Dennis Head lighthouse of 1854 had prevented any further stranding of ships on North Ronaldsay. At least thirty sail or steam vessels have grounded or sunk in the vicinity since that September night when Allan Stevenson's newly completed tower began to send out its warning beams. It must in fairness be added that most of these ships ran aground during dense fog, bad visibility, or when the light was obscured in the 1914-18 and 1939-45 wars.

The comparatively few instances when Dennis Head lighthouse failed to give adequate warning must be weighed against the thousands of occasions when it has flashed out a timely signal. One of the early disadvantages associated with Dennis Head was something entirely independent of lighthouse design. North Ronaldsay remained unconnected to the telegraphic system until a year or two before the 1914-18 war: a situation which in effect isolated Britain's highest headland-sited lighthouse from the lifeboats and other organisations brought into being for the greater safety of life at sea. How many more years it might have taken to bring this link-up had there not been the tragic loss of the "Isle of Erin" must always remain problematical. In actual fact, this stricken sailing ship remained within sight of the lighthouse for over seven hours without the lightkeepers being able to summon aid, and she eventually foundered, with the loss of 19 lives.

The subsequent Board of Trade inquiry strongly recommended that North Ronaldsay be linked to the existing telegraphic network at Sanday. This followed in the form of a low-powered wireless station operating from the island post office. The developments of the next decade or so made the advantages of wireless communication so evident that all the Northern Lighthouses were directly connected by a radio telephonic link.

By 1932, it had also become apparent that a sound warning could be more important than a visual one when banks of summer fog build up in the locality. So that year saw the installation of a fog signal and a radio beacon. Post-war discoveries in the field of lighthouse engineering have brought other improvements. Experiments designed to overcome the uneven radiation of sound during fog have resulted in a new warning system, an arrangement in which fog horns of different sizes and pitches are spaced so as to project their combined blast in a way calculated to eliminate the areas of poor reception that have hitherto been an obstacle to the provision of an efficient fog signalling system.

Nine years have passed since the last stranding of a ship on either the island or its off-shore shoals, and thus it would seem that modern science has removed most of the hazards of this coastline. There can, however, still be the rare occasion when a navigator places too much reliance on his 'push-button helpers' and finds the island as solid as ever!

But generally speaking, the shipping going eastward, or westward, past Dennis Head now has a greater margin of safety than the most optimistic seafarer could have foreseen a century ago. The story of North Ronaldsay's two lighthouses, covering nearly the whole period of Scotland's Northern Lighthouses, also helps to show the part that the lighting of the coast has played in reducing the risks associated with the transportation of passengers and goods by sea.

A former island minister, when announcing the singing of the usual first six verses of Psalm 119, liked to add: "Let our tower with its 167 steps (which, by the way, is the same number of steps as there are verses in this psalm) continue to guide the seafarer wherever it be Thy will to lead him."

15

Religion and the Churches

. . . pagan rites, the standing stone, archaeological relics, evidence of Celtic missionaries, early chapel sites, the Auld Kirk, lists of Ministers and Readers, Disruption, the New Kirk, list of Free Kirk Ministers and Lay Preachers Re-union and how the Church fares today . . .

Pagan rites and Christian forms of worship must have co-existed in Rinansay for a long time before 995 A.D., the year when the Norwegian King, Olaf Tryggvason, forced Earl Sigurd to adopt the Christian religion for his earldom as the only alternative to having his son put to death on the spot.

Whatever may be thought about the merits or demerits of this compulsory mass-conversion, there seems to be ample evidence that Celtic missionaries from either St. Ninian or St. Columba had reached Rinansay and other outlying islands of Orkney as much as three or four centuries before the Norsemen began to colonise them. Excavating at the ruined Broch of Burrian and elsewhere on his estate, the late Dr. Traill recovered a number of relics in which the Cross and pagan symbols are equally evident.

These finds are preserved in the National Museum of Antiquities of Scotland, Edinburgh. The two most important ones are a Celtic church bell and an inscribed ox bone. The latter is marked with a designmade by intertwining Christian and Pictish symbols, showing how the new religion was grafted on to the trunk of old belief. Watching over this growth, the first Celtic missionaries would probably meet with stiff opposition. The idea that their chapel could ever make a better 'place of inspiration' than the standing stone, that had never failed to foreshadow the Seasons, would not readily take on!

This thirteen-foot-high monolith with its sighting hole would provide the right setting for the leader and 'wise ones' to give out edicts, or instruct their followers as to what would be required to placate the Gods and bring a good crop. It would also mark the place where younger members of the community could stage their ritual dances on a bright night when the full moon lit up the countryside. According to the Rev. William Clouston, parish minister of Cross, Burness and North Ronaldsay from 1773 to 1793, a modified version of this time-honoured custom survived down to the beginning of the eighteenth century, when New'e'r Night dancing was still held at the stone.

It may also have been the place where all important promises and vows were made. In this connection it must, however, be pointed out that the circular hole in the stone is scarcely large enough to have allowed the contracting pair to shake hands in the manner described by Sir Walter Scott in "The Pirate." This does not make the lichen-crowned sentinel any less impressive. The waving grey tufts of fungal hair convey the impression of a very old man, a man who has looked out over the land and the sea for such a long time that he has seen most of the island's history being made. His recollections could cover coracles and longships as well as the small aeroplane coming in to land in the next field. And looking towards the Auld Kirk, and the New Kirk, this Standing Stane might be excused if it claimed to be the first symbol erected in order to placate the "Unknown" and the "Feared."

With the coming of the Celtic missionaries, small Christian chapels seem to have been set up in two or three different parts of the island. Traces of these cells are, or were until very recently, evident at Cross Kirk, near Sholtisquoy, where there is also evidence of a burial ground.

This claim seems to be strengthened by the presence of the Old Norse place-name Griö, meaning peace, sanctuary, or security. Another place of early worship is indicated by the name Bride's Kirk, at the south-east corner of the island, while Rinar's Hill, now the Kirk Brae with its Parish Kirk and island burial ground, is also likely to have been a religious meeting place from a very early date.

The manner in which Christianity fared in Rinansay after Earl Sigurd had to adopt it as the religion for his Earldom remains a matter for conjecture. It is unlikely that there would be any sudden rush to the Galilean creed, but it is also feasible that Ragna and her son Thorstein would play safe by setting aside some corner of the Bu at Kirbest as a chapel, while also remembering the power of such well-tried Gods as Thor and Woden.

This slow replacement of the old religion by the new may have paralleled what was occurring in Norway. There, many of the people, reluctant to sever entirely their links with a pagan past, paid lip-service to both the old gods and the new.

North Ronaldsay, in common with the remainder of Orkney, would have contributed its quota of labourers for the building of St Magnus Cathedral. There is a tradition that the islandmen collected the nickname 'Selkies' because of the seal steaks by which they nourished themselves while engaged in this work. Possibly they returned home with an appreciation of what can be accomplished by planning and united effort, and in the mood to build a small church of their own.

Such a place would only be built on a modest scale and be no more than a simple stone erection, perhaps having a thatched roof and only a slightly larger version of the other island dwellings. It must have been difficult to secure enough kirk lands to support a minister or reader. Without such maintenance, it would have been unreasonable to expect anyone of education and ability to pursue his calling in the island.

Ecclesiastical records do, however, show North Ronaldsay as an old parish, but one which was for long considered too small for separate status. It is mentioned as part of the Chancellor James Annand's benefice, centred on Lady Kirk in Sanday, but which included Cross Kirk (also in Sanday), the benefice of Papa Westray, and St Colm's (or St John's) Kirk in North Ronaldsay. In such a scattered group, it was inevitable that Annand should require the assistance of local Readers and Exhorters.

By 1567 Chancellor Annand was either assisted, or succeeded, by John Graham of Sanday's Lady Kirk. He had as a reader Thomas Tailyour, who helped in both Sanday and North Ronaldsay at that time. Twenty-four years later, in 1593, North Ronaldsay is again mentioned. On this occasion the island had its own minister, John Bonar A.M., who obtained his degree at the University of St Andrews in 1582. As it is thought that he held the charge of Abbotsrule at or about the same time it is unlikely that he devoted much of his time to his North Ronaldsay congregation.

After a brief spell of this fully qualified minister, the island by 1615 had become part of yet another re-grouping; this time it was absorbed into a viable unit with the Stronsay and Eday parishes where Magnus Paplay and James Oswall acted as readers. Then, around 1673 when James Strachan had been appointed to Cross and Burness, it was again thought more convenient to have North Ronaldsay linked with Sanday, making it the Parish of Cross and Burness and North Ronaldsay. By 1691 a John Tulloch is listed as Strachan's reader in North Ronaldsay.

It was also during the period covered by the preceding paragraph that the Rev. Alexander Smith A.M. was outlawed to North Ronaldsay as a punishment. His covenanting activities and disrespect for Archbishop Sharp's edicts had resulted in his being removed from his church in Colvend, Dumfriesshire. He had been involved in a previous banishment to an uninhabited island in Shetland, from which he had escaped before being transported to North Ronaldsay in 1668. Correspondence between Alexander Smith and Sheriff Blair shows that Mr Smith preached to the people of North Ronaldsay, but his stay in the island cannot have lasted very long as records confirm that he was allowed back to Edinburgh, where he died

It is amazing that around 1681 the then minister of Cross and Burness and North Ronaldsay failed to pay his Reader, John Tulloch, any salary for over 3 years. As the amount claimed for this North Ronaldsay service was only £28 Scots, Tulloch's pay could only have been under 4d. per Sunday in English money. The Bishop and Brethren ordered Mr Strachan to pay the due amount of £28 Scots by Hallowmas, adding that this was for bygone services, and that for time to come, John Tulloch might keep the marriage money together with any penalties that might be got in the island.

Following Mr Strachan, the ministers of the united parish, for the better part of a century—until 1772—numbered six. They were:—

Richard Mein, A.M.............................1683 to 1703
Murdoch McKenzie, A.M. ....1704 to 1710
Thomas Covingtree, A.M. ....1711 to 1744
James Tyrie ....1746 to 1747
John Scollay, A.M.............................. 1749 to 1766
and Hugh Sutherland ....1768 to 1772

During this period the Sanday based ministers probably visited the northern part of their parish only occasionally, leaving the routine duties to their local Readers, who on the whole, seem to have carried out these tasks in a satisfactory manner.

The next Cross-Burness and North Ronaldsay minister, the Rev. William Clouston, left behind a very accurate and detailed account of North Ronaldsay in the form of notes on the island contributed to the First Statistical Account of Scotland, published between 1791 and 1799. Mr Clouston's successor, the Rev. William Grant, A.M. held the Cross and Burness charge for 54 years. He was 89 years of age at the time of his death, and had been unfit for such strenuous undertakings as crossing the North Ronaldsay Firth for a long time before that. Under these circumstances, North Ronaldsay was again allowed to have its own minister.

It was about the same time proclaimed a separate parochial Church. This took place in 1830, and North Ronaldsay was declared to be a quoad sacra parish by Act of Assembly, 25th May, 1833, and designated as such by the Court of Teinds on 2nd June, 1847.

The Rev. Patrick Fairbairn was the first minister to hold this charge after it had been given the status of a parish in its own right. He ministered to the island from 1830 to 1837, when he was translated to Bridgeton in Glasgow and after that to Salton in Haddingtonshire. He seceded at the Disruption and continued as minister of the Free Church there. In May, 1853, he was appointed professor of Theology in the Free Church College, Aberdeen. In 1856 he was chosen for the same chair in the Free Church College in Glasgow, where he was raised to Principal the following year. Professor Fairbairn was the author of several religious books including the 'Imperial Dictionary of the Bible.' He was Moderator of the Free Church Assembly of 1864.

The Rev. Adam White, A.M., who gained his degree at the University of Edinburgh, held the charge of North Ronaldsay from 1837 to 1843, but on joining the Free Secession in the latter year and signing the deed of de-mission, he was declared no longer a minister of the Church of Scotland. He was admitted to the Free Church in Harray and Sandwick in the same year, ministering there until his death in 1873.

Although Mr White led the majority of his congregation out of the North Ronaldsay state church, he was not, for some reason or other, elected by the seceders as their minister. It must, however, be stressed that Mr White's independence of mind throughout his six years' ministration has left a lasting impression. He was responsible for compiling the "New Statistical Accoun" of the parish of North Ronaldsay in 1840, and for initiating the Free Church movement that subsequently attracted other able preachers and good organisers to the island.

With the prospect of another church and manse to be built, this seems an appropriate place to give a brief description of the island's Kirks, before resuming the list of ministers who follow Mr White.

The present Old Kirk, which was formerly the Established or State Church, was built in 1812. Earlier than this a smaller thatch-roof building sited near the middle of the kirkyard provided a place of worship. This building faced the east and confirmation of its existence was provided when the late Mr W. H. Traill's grave was dug up in 1924 and the old foundations were unearthed. It appeared that a considerable number of people had been buried inside this church; some well-preserved skulls of above average size were exposed and had to be re-buried. The manse of the Established Church was built in 1829 and continued in use until 1912, when it was replaced by a modern building more in keeping with the needs of that time. The old manse, renamed "The Bungalow," continued to be of service to the island as the home of the local doctor for many years after that, but it is now demolished.

The New Kirk was built near the centre of the island at the time of the Disruption. Both this former Free Church and manse are in good state of preservation, although they are now 126 years old. The Old Kirk and the New each have bells which are still rung, to summon people to church or to celebrate wedding and similar occasions. The bell of the Old Kirk was presented by Mr W. H. Traill in 1906, and hung in a specially built tower resembling a Norman keep; the bell of the New Kirk, said to have come from a ship which was wrecked on the island, is hung in the arch surmounting the end gable.

The next appointment to the Established Church, after Mr White had seceded to the Free Church with a considerable part of his congregation, was the Rev. Robert Waugh. He was ordained and inducted by the Presbytery in 1844, but seems to have been transferred to a parish in the South shortly afterwards. The vacancy left by Mr Waugh was filled by the appointment of the Rev. John Keillor. He held the charge from 1847 to 1866, when he was translated to Walls and Flotta.

It so happened that a German emigrant ship grounded on the island during Mr Keillor's ministry, and he is said to have exhorted his congregation to get this vessel refloated at all costs. They responded so well that by the time she had been kedged off the rocks her false keel floated up by her side. She set out for her American destination afresh, but neither the ship nor any of the 300 people on board, who included many women, were ever heard of again.

The Rev. Thomas Kaye was elected to fill the

vacancy left by Mr Keillor and thus became the fifth minister after North Ronaldsay had been made a parish of its own. He held the charge from 1866 to 1876. The Rev. D. McOwen followed in 1877 and continued to hold the charge until his death in 1885. Next came the Rev. George Grant, who was a graduate of Aberdeen University. He ministered to the Established Church from 1885 to 1898, when he received and accepted a call from the parish of Ord, in Caithness. After Mr Grant, the Established Church elected its eighth minister, the Rev. R. Grieve, who held the charge from 1898 to 1904, when he likewise went to Caithness to the parish of Berriedale.

At this stage the Established Church had 139 members, while the stipend was £120 with a manse. The Rev. Robert Wilson accepted the call to the vacancy left by Mr Grieve. He had previously been assistant minister in Airdrie parish and held the North Ronaldsay charge from 1905 to 1910. Mr Wilson was followed by the Rev. William Augustus Forbes, M.A., B.D., who occupied the pulpit for the next ten years.

The eleventh minister, the Rev. William Scott, followed in 1921 and ministered until 1929, when the United Free Church and the Established Church of Scotland again re-united as a single congregation under the same minister.

The ministers who served the United Free Church in North Ronaldsay during its 83 years of existence were: Mr White, who was parish minister at the time of the Disruption, and led the seceders from the Established Church. The Rev. Robert Wilson, M.A. was elected as the first minister of the new Free Church, and held the charge from 1846 to 1877. He was followed by a series of six ministers and several lay preachers. Of these, the second appointment was the Rev. J. Grant, M.A., who was in his turn followed by the Rev. James Cheyne, M.A. The Rev. William McPherson, M.A. was fifth in the series and he was succeeded by the Rev. Alexander Y. Bisset, M.A., B.D. Mr Boyd, a lay preacher, then officiated for some time in a temporary capacity. The next minister to hold the charge was the Rev. Robert Munro, who resigned in 1928 owing to failing health. After that the vacancy could only be temporarily filled by lay-preachers until the time of re-union with the Church of Scotland in 1929.

Due to an acute shortage of ministers and the continuing island depopulation, even this event of re-union made it difficult to find successors to its first minister, the Rev. William Scott. Briefly, the record since then is as follows:—

The Rev. MacKenzie Gordon held the charge from the early 1930s to 1939 or 1940. He was followed by a lay preacher. The Rev. Donald S. MacAlpine, who was appointed after the end of the 1939-45 war, served for a year or two. Then after another gap in the continuity, Miss Currie, a Church Sister from Aberdeen came to fill the vacancy. Appointed as Deaconess she officiated until Mr Gordon, a lay preacher, succeeded her for a period of about two or three years.

After another vacant spell during which Miss Currie, already retired, continued to help out on a temporary basis, another determined attempt to fill the vacancy was made. On the charge being advertised, the Rev. T. Arthur Tulloch, M.A., minister of Whitekirk, East Lothian, who had shown some interest, was approached on behalf of the North Ronaldsay congregation. He eventually accepted the vacant post and was inducted to the parish in 1968.

The appointment promises to be an interesting one, for Mr Tulloch's grandparents left North Ronaldsay to make their home in the neighbouring island of Eday sometime after the middle of the nineteenth century. In view of this, North Ronaldsay might now be said "to have a real minister of their very own." This could therefore be an interesting experiment capable of creating a renewed enthusiasm for church matters, and perhaps improving the attendance. It is being tried out in an island which has not had an ordained resident minister for more than twenty years.

Owing to the very high proportion of elderly people in his congregation, Mr Tulloch is faced with a fairly constant need to visit his members who are no longer able to come and hear him preach, but a pre-recording of the service could perhaps enable his Elders to assist by replaying the tape to those who are housebound. Anyway, there will not now be any need to look up medical text books, and keep a reserve of diluted carbolic acid, with other medicines, in readiness to cope with accidents and illnesses, as many of the earlier island ministers had to do when there was neither a resident doctor nor trained nurse. Yet, there is every likelihood that Mr Tulloch will find plenty of opportunity for the use of a trained mind, and his counsel and organising ability can be employed for the good of everyone in this small community.

16

Education

*. . . and a look at island schooling throughout
the years . . .*

It is likely that the earliest efforts to make
education available in North Ronaldsay as elsewhere
took place under the auspices of the church. Most of the
island's nineteenth century ministers held the degree of
M.A., and it would be strange if some of these
'gentlemen of the cloth' did not shed a little of their
educational enrichment as well as preaching a Sunday
sermon.

But even with this possibility it must also be
admitted that there is no firm evidence that either of
the two North Ronaldsay men, who became deep-sea
captains during the second quarter of the nineteenth
century, had received their early education from a
minister. There is instead, an oral tradition that
lessons in arithmetic and elementary navigation could
be had from a man who lodged at Peckhole during the
period 1810-15. This opportunity to learn the
rudiments of navigation meant that any smart boy
could take up seafaring with a better chance of
promotion in what was likely to be the only occupation
then open for those having to leave an over populated
island.

The fog enveloping educational matters began to lift
around 1837. William Fea, the island's first resident
schoolmaster, had by then been teaching for a few years
and set the course he intended to pursue. A stern
disciplinarian, he worked unremittingly at teaching the
Bible and the three Rs. Driven on by his tawse the
abler pupils made good progress while the others, with
constant fear of punishment, would long for the day
when their schooling would be finished. Like Pooh-Bah

in Gilbert and Sullivan's opera "The Mikado' Mr Fea held nearly all the official appointments in the island.

He combined the duties of teacher, scripture-reader, postmaster, and registrar during most of his working life, which extended over fifty years.

Whatever harm Mr Fea's tawse may have done to the less bright pupils, he had by the middle of the century turned out more than a dozen scholars who could write in an almost copperplate style. Evidence of their firm well formed signatures can still be seen in the Register of Births, Marriages, and Deaths, kept at the Register House in Edinburgh. This is rather remarkable in that the instruction was given in a small, remote island as much as nearly forty years before The Scottish Education Act of 1872.

It happened that the island girls were also receiving some separate instruction before the Education Act came into force. This combination of ordinary education, Bible subjects, and sewing was provided by the Misses Wilson, daughters of the Rev. Robert Wilson, minister of the Free Kirk from 1846 to 1877. The school they founded must have existed in addition to Mr Fea's during the latter part of his time as island schoolmaster, for it is still said that both boys and girls were equally certain to get the tawse if he suspected the slightest relaxation of effort.

The small building where William Fea laboured so long and so unremittingly can still be seen standing in the playground of the present school. In his time it had a thatched roof, small windows, and no heating except a peat fire that depended on fuel brought by the pupils. Each scholar had, in turn, to bring a peat to school. The fact that the pupils relied on goose quill pens and odd bits of paper did not hinder some of them acquiring a good style of handwriting. A sentimental regard for earlier times may have helped to preserve the old school building, which first served as a coal store for the present school, and now contains the electric generating plant.

Anyone who attended school around the beginning of this century, or even earlier, may still re-capture the sensation of climbing over the 'skule stile' and walking along the narrow pathway. This access was formerly used by all the children who lived north of the school, while a wider, but equally muddy, approach road was provided for those living to the south.

Going to and returning from school, meant a long, unpleasant journey for some of the children, for the building was nearer to the south end of the island. Young children in the extreme north were not considered able to undertake the three-mile trek until they reached the age of seven, and therefore, started a year later than the 'south-enders' or others nearer the school.

In the winter season, high winds and driving rain often soaked both clothing and footwear long before the school was reached. So it was no unusual sight for overcoats and other articles of clothing to be hung on the fireguards to dry out in time for the return journey. The rising steam sometimes made a very realistic fog around the map of Newfoundland, which hung on the wall directly above the fireplace. Perhaps, one of the teachers having more than an average sense of humour may have looked on this phenomenon as a ready-made demonstration designed to illustrate what happens when the Gulf Stream meets the cold Labrador Current at the Grand Banks!

Mr Fea's long period of service as island schoolmaster was not equalled by his successors, some of whom stayed such a short time and left so little mark that their names and dates can only be found by searching through old directories. In view of this difficulty, it has been thought that it would be helpful to include as full a list as possible of all teachers.

Subject to any further information coming to light, a full list of North Ronaldsay's Head Teachers and Assistant Teachers is as follows:—

Year	Head Teacher	Assistant Teacher(s)
1835c.	William Fea	None
1874c.	G. Learmonth	"
1878	John Sinclair	"
1881	George MacKenzie	"

Year	Head Teacher	Assistant Teacher(s)
1883	Robert Gibson	None
1884	Robert Smith	,,
1886	Robert Curr	,,
1888	George Mackenzie	,,
1895	James McPherson	Miss Mary A.Wood (1891-1896)
1900	Colin Campbell	Miss Fotheringhame (1897-1900)
1902	Robert Gillies	Miss Sarah Muir, Waterhouse (1900-1904)
1903	C. Sutherland	Miss Sarah Muir, Waterhouse (1900-1904)
1904	Chas. B. Robertson	Mrs Robertson & Miss Sarah Muir, Midhouse (1905-1908)
1907	James Thomson	Miss Sarah Muir, Midhouse
1908	Fred Robinson	Mrs Robinson & Miss Sarah Muir, Midhouse
1914	G. F. Robertson	Mrs Robertson
1917	J. S. Glass	Mrs MacKenzie, Midhouse
1922	Mrs MacKenzie	
1923	Thomas Myles	Miss Ivy Johnston (1923 1932)
1933	Robert Flett	Miss B. Sandison (1933-1934)
		Miss E. S. Inkster (1934-1936)
		Miss Vera Matheson (1936-1938)
1940	Mrs R. G. Scott	Mr J. D. MacKay (1941)
1942	John D. Mackay	Miss Lennie (1944-1946)
1946	Rev. D. MacAlpine	
1947	Miss M. Tulloch	None
1948	Alex Walker	Mrs Walker
1953	Donald MacInnes	None

Year	Head Teacher	Assistant Teacher(s)
1956	Mrs Isobel Mainland.	None
1960	Mary A. Thomson (Temp. Appoint.)	,,
1961	Oliver W. Scott	,,
1965	Mrs Ivy Gordon	,,
1968	Isobel M. Bews	,,
1968	Miss Shena L. Henry	,,
1970	Mrs J. C. Swanney	,,

The Society School in North Ronaldsay was founded around 1817 by the Society in Scotland for propagating Christian Knowledge, and supported by them to the extent of £15 yearly. In 1837 the school had 43 male and 31 female pupils: total 74. These were between the ages of 5 and 15 years.

The school was under the superintendence of the North Isles Presbytery. It was inspected regularly by the parish minister, and annually by a committee of the North Isles Presbytery. There was one teacher, male, appointed by the S.S.P.C.K. He had a salary of £15 a year. The fees were 1/- a quarter for reading; 1/6d. a quarter for reading and writing; and 2/- for reading, writing, and arithmetic.

The text-books used were:—English—Dr. Thomson's series of School books; Arithmetic — Gray's Religion— Bible; Catechism—The (?) , Shorter and Proof Catechism.

School times were, 10 a.m. to 1 p.m.; 2 p.m. to 4 p.m. Holidays—A week at Christmas and three weeks in September.

Prizes or Rewards—The esteem of their teacher and emulation in the class.

Punishments—Occasional confinement in school, and sometimes corporal chastisement.

The schoolmaster, William Fea, was educated at the Manse of Cross parish, and the parochial school of Sanday. (The above compiled from Returns related to non-Parochial Schools in the Orkney Isles, published in 1841.)

Old Statisical Account 1795c. (Rev. W. Clouston—)

There was no school in the isle of North Ronaldsay for 25 or 30 years past; and yet almost all the young people can read, and upon examination, appear to be well acquainted with the scriptures and principles of Christian religion, as they are in many places where regular schools are instituted. As the farms there are small they have a great deal of spare time, and the parents then teach their children to read.

Of those teachers who held the post of Schoolmaster between Fea's time and the outbreak of the 1914-18 war, Learmonth, MacKenzie, MacPherson, Robertson, and Robinson are all credited with turning out well taught children. Other teachers, some of whom were in the island for comparatively short periods, have their names recorded as Curr, Gillies, and Sutherland.

A native, Mr James Thomson, Bridesness, held the post of temporary teacher over a long span of years. As such he filled the recurring gaps between successive schoolmasters. By reason of his frequent spells of duty, Jimmie turned his title of Temporary Teacher into something of a misnomer for he was often called upon to pllay the part of local dominie.

As can be seen, the island population remained high during the whole nineteenth century and continued so until after the 1914-18 war. The average number of children attending school throughout this time was about seventy. The beginners and those in classes one, two, and three were accommodated in the southern half of the glass-partitioned school-room and taught by a female teacher. The older children from classes four, five, six, and supplementary, or ex-six occupied the northern half and were taught by the schoolmaster.

Both teachers sat at elevated desks which enabled them to keep an eye on all that was going on in their class rooms. The sliding glass partition between also afforded the schoolmaster an overall view as well as ready access to any pupil whom he suspected of not working to capacity.

But Fred Robinson's cane, which had by this time replaced 'Ald Fay's tawse", became more and more of a deterrent than a reality. It was, on the whole, only used when it was fully merited. Fred, an Englishman, from

Wigan, had a highly developed sense of humour, but often used irony or ridicule to drive home a point. In this connection most of his pupils who are still alive will recall an occasion when he became irritated with the way in which the boys and girls of a particular class were reciting a poem 'The Landing of the Pilgrim Fathers.'

Each pupil had to recite a verse in rotation until the poem was completed. As might be expected, the newly learned piece developed into a meaningless jingle which from the opening lines became a singsong with the punctuation and emphasis completely misplaced.

After listening to the broken image:

The heavy night hung dark

The hills and waters o'er

Fred could bear it no longer, and dramatically shouted, "Stop! Anyone listening would think the poem was about David Knight taking a dislike to some small boy called Dark and acting the hangman." David Knight happened to be one of the larger boys attending school at that time. This vivid way of calling attention to our errors must have had the desired effect, for the whole incident immediately sprang to mind when I had the fortune to visit the 'stern and rockbound coast' in 1970 and also to see full scale replicas of the three ships that had carried 105 English settlers to Jamestown, Virginia, in 1607, some thirteen years before the Pilgrim Fathers landed at Plymouth Rock.

Another highlight of this visit to the United States and Canada more than half-a-century after I left school in North Ronaldsay, brought yet one more of the poems that I had learned to mind, when a sightseeing tour halted at Barbara Fletchie's home, where the 'Old Glory' still flutters from a flagpole sticking out of the attic window.

Let me quote yet another final extract reminiscent of schooldays recalled on that same journey when viewing the 'Statue of Liberty' with the inscription thereon:—

"The New Colossus" by Emma Largaras:—

"Give me your tired, your poor,

 Your huddled masses yearning to breathe free,

The wretched refuse of your teeming shore,

Sent there, the homeless, tempest toosed to me:

I lift my lamp besides the Golden door."

Quite a number of the seventy pupils who made up the average school role in former times had to leave the island in order to make a living. Most of them seem to have found the educational foundation which they received at the island school suitable for the work, or further training, they had in view.

Some of the young men of this period managed to qualify for professional careers. Others were attracted to seafaring and lighthouse keeping. To become a ship's captain had always been considered in North Ronaldsay a very worthwhile job. John Tulloch of Veracott had commanded a sailing ship at the middle of the nineteenth century, and the news that Willie o' Breck, a third generation descendant from another branch of these Verecott Tulloch's had gained his Master's Ticket in 1909 was received with what might be described as general acclaim.

Young women of this period, has little choice of occupations. The more ambitious might become nurses or teachers, but for the others domestic service, either in the home country, the United States, or the colonies was the only available career.

All the girls who took up nursing and teaching were successful.

The most outstanding was Miss Anne Tulloch O.B.E., Matron of Stobhill Hospital, Glasgow, and Senior Examiner for Scotland, who died in North Ronaldsay in 1970 at the age of 84 years.

A North Ronaldsay man Mr John W. Muir, also, without the privilege of a Secondary education, managed by his own initiative to reach the post of Wireless Engineer, with G.P.O. endorsement.

The post-war years have brought many changes in the pattern of island schooling. The roll of seventy children which was maintained during the early part of this century, began to drop after the first world war, and this downward trend has continued until less than twenty attend school at present. The last decades have also brought educational centralisation and specialisation. Promising youngsters of over eleven years are all sent to Kirkwall Grammar School. While this may be, and probably is, good for the boys and girls concerned, there are grave local doubts as to whether an ageing and dwindling island community can withstand the system for long. Some of the older people suspect the theme song, "More Highers bring better Opportunities," of being a new version of the lure of the Pied Piper of Hamelin had on the children there.

However, from the academic point of view, this new system is already proving itself a success. Out of the greatly reduced school output of post-war years, more boys and girls than ever before gain academic distinction. Two recent instances worthy of mention are David K. Scott and Marion Tulloch, who are both Doctors of Philosophy. There have also been other degrees including several Bachelors of Science and a number of Masters of Arts, but the most original achievement, by a pupil of North Ronaldsay school are the paintings and sculptures by Ian Scott. His statue of a lifeboatman looking out to sea from Osmandwall Cemetery was commissioned by the R.N.L.I. as a memorial to the eight man crew of the Longhope lifeboat, who lost their lives while going to the assistance of the Librarian ship "Irene' on the 17th March, 1969. It was unveiled by the Queen Mother on the 9th August, 1970 in the presence of one of the largest and most distinguished crowds over assembled in Orkney.

How far the island libraries of the past and present have helped to inspire this desire for knowledge and learning is often commented upon by visitors, who find the average North Ronaldsay person to be well informed on a wide variety of subjects. There is no doubt that credit is due to the Church, to Coats of Paisley, and to Mr MacGillivray, the County Librarian, all of whom have striven to make a good selection of reading matter available. Radio and television, too, must be included in the list of media that stimulate and help to satisfy that curiosity about world affairs which is so characteristic of men and women born in the northmost island of Orkney.

17

Malt Making and Brewing

. . . in former times

Maltmaking and brewing were already well established in the Outer North Isles of Orkney in Viking times. Proof of this is contained in the Orkneyinga Saga where it describes how Rognvald Brui's son was surprised and killed by Thorfinn at Papa Stronsay, while he was in that island for a cargo of malt. This malt had been required for a great feast which Rognvald had planned for the Yule of 1046. The production of good crops of bere to make into malt seems to have increased as the years went by, for another old record shows North Ronaldsay and Papa Stronsay as helping to supply the needs of Norway.

The entry anent this takes the form:—

"On the 28th May, 1633, Harie Henrysone chartered the bark callit 'James' of Kirkwall to come to the most convenient port of North Ronaldsay and lie four wark wetherly days for the taking in of twenty chalder of beir." After that the "James" was to go to Papa Sound to be loaded up by Harie's brother, and thus freighted to proceed to Bergen and lie eight days to discharge. For this the brothers were to pay £210 Scots "within the space of fortie aucht houres efter the delyverie of the same loading."

Again, four years later, in March 1637, a further record shows that David M'Lelland, who came to Kirkwall as "servitor to Mr John Dick," and afterwards became proprietor of the Woodwick and North Ronaldsay estates, bought one-third of "the bark callit the 'Lamb of God,' for 176 rix dollars, at 58 shillings Scots money the piece." It is very likely that this vessel, too, was meant for carrying grain and malt to Norway.

Of the grain that was left, a good proportion had to

be set aside for malt. No household of that time, or even of a much later date, would break the custom of allocating the best of the year's crop for this purpose. The tradition was so well established that brewing was just as important as baking, and the amount of grain used for malt could sometimes make inroads on that which should have been reserved as seed-corn.

Such improvidence is in some ways understandable, for home brewed ale had many uses. The brown liquid might be made strong, or weak, depending on the intentions and resources of the brewer. Made with a specific gravity which was only slightly above that of water it was given the name of 'plink.' This anaemic ale was only worthy of such down-to-earth uses as a thirst-quencher, and for supping with porridge when milk was scarce. Strengthened until it became syrupy, like a good liqueur, it was sometimes credited with having aphrodisiac properties that could be utilised by mothers who had too many daughters of marriageable age left on their hands!

Ale of a strength between these extremes often took the place of tea, or coffee. Cold outdoor tasks, such as bringing in loads of turnips for the cattle might be rewarded by "a kon o' ale t' warm thee ap." But it was during the three weeks of Yule and New 'ear, when every household had a plentiful supply, that house to house drinking helped to make the short, dark days and long winter nights not only tolerable, but an eagerly anticipated season.

The spirit of neighbourliness and merriment displayed at this time of year can be appreciated from the sentiments expressed in the *New 'ar Sang*. This vocal effort ran to thirty-three verses and covered all the facets of island life in former times. It was sung by the stravaiging groups of menfolk as they strolled from house to house on New 'ar eve. Their destination reached, it acted as a pass-word. After admittance, the appropriate verse could always be used in order to suggest, and speed up, the order of merrymaking.

> *"Gudwife gae to your geelin vat*
> *An' draw us of a skeal o' that,*
> *O' draw us ane, draw us twa*

An' we'se be merrier, or we gae awa'
O' draw us twa, draw us three
An' aye the merrier we will be "

So, all in all, only fat, well ripened corn taken from the Toomal or most fertile field on the croft was earmarked for the Yule and New 'ar festivities. In a non-vintage season, man could but strive to extract the alcoholic properties that Providence had begrudged and herein lay the real art of maltmaking and brewing.

To begin with, the corn had to be thoroughly steeped in water for forty-eight hours. This might be done in different ways, but the most popular method was to use the same vats and barrels that would be needed for the brewing operations once that stage was reached. Scrubbed clean, inside and outside, the wooden containers were aired to remove any musty smell lingering since they were last used. The barrels would then be set up wherever convenient in the barn and partially filled with corn to allow space for the addition of sufficient water to saturate the grain completely for two days.

The same result could be obtained by sinking the sacks of corn in a well, or deep pond, and it was said that Tammie o' Conglabist, who was credited as being one of the best maltsters and brewers in the island, always steeped his corn in the brackish water of Trolla Vatn. This may have helped to give the Conglabist Ale a special flavour, in the way the peat-dried malt of Islay produces the world-famous Laphroaig whisky.

After the excess water had been drained off, the soaked corn was next heaped on a floor and left for germination, before receiving further attention. Once it showed signs of growth and increase of temperature it had to be spread out in order to slow down the process, as a too rapid germination was detrimental to a proper conversion of the starch content into sugar. In this connection, an earthen floor made of hard-packed clay was generally thought to be better than a stone or concrete floor. Tammie o' Conglabist and most of the malt makers of his time allowed a period of three weeks to elapse from the time the malt was first put on the floor before it was considered to be ready for the kiln.

During this time the germination was allowed to proceed until all the puckles of grain had 'twa three taes,' that is, showing the beginning of a root at one end and signs of a shoot at the other. The growth had to be carefully regulated by controlling the temperature of the malt. The heat, which should be slightly warmer than the malt maker's hands, was kept steady by turning over the spread every twenty-four hours, or oftener if the weather happened to be warm. If the growth became too rapid, the individual roots tended to interlock forming lumps of moist grain. This had to be guarded against by breaking up any such lumps and also rubbing off the excess growth during the daily, turning-over operation. Again, by increasing, or decreasing the thickness of the spread, the experienced maltster could achieve the exact rate of development he wished to maintain.

At the completion of this slow, drawn-out process, or about the twentieth day, the malt would again be shovelled into a compact heap, covered over by sacking, and allowed to lie another day so that any remaining starch might be turned into sugar. This final process on the malt-floor was called 'putting the malt in sweet bed.'

It was then ready for drying in a kiln, and this had to be done immediately. Up to the beginning of the present century, and in some cases much later, every croft and farm had its own kiln. This grain-oven might be either rounded or square and always formed one end of the barn of which it was an integral part. It was separated from the main part by a stone wall, which had two doors placed one above the other. The smaller, or lower opening led to the 'kiln hoggie' or draught tunnel and furnace whence the heat could rise and dry the malt. The upper door provided the entrance to the drying floor on which the grain or malt was spread. It would usually be four or five feet above the fire, and at this height, the circular building would have widened out to a diameter of ten feet, or more. The greater width allowed for a wall-ledge to support the outer ends of the 'kiln-sticks,' the inner ends being laid on a square wooden beam, built into the walls at either end. This beam crossed the building at exactly the same level as the ledge, and was known as the 'kiln-laece.' The 'kiln-bedding' of straw was spread over this fan-shaped arrangement to allow the rising heat to dry the malt to the desired degree of crispness. The smoke from the fire and the moisture from the drying malt escaped through the wide chimney in the domed top of the kiln which always rose a few feet above the barn roof. As there was always some danger of the 'kiln-bedding' igniting, the fuel used for drying the malt had to be of a kind that was unlikely to produce sparks, or any sudden flare up of gases, such as happens with some sorts of coal. Peats, coke, and small logs of oak which were free of tar, might all be used with safety provided the clearburning fire was fed with small, regular amounts of these fuels.

It generally took around six to eight hours to dry the eight to twelve bushels of malt that might be used in the Yule and New 'ar festivities. During this spell, the minder-of-the-kiln had to be on the lookout, as part of the kiln would be overheated on the side nearest the fire and chilled on the opposite side by a strong draught from the open barn door. While this uncomfortable air stream was inclined to leave the kiln-minder with a developing cold, coughs and sneezes were never looked upon as too high a price for the forced-draught that kept the kiln-fire burning bright and clear.

The warm glow of the 'kiln-hoggie' could be depended upon to attract a small group of menfolk, neighbours who had dropped in to yarn about shipwrecks and other happenings of former times. Children from the nearby houses might also find their way to the dimly lit barn, to while away the evening by playing hide-and-seek amongst the sacks and straw or, tiring of their childish games, they might absorb some scrap of information about events that had happened several generations earlier. Whether the children were sufficiently impressed to retain and preserve these stories was yet another matter, but the future of maltmaking was at the same time at stake. Unless these boys watched, and were in their turn able to hand on the art of maltmaking, a time would surely come when there would be no ale for Yule !

After the malt had reached the right degree of dryness being sufficiently crisp to break easily bitten, between one's teeth it was considered ready for removal from the kiln. If it was intended for immediate use, it had to be bruised, or coarse-ground as a final preparation for brewing. This course-grinding was formerly done at home on a hand-quern. Every house employed one of these until early in the present century, but they then went out of date when a new meal mill, powered by an oil-engine began to provide a better and quicker service.

Brewing day nearly always brought a complete change of scene, for the 'men's-wark' was finished once the malt was handed over. From then on it was up to the womenfolk who called upon their men only for the labouring jobs connected with brewing. Although there may have been some exceptions to this, it could generally be claimed that most of the secrets of making and dispensing a strong brew belonged to the division of skills known as 'women's wark.'

The 'brewing-veshals' which had already been used for steeping the malt would again be washed and aired. Other preliminaries included the provision of a good reserve of fuel and well-water. The actual brewing might commence as early as six o'clock on a dark winter morning. Amid the hustle of activity going on in the lantern-lit barn, a fire would first of all be kindled. Then a large twelve to twenty gallon pot, or boiler, of water would be boiled as quickly as possible and this liquid thereafter 'owsed' or baled out into one of the barrels already placed alongside. A clean sack and wooden lid would also be set at hand for covering this barrel, as the contents had to be kept hot until another pot of water could be brought to boiling point.

When this stage was reached, the 'first masking' could take place. A 'masking-vat' was always the largest of the brewing utensils and generally shaped like an elongated tub, with a tap at the bottom end. The masking as considered to be the most critical part of brewing. Not only did it control the strength of the brew, but was also beset by such dangers as a chocked-tap, or 'stuck wort' unless certain precautions were taken

A rough-and-ready sort of filter was generally improvised to keep the meal-content of the malt well away from the inner aperture of the tap. This consisted of a bunch of clean oat straws arranged as a strainer held in position by a semi-circular stone. This arrangement might also be made more efficacious by sifting and removing all the meal-content of the malt round about this straw-strainer. The clogging effect from the addition of too hot water might also be avoided by mixing the newly boiled pot of water with the first one that had been set aside in the covered barrel.

As in the making of tea, the malt and water had to be given sufficient time in which to infuse properly. The length of time allowed may have varied according to the preference of the particular brewer, but was considered by many to be two hours. The right ratio of malt to water was another variable that had to be decided according to the views of the brewer. But there was general agreement that a good average ale would result from a mixture in which the 'masking sheul' could almost stand upright when unsupported. Should the brew be required for some very special occasion, the ratio of malt to water might be still further increased by hanging a hat of the top end of the 'masking-sheul' which had still to remain erect. The 'masking-sheul' was a length of wood for use in the vat. It was like a paddle, flat at the bottom and rounded towards the top. Its purpose was to stir up the malt in the vat, similar to a teaspoon in a teacup.

When the raw wort was drawn from the masking vat it was ready to be boiled with hops. The best results were obtained by boiling it for two hours, by which time it would have become slightly sticky like extract of malt. The brew would be mild, or bitter, according to-the amount of hops used. The first pot of wort was always thought to be the best. It could either be kept separate or mixed with the subsequent pots, which were made in exactly the same way after more water, and perhaps more malt, had been added to the masking vat.

Once the wort had cooled down to about bloodheat it was ready for barming. This process required the addition of the right proportion of brewer's yeast to start fermentation if an average quantity of ale was to be made ready in a hurry. Barm of this amount was seldom available in the pre-Yule rush, and there were seasons when a single spoonful had to be encouraged to grow on a small amount of whisky and wort for several days before it could suffice for a few gallons of wort.

While the womenfolk, who traditionally attended to the barming, bottling, and serving of the ale had the patience needed for nursing these small amounts of barm, there is a story of one drouthy worthy who found this waiting period too much. After nursing his drop of barm to which a full glass of whisky had been added, as well as some wort, right through a long winter evening, a midnight inspection showed no progress. Then one of the youngsters who had been watching heard him say: "Bi-me-soul,' I'll no waste th' whisky onyway"and immediately matching his actions to this statement of intent, he swallowed the lot!

That was many years ago, and times have changed. So for that matter have the time-honoured customs that were associated with maltmaking and brewing. The 'brewing-veshels 'the masking-sheul,' and 'the-muckle-three-toed-pot,' are now, like the men and women who used them, 'no more'! The generations which have grown up since the war are sharing in all the benefits that come with the use of modern machinery and organisation, but their malt is now made and dried in Edinburgh, or Copenhagen, and their Special Brew for Yule has to be bought across the counter at the licensed grocer!

18

Going to the Wars

. . . the Ward Beacons, the Press Gang, the Derby Scheme, and finally Conscription, have all in their turn shouted, "The King and Country needs You." . . .

We are told that Thorstein's warning beacon was set alight for the purpose of summoning the young-and-fit to assemble at Kirkwall under the leadership of Earl Paul. This call-up of 1136, contains perhaps the earliest recorded mention of North Ronaldsay men being mobilised for defence. There were, of course, other battles like those of Clontarf and Stamford Bridge into which some of the islanders may have been drawn, but their presence is not recorded.

Neither is there any tradition of a well-handled battleaxe being wielded at Largs, nor even of participation in the victory over the Caithness men at Summerdale. It needed Napoleon, with his blocade of the English Channel, to bring the British Navy into northern waters and to make this island of strategic importance. The move also led to the setting up of Naval Press Gangs, so that there might be no shortage of sailors for manning these ships-of-war.

Experienced seamen, already serving on coasters and merchantmen, were often seized and incorporated into the crew of any warship that might be short of hands. Naval parties also landed on the islands in order to compel any young man they could lay hands upon to join the armed forces. The fittest were usually claimed for the navy, while the less agile and those with poorer eyesight found themselves in the army.

This system of recruiting was very unpopular, and the mention of it can still be depended upon to bring forth strong condemnation.

Many stories are told about the armed landing parties being outwitted by the islanders, but some of these yarns are obviously embellished, and there is little doubt that many escapes were due rather to the sympathy of the pickets than to the ingenuity of the men. The first man to be press-ganged in North Ronaldsay may have been a John Tulloch from Senness, but he seems to have taken to soldiering and served through the American War of Independence before returning to the island. It appears that the Laird's representative, who controlled the allocation of crofts, took this war service into consideration, and placed John Tulloch's three sons in substantial holdings. John got Ancum, Tom went to Hooking, and William had the tenancy of Senness, which was then one-seventh of the Easting.

Another man who served during the latter part of the eighteenth century, was a Swanney from Claypows. It cannot now be ascertained whether this sailor was pressed direct from the island, or taken off a ship. He was apparently entered on the naval roll as Swan. Combining ability with an aptitude for enforcing discipline, he finished up as a Master of Arms. His tombstone in the local kirkyard, shows that he lived to an age of 82 years, and died in 1836.

How different this John Tulloch was from Peter Swanney of Claypows is illustrated by the tradition that the sailor returned with savings of three-hundred pounds, while the soldier brought back only a clock and sixpence!

From Viggie came another Swanney, who may have been a relation of the Master at Arms. This man's story, published in an American magazine and told recently in a B.B.C. programme, likewise belongs to the Press-gang period. Either voluntarily or through persuasion Swanney was serving in a ship engaged in bringing home to England some of the victors of Waterloo. He had risen to the position of ship's bosun and as such had some freedom to befriend those he considered to be in need of help.

It so happened that a wounded soldier under his care was rapidly weakening in spite of all that

Swanney could do for him. The soldier realised that he was dying and asked for his haversack to be brought and opened, so that he might give the friendly sailor a keepsake. He told how on being wounded he had somehow managed to drag himself to an abandoned carriage. Noticing the "N" monogram on one of the windows he began to realise that he was inside Napoleon's personal coach. By using his bayonet, he prised out the pane of glass and carried it away as a souvenir.

When Swanney returned to his island and built himself a house, this monogramed pane was used as a skylight, but it is now however, in America as a prized showpiece at the office of the "San Francisco Examiner." How it got there is another interesting story, but one which does not belong to this chapter.

A record concerning a family named Donaldson, thought to have come to Scotsha' from Shetland describes one of them, Peter as a Professional Soldier. As his son Samuel was born in 1791, it is probable that the father had finished his period of service before that date.

The nest burst of activity by the Press-gang occurred three years before Waterloo, when three more men were taken away to the wars. They were John Muir, Sholtisquoy; Thomas Tulloch, Garso; and Peter Turfus Skelperha.' All three were drafted to the navy, and were said to have been locked up in the storehouse of Hower overnight to ensure that they would be ready for the vessel which was to collect them. Of the three only Thomas Tulloch survived his active service. John Muir was taken prisoner and died in a French goal. while Peter Turfus was killed in a naval action. When Tom Tulloch never returned home after the War, he was assumed lost, so the island's Bailie—"Beyle"—as recompence offered Peter, Tom's youngest brother, any holding in the island. He would not accept the offer, as it would have caused the displacement of some family, but he always remained on very favourable terms with the "Beyle" and his family ever afterwards. At that time Peter was far more interested in the fishing than in the land.

On one of his fishing trips along with Willie o' Senness they boarded a ship and were well received. The Captain spoke to them and asked them for certain old people in the island, an inquiry which they thought very strange. So they in turn tried to question him, but, very averse to answer very much their queries, he made for his cabin and did not appear again. When they went on board their own boat it was well stocked with provisions of every sort. After they returned to the island relating their story with a description of the Captain, it was eventually proved beyond doubt that he was Peter's own uncle, who had left the island as a youth, never to return. On another occasion when out fishing in Dennis Roost along with John of Ancum, the wind increased suddenly from the South West and they had to run before it to Fair Isle, where they were storm-stayed for a week. The people at home gave them up for lost, but they turned up towards evening of the eighth day, none the worse of their escapade.

Although Peter's brother Tom grew increasingly fond of the sea, his loyalty to a mate made it impossible for him to return to it.

It so happened that Tom and his friend were serving under an officer who often handed out severe punishments for trivial offences. To make matters worse this young lieutenant took a dislike to Tom's comrade, and soon found an occasion to have him flogged in front of the crew. Looking on with the others, Tom made up his mind that he would somehow give this bully a dose of his own medicine.

The occasion presented itself when Tom was selected to be one of the boat's crew detailed to row this officer ashore at Aberdeen. The official and social calls took so long that darkness was beginning to fall before the party reached the harbour to be taken back to the ship. There was sudden consternation when a roll call showed two of the party to be missing. An immediate search soon revealed the Lieutenant in so dazed a condition that he could only remember being challenged to fight ! It is hardly necessary to stress that Tom could not be found.

News of this happening only reached North

Ronaldsay many years later, when Peter, Tom's younger brother received a letter from a Thomas Taylor resident in Aberdeenshire. Taylor was the name his brother had assumed in order to baffle the authorities in their search for him as a deserter from H.M. Navy. When Peter eventually went to visit him in 1843, he found him married, settled down and in fairly prosperous circumstances. At any rate, Tom bore the 'Beyle' and others who had helped to have him pressed into the navy no grudge. He even thought they had inadvertently done him a good turn.

The account of what befell him after he went 'on the run' follows the course of a romantic novel had there been a Dumas to record it. On deserting, Tom made for the country side and slept in hay-stacks. Luckily, at last, he picked a place where the farmer's wife was willing to assist and to bring him food until the search was called off. By this time, he had become friendly with her daughter and this friendship soon ripened into matrimony. Tom undoubtedly belonged to the same breed of fearless adventurers as the 'Three Musketeers' and this assessment is supported by subsequent generations of relatives, who have shown that no Press-gang is necessary when the country calls for fighting men.

Paradoxically, there is also another aspect of this 'pressing' and 'desertion' incident. When Peter visited Tom in 1843, there was at that time very little contact between the remote homeland and the Scottish Mainland. So Peter's report about the Disruption was eagerly awaited. Such key churchmen as Mr White, the Parish Minister, Charles Thomson of Howar, and the Keldays of Holland, required only to hear about Dr. Chalmers' convincing case, and success of his act of defiance, combined with the news that Tom, too, had opted for the Free Kirk, in order for them to break away from the Established Church and form their own congregation, in which Peter became one of the founder elders.

"Three more Musketeers" appeared in North Ronaldsay some time before the turn of the century, when John Tulloch, Upper Linnay; John Thomson,

South Ness; and Peter Tulloch, Garso; joined the Royal
Naval Reserve. They had all completed their period of
engagement before the outbreak of the 1914 war.

As the first group of reservists from the island, they
seemingly felt the need to demonstrate the art of
fencing to their pals who had not had the benefit of a
training at Fort Charlotte. The outcome of this
escapade was so amusing that it must be included.

After an explanation of the various evasive
movements which could be used, it fell to John
Thomson to take on Jimmie o' Nether Linnay, one of
the 'untrained.' In the excitement of the make-belief
sword play Jimmie forgot the rules, and taking
advantage of his long-reach came in over Thomson's
guard to give him a smart rap across the knuckles.
With his fingers temporarily paralysed, Thomson had
to concede a victory to the 'untrained,' whereupon one
of the watching spectators, Jimmie o' Holm, voiced the
general reaction in his terse comment:

"Bi G— if that's all your training has done, I don't
think much o' hid."

The only other contribution that the island made to
the pre-1914 armed forces, were two or three young
men who left to do farm work in Shapinsay, or on the
Mainland of Orkney. Most of these farm-hands became
part-time soldiers by joining the Orkney Territorials. A
Hugh Tulloch of Liverpool, but originally from Hooking,
North Ronaldsay joined the regular army and became
an N.C.O. in the Scots Guards before the Expeditionary
Force was sent overseas in 1914, and was in the retreat
from Mons. Another Hugh, this time a Hugh Swanney
from Glasgow, who had originally come from Westness,
North Ronaldsay, had also joined the Royal Navy on a
21 years' engagement before 1914. He served
throughout the whole period of the 1914-18 war, and
survived the sinking of H.M.S. "Majestic" at the
Dardanelles in 1915.

The year 1914 was hardly out before the need for
men became just as urgent as it had been in the time of
Napoleon, when recruiting was left to the Pressgang.
But now the country had discovered more subtle ways
of gathering the 'rookies' needed to maintain its

growing battalions. From a monthly return by the local Registrar the Authorities knew the resources of manpower available to the Navy, the Army, and the Air Services. And urged on by a persistent flow of propaganda from Press and pulpit, the youth went either willingly or reluctantly to the various branches and theatres of war.

In the years 1914-1918, over thirty men and women found their way into uniform. Of these who had already left to find work and settle in other parts of Britain and elsewhere, an even greater number answered the call. The new style of recruitment began with a stirring exhortation to "save little Belgium."

The Derby Scheme followed, with the suggestion that if men "signed on now" the chances were they would never be needed. Finally, with conscription, the appeal hardened into "Come before we fetch you." Judging by results, that modern form of recruiting worked much better than any "Press Gang."

The call-up notices, or slips of paper delivered by the postman, took away every second man between the ages of eighteen and forty, whereas the Press-gang of former days managed to round-up only one man in twenty of the equivalent age group. Regarding the service-men of the 1914-18 war it must in fairness be said that the 'fighting spirit' evinced in earlier wars by John Tulloch, Senness, and by Tom Tulloch, Garso, had not entirely died out. Another Garso man, or rather boy, John W. Tulloch, was so anxious to 'do his bit' before the war finished, that he volunteered and was accepted as a Boy Signaller in the Royal Naval Reserve (Trawler Section) at the early age of 16 years.

With an island upbringing it is understandable that most of the young men should try to get into some branch of the sea-going service. Both the Merchant Navy and the Trawling fleet carried a number of North Ronaldsay men as officers and as members of the crew before the 1914 war broke out, and these were supplemented by fresh recruits right throughout its duration.

In August, 1914, those already at sea were: Merchant Navy-Capt. William Tulloch; Marine

Engineers—John Muir, Thomas Swanney, and Hugh
Tulloch; Seamen—David, John and Thomas Thomson,
John and Peter Swanney. There were also some others
sailing on Orkney coasters and on herring boats, but
these were soon channelled into the R.N.R. and are
listed under that heading. The same may be said about
the various Swanneys, Thomsons, and Tullochs who
were sailing as skippers, as members of the crew on the
pre-1914 trawlers fishing from Dundee, Leith and
Granton, and who found themselves in the R.N.R. (T)

Of these, the first North Ronaldsay man to take up
trawling was a Thomas Tulloch, whose mother's
maiden name was Cutt. He settled originally in Leith
and fished from there, encouraging several of the
Swanneys and Thomsons from North Ronaldsay to
follow his example. Tom soon became a skipper, and his
relatives also took to the life. His next move was to
transfer his services to a Mr Hay of Dundee, who had
only a single trawler at that time. Together, they built
up the business until they had the largest trawler fleet
fishing out of Dundee, by which time Mr Hay had
become a leading figure and Provost of the city.
Meanwhile, all the Swanneys and Thomsons of Leith,
or Granton had also become trawler skippers.

Most of them took part in the First World War as
members of the R.N.R.T., and Thomas Swanney,
formerly from Holm, Charles Thomson, from Cursetter,
and John Thomson, from Howatoft along with John and
Thomas Thomson, Quoybanks lost their lives in the
service. James Thomson from Howatoft held the rank
of Commodore of the Granton Trawler Fleet and was
invested at Buckingham Palace with a D.S.C. for
sinking an enemy submarine. When the war was
finished, all the trawler men went back to fishing. They
were very successful, and one of them was Willie
Thomson of Cursitter shown to be worth £20,000 at the
time of his death.

The following were drafted into the Royal Naval
Reserve (Trawler Section) during the 1914-18 war, and
all of them joined direct from their respective homes in
the island:—Robert Tulloch, Longar; John Tulloch,
Scottigar; William Muir, Waterhouse; John Tulloch,

Upper Linnay; (who was mentioned in the London Gazette); Robert Tulloch, Cott; Thomas Thomson, Quoybanks; John and Tom Tulloch, Purtabreck; John Tulloch, North Ness; William Muir, Scotshall; William Tulloch, Cruesbreck; and John W. Tulloch, Garso.

John Tulloch, Hooking, was drafted into the Royal Naval Reserve (Armed Merchant Ships) and was aboard the Armed Liner "Moldavia" when she was torpedoed in the English Channel. The island minister, the Rev. William A. Forbes also served in the Army as a Chaplain.

Those drafted into the Army, or into the Air Services were distributed as follows:—Seaforth Highlanders: John R. M. Tulloch, Greenwall (Military Medal); William Tulloch, Upper Linnay; William Cutt, Greenspot; James and Peter Swanney, North Gravity, and William Tulloch, Phisligar. All six served on the French and Belgian Fronts, with the exception of William Tulloch, Phisligar, who served in the Near and Far East, taking part in General Allenby's campaign in Palestine 1917-18. William Tulloch, Upper Linnay, a promising young man of 21 years, was killed in action in France during the 1918 German offensive, while William Cutt, Greenspot was wounded and taken prisoner. Cameronians (Scottish Rifles): Willie Cutt, Gerbo, and Willie, Tulloch, Sandbank. Scottish Horse: John W. Muir, Burray. Royal Garrison Artillery: Peter Cutt, Greenspot; Dan and Willie Laverty, Barrenhall; John Cutt, Parkhouse, and John Scott, Westhouse. All these, except John Scott, Westhouse, served in the Near and Far East. Royal Field Artillery: Thomas Scott, Westhouse. Royal Army Service Corps: James Tulloch, Kirbest. Women's Army Auxiliary Corps: Tomima Tulloch, North Ness.

Of these 32 who are listed as having been recruited direct from the island, only 15 resettled there on the cessation of hostilities. The others either emigrated to Canada, the United States of America, or Australia, or found employment in the British Isles. Such a mass exodus influenced others to follow, and the trend towards depopulation became more obvious as the 1920s continued into the 1930s. So, with an already greatly reduced population, the island could not provide so many men for the 1939-45 war.

The names of those who joined direet from the island together with their respective units, for the 1939-45 war are as follows:—Seaforth Highlanders: John Seatter, Howar, who served with the 8th Army in North Africa and afterwards in Southern Europe. R.F.'s: Alexander Thomson, Howatoft, who returned home from Canada at the beginning of the war, served throughout the Normandy Landing and was killed in action at Luscux on 22nd August, 1944.

Royal Army Service Corps: John Tulloch, Senness, who served with the 14th Army in Burma. Royal Garrison Artillery: William Swanney, Claypows. Royal Engineers (Transport Section): William Tulloch, Twiness. Royal Air Force: Hugh Swanney, Trebb and Alfie Swanney, North Gravity. John Swanney, North Gravity was serving on a Regular Engagement in the R.A.F. before the war broke out. He was stationed in Java, and was made a prisoner-of-war by the Japanese, to be held by them until the end of the war. Royal Navy: Tom Seatter, Howar, who served as Petty Officer on the battleship H.M.S. "Malaya." The vessel was badly damaged by air and submarine attack and had to go to an American dockyard for repairs. This lengthy stay in the United States enabled Tom to visit his relatives out there. William Muir, Waterhouse, served in the R.N. as a Wireless Operator.

Auxiliary Branch R.N.: John Muir, Waterhouse, and Thomas Thomson, Howertoft. Essential Civilian Warwork (London Blitz): Thomas Tulloch, Garso, served voluntarily during the worse phase of this— aerial bombardment. Women's Services. W.R.E.N.: Mabel Thomson, Howatoft as P.O. W.R.A.F.: Janet Tulloch, Sandback as L.A.W. Merchant Navy: James Swanney, Trebb and Hugh Thomson, Bewan.

In addition to those listed above, special mention must be made of some veterans of the First World War who continued to serve in or return to the Merchant Navy. Constant exposure to air, surface, and underwater attack made this one of the most hazardous of the wartime services. John Tulloch, Stromness, and

formerly from Upper Breck, served throughout both
wars, as well as in the years between, on the Northern
Lighthouse Tenders. He was awarded an M.B.E. Tom
Tulloch, Purtabreck, also remained constantly at sea
throughout his whole career, and still did occasional
relief-duties after well over half-a-century afloat.
Without State assistance he studied and succeeded in
qualifying as a Chief Marine Engineer, with Motor
endorsement. In this capacity, he sailed as Chief
Engineer in most parts of the world. He was familiar
with a range of different vessels that included tramps,
tankers, and passenger-carrying ships, and he
completed a lengthy spell of service as Commodore
Engineer for the North of Scotland Shipping Company.

The late John W. Tulloch of Washington, D.C., who
has already been mentioned as a Boy Signaller in the
R.N.R. during the 1914-18 war, was another North
Ronaldsay born veteran who returned to sea. He left
his business of painter and decorator in order to serve
the country of his adoption. Joining the United States
Merchant Marine, John served in every theatre of war,
from Europe to the Far East. He was wounded and
decorated while serving in the Mediterranean. Later,
he was awarded a Merchant Navy Unit Citation while
on duty in the Pacific.

Speaking about his experiences, he always stressed
the fact that he had seen more destruction in a few
minutes of the second war than he had witnessed in the
whole of the first. And in reminding his father of an
extreme danger unknown to him during his time of
service he always finished with the words, "There was
no make-believe about the 'Kamakse' Japanese pilots as
they dived to certain death in order to sink an enemy
ship."

19

Yarning through the long winter months

. . . where mill, shop, and smithy become
meeting places, or island parliaments . . .

In the North Ronaldsay of bygone days, mill, shop, and smithy, were more than places where grain was ground, groceries bought, and horses shod. They were places where men met on the long winter evenings to talk and tell stories and fanciful tales. All sorts of subjects were discussed, but the conclusions arrived at generally rested on the wisdom that is supposed to come with age. Mere boys, and that meant anyone who had not reached his late twenties or early thirties, were rated as innocents and not considered likely to have anything worthwhile to contribute to this old men's parliament.

The First World War, which quickly changed the age old pattern of social life and incidentally, this reverential attitude to age and experience, had scarcely begun, when a meeting convened by William Traill the island Laird instituted an all night beach patrol.

The shores were divided to correspond with the various districts, or townships, and double sentries carrying heavy-sticks posted to watch for enemy landings, or any other suspicious happenings.

This embryonic attempt to set up a Home Guard was something new, and the duties imposed were willingly carried out for the first few weeks. Then with the harvest work making increasing demands on their time and the nights quickly lengthening and darkening, doubts about the value of the exercise in 'men o' war's wark' began to spread. Soon only the elderly, who had been excused from active patrolling, continued to see any merit in 'playing at soldiers.' The detailed reports, which had at the beginning been sent to Naval Headquarters in Kirkwall, became fewer and soon ceased altogether.

While mill, shop and smithy were thus deserted, the traditional exchange of views and prejudices was greatly hindered. Sunday provided the only opportunity for discussion and debate.

It must have been shortly after the beginning of the war that the residue of men and boys, making up one of these all-male groups, got round to discussing the value of the round-the-beaches patrol. The confused arguments had raised nothing of any value when Willie, well known for his illuminating remarks, settled the walking-staff versus gun argument for all time.

"Id's like expectan' an egg-shell t' withstand a lunder fae a fourteen pund mell."

Although the logic of this might be thought sound enough, it must have been voiced too soon after the previous week's sermon, in which the minister had declared: The three Ms—more men—more money—and more munitions will be needed in order to win the war.

This must have impressed one of the Kirk Elders from the North Yard, who must have thought the staff versus gun remark bordered on frivolity and that he must uphold the State. So, straightening himself to his full height and speaking in an authoritative tone, he let the youngsters know what was expected of them, "There's no justice like British justice, and it must be defended."

But war or no war, the island's workaday activities had to go on. The lobster fishermen gradually began to pay less attention to the Defence of the Realm Regulations. The more venturesome were soon ignoring the rule that all boating must be reported to the naval authorities in Kirkwall. Surely these instructions were never meant to prohibit the setting of a few creels in the geos and creeks on the west side of the island? So praams and other small boats began to be dragged overland to test whether the enforced lull in fishing had encouraged more lobsters to this part of the shore.

With good catches and rapidly rising prices, due to

the presence of naval personnel in Scapa Flow, even more than the usual amount of these crustaceans were being served in salads in the Kirkwall hotels. But this local windfall could hardly be expected to last for long.

As the months and years went by, most of the lobster fishermen found their way into uniform with the Naval Reserve. There, in trawlers temporarly transformed into mine-sweepers, they would sometimes pass and re-pass the Altars, the Sealskerry, and the Reefdyke, all shoals around which they had formerly set their creels. Or again, when patrolling further off shore, they might be sailing over the very same fishing grounds where a fine settled summer had lured them in search of cod, or haddock.

Others who failed to convince the recruitment officers that an island birthplace automatically conferred the right to a place in the Navy were shunted into the various branches of the Army, or into the Air services. Army canteens and Y.M.C.A. rooms gradually took the place of the island shops, but the tales told in a wide assortment of English, Scottish, and Irish dialects completely failed to arouse any interest. They had little of the bite and savour of the island yarns, which had been turned into works of art by generations of telling and retelling. One bizarre tale of courage fortified by sorcery, told at a North Ronaldsay story-telling session, ran something like this:—

"Bi me sa'l t' first sodger t' fight in any o' t' wars cam' fae Senness, unles' I'm misinformed. His ald gran'mither must ha'e kenned her Saga, for sho wus sae determined that if this gran'son wus unlucky and got wounded t' injuries wud never be on his back. So tellin' him never t' let doon his side, sho wus said t' mak' him drink a courage-given' measure o' cock's blood."

Whether this magic potion had the desired effect was left untold, but other contributors to the discussion helped to confirm that he took to the army life like a duck to water. He also lived to return to his birthplace, little the worse for soldiering in Europe and taking part in the American War of Independence. Also, as mentioned in the chapter "Going to the Wars," he was

said to have come back home with only a clock and a
sixpenny piece. Once back in the island he seems to
have developed a hunger for land and had before long
been given a sizeable holding for each of his three sons
as well as having to employ four labourers at Senness.

With so many islanders away on war service in the
latter part of the 1914-18 war both the frequency and
the attendance at these gathering places became less.
Even the wireless bulletins of official gains and losses
were being accepted with scepticism, but the comedy
and tragedy of war are always closely linked. One of the
islanders, on hearing of the loss of H.M.S. Hampshire
with Lord Kitchener and his Staff, commented, "Aye; t'
mon and t' warship will be a great loss, but I'm dashed
if I understand t' fuss aboot his cudgel."

By the Summer of 1919, most of the service men had
been demobilised and returned to the island. In many
cases, this was only to see their folks before planning
what they were to do next.

The shops and other gathering places became
crowded again, but the mood of these discussions had
changed. There was less patience with those who might
be described as 'long-winded blethers' and scarcely
concealed boredom for trivial, round-the-door
happenings. Europe, the Middle East, and other Far-
away places were no longer something in a book. They
had become realities, countries and peoples where a
good proportion of the ex-service yarners had sampled
Vin Rouge, or haggled with the Stall-Holders in a
Baghdad bazaar.

Only a good storyteller like Willie, or someone with
a stock of general knowledge such as John Scott, could
be sure of an attentive hearing. Those who had been
ordered about on the parade grounds had, perhaps
unconsciously, taken a distaste to authority. Anyway,
the idea that age conferred superior wisdom no longer
held. This simmering revolt, cannot be better described
than in the words which someone taking part in the
discussion claimed to have read,

"This rebellion is world wide. Even the most remote
of small, Pacific Islands are beginning to question the
authority of their Headmen."

In the similar isolation of North Ronaldsay, this mild discontent went no further than a threatened strike by the kelp workers owing to poor returns. In accordance with custom, a meeting for the purpose of drawing up a round robin to the Laird only got properly started around ten o'clock one Autumn evening. The island had towards the end of 1919 acquired a Memorial Hall, in the form of a large army hut converted into a Community Centre, where meetings were beginning to be held instead of in the shops and smithy.

The regulations for the Memorial Hall had fixed the closing hour as 10 p.m., and the meeting had only just got down to work when the caretaker insisted on putting out the lights and locking up for the night. As might be expected, this hasty action aroused more heat than the low kelp prices! The storm of angry shouts and protests were overheard by the island's Justice of Peace, who lived near by. The row must have considerably upset this peace-loving man. In his capacity of shopkeeper he mentioned it to those of his customers whom he suspected of being there. His mild reproof took the form: "Have you ever read Carlyle's French Revolution? If you have, I don't need to tell you how dangerous a mob can be."

This storm in a teacup soon settled down. The laird tactfully conceded a slight price increase and no mob ever got out of hand. But another amusing event soon followed to show that Youth did not altogether accept the dictum that 'age and experience'should be left at the helm all the time.

The summer of 1920 brought a long spell of fine settled weather which allowed all the small boats to go out in search of cod and haddock. A whole seven years had gone by since the good fishing year of 1913 and the grounds had also had a rest from intensive trawling during the four years of the 1914-18 war. There was every prospect that flsh might again be plentiful. This proved to be the case, but on this occasion, instead of cod, it was haddock which had come to the west side of the island in considerable numbers. Soon every boat that could float, or that only leaked within baling limits, might be seen approaching the grounds from both the north and south ends of the island.

Ironically, the seven years which had allowed the stocks of fish to improve had caused the boats to deteriorate. Many of them were rotting away where they stood shored up in the boat nousts. As a result, there were more potential fishermen than seaworthy boats.

It happened that one particular skiff had been repaired for pleasure sailing but not to use for fishing. Consequently the crew consisted of only two inexperienced youngsters. As might be expected in a situation where the men outnumbered the boats, it was thought that these greenhorns should not be allowed to risk their lives on a fishing trip without an addition of at least a couple of veterans. So two older men made it their business to put themselves in charge and set about planning every detail, including the time of sailing for the fishing grounds each morning. The arrogance which led to this underrating of youthful aspirations soon received a check, for less than a week of fishing had taken place when the two older men arrived just in time to see the skiff disappearing beyond the Green Skerry and heading in the direction of the fishing ground without them!

This story symbolises the eternal conflict between age and youth and would be incomplete without the sequel.

Nearly fifty years were to pass before the two rebels met again in North Ronaldsay. Both of them —John o' Burray and John o' Garso—had left the island in 1921. When they looked together over the same stretch of water in 1967, they momentarily relived that morning of long ago, but, somehow, with the victims of their practical joke dead for many years and one of themselves only two years from his own passing, the oft repeated tale has ceased to be amusing.

Another war, Hitler's, helped to intensify the split between youth and age, even creating an atmosphere where post-war candidates for the North Ronaldsay District Council were considered too old if they were on 'the wrong side of forty.' It may be thought that only the young and fit are able to argue forcibly enough to bring all the bonuses that go with a Welfare State. The irony of this view is that all those who were demobilised in 1945, after winning the war for democracy, are, themselves, now too old to be eligible for office! Like King David, they are condemned out of their own mouths! Worse still, a population of under one hundred and fifty does not allow much choice in 'under forties' with the qualifications and will to work for the public weal.

20

Looking Ahead

*. . . is depopulation likely to break the continuity
of this island story? . . . will the lack of manpower
eventually destroy a unique way of life, to which
as many as two hundred generations may have
contributed?*

Any attempt to forecast North Ronaldsay's future
must be in some respects an invitation to be proved
wrong by subsequent events. On the other hand, there
are always straws in the wind to provide some guidance
for those who are curious about what the years ahead
have in store. In this connection, any examination of
developments since 1914 generally shows that it has
been external events, rather than locally made
decisions, which have brought all the major changes.
Moreover, this tendency is likely to continue, for at
least the immediate future, as the policy of central
planning with ever larger units is still very much in
favour.

No doubt intelligent and industrious farming and
fishing will, as always, remain the mainstays of the
island's economy. The discovery of extensive oilfields in
the North Sea is also a factor which could have an
indirect infiuence on what happens in the next decade.

The lack of any natural harbour combined with the
absence of deep water approaches will prevent the
direct location of oil plant on North Ronaldsay, but this
does not provide protection against possible pollution.
If, for instance, a laden oil tanker were to rip open her
hull on the off-shore Reefdyke, the spillage would be
almost certain to poison the seaweed that provides
most of the food for native sheep. It might also destroy
large areas of growing seaweed which acts as a natural
breakwater for the low-lying island.

Even if this sort of major catastrophe should never happen, the proximity of the oilfields and possible landbased maintenance work in connection with the industry could make itself felt. On the credit side, there would most likely be some recruitment of schoolleavers who would otherwise have to leave Orkney to find suitable jobs. Conversely, the departure of anyone who is presently engaged in agriculture or fishing can only be seen as a loss to a small community that can ill afford any further diminution.

With regard to some trends of the past sixty years, many of the improvements and higher standard of living can be seen as 'dividends of the machine.' The rapid development of the petrol engine, following the First World War, gradually enabled many of the everyday tasks to be speeded up and done with far less effort.

The ferry-boat, which had to the early twenties depended on sail, was fitted with an engine. This changeover to the new source of power brought so many benefits that a desire to modernise and keep in the forefront of mechanical advancement has remained an island characteristic ever since.

This march of progress may have been inevitable, but one would be very insensitive indeed not to feel some pangs of regret when the inter-island air service made both the ferry-boat and her crew redundant. It would also be ungrateful to forget 'Big Johnnie' or any of the other boatmen who preceded or followed him in the dangerous calling of ferrying mail and passengers across the North Ronaldsay Firth.

Johnnie was the last of 'The men o' Ness,' a family of boatmen who had for three generations continued to cross the Firth in all sorts of weather. This stoic endurance of hardship had by Johnnie's time been inherited from an ancestry of at least four generations of seafarers. His great-grandfather, the first of 'The men o' Ness,' served as a sailor aboard the "True Love"of Hull. This vessel, built as a New Bedford whaler, was afterwards under British ownership and used as a Hull whaler for many years before she was again returned to American ownership.

On returning to his island, this Thomas Tulloch again took up crofting and fishing. He is remembered as the only North Ronaldsay man who ever stood on the Reefdyke dry shod! This feat was accomplished by wearing full-length seaboots and waiting for the lowest water of a spring ebb-tide before he stepped over the side of his lobster boat that had already been carefully positioned over the shallowest part of this submerged ridge.

About 'Big Johnnie' too, there is a story that will help to keep his memory green.

It happened around Lammas, on a day so calm and sunny that it might have been summer taking her final bow!

Johnnie may have been thinking that he would soon be contending with another eight months of wintry conditions. So, why shouldn't this ideal day be used for de annual ceremony of 'bidding goodbye to summer'?

Anyhow, slack-water, the best time for a quick return run, had been missed by the time his passengers had all assembled at the Black Rock. Normally, this delay might have been annoying, but in the circumstances it suited exactly. Johnnie looked at his passengers, who included the island doctor on his way back after a holiday. Then putting on a worried expression, Johnnie said:

"Weel folk, the ald engine'll no' tak' us back without a new sparkin' plug. So, I'll awa' doon t' Kettletaft t' get ane."

Johnnie could not have foreseen how the medico was to react. The well-meaning doctor opened up a small parcel and handed over a brand new sparking-plug, explaining that this would save time. No gift could have been more unwelcome, but Johnnie proved equal to the occasion. After taking a good look at his unexpected gift, he pushed the new plug well down into his trouser pocket and addressed his benefactor:

"Na, na, doctor, the ald worn engine'll do far better wi' a second-hand ane that's been 'braken-in' on a tractor." He then mounted an old bike and hastened away to Kettletoft Hotel. There, in the bar amongst his cronies, hours went by as if they had been minutes.

Then, after 'a final one for the road,' Johnnie reckoned that the flood-tide had spent its strength and that conditions would be just about right for a quick run home!

The motor-driven ferry-boat continued to carry the mail and passengers for many years after Johnnie's time. His successor was Hughie Thomson of Bewan, who had formerly served in the Merchant Navy. The lack of any safe harbour proved such a handicap that he decided to give up after a few years' experience. The contract was then given to his nephew, Henry Thomson, who by operating from Otterswick Bay on the Sanday side of the Firth, managed to run a very satisfactory service. This enterprise was, however, fated to become a victim to the onward march of progress. The advantages of air transport had, by the late sixties, become so apparent that The Orkney Islands Shipping Company thought it prudent to introduce a subsidiary air service for any of their passengers who wished to travel by this means.

Loganair started to operate in 1967-68 and was soon carrying nearly all the passengers who had formerly used Henry's ferry-boat. The contract for carrying the North Ronaldsay mail was also transferred to Loganair early in 1971.

As might be expected, there was a lingering nostalgia about the passing of the ferry-boat. The whole island was also soon to be grieved by the sad tidings that Henry had been drowned when his boat "Northern Isle" had foundered off the Start Point, Sanday on November 15, 1971.

Petrol- or oil-powered engines have also taken over many of the tasks connected with farming and the dried-tangle industry. Tractors and motor vehicles of increased size and power are now in universal use. Many islanders regard this as proof of progress, but others are not so sure that such a full commitment to the tractor is an entirely unmixed blessing. The constant production of new models makes it difficult to obtain replacement parts for the older machines. The tractor is also under-employed on the smaller crofts, where it may stand idle for days on end during most of the year. Neither can it reproduce itself like the horse, which has, alas, completely disappeared. Other new inventions in the form of sound radio and television have come to take the place of the island singers and fiddlers of bygone years. This receipt of news, immediately it has happened instead of only after long delays, whenever the old ferry-boat was storm-stayed, has its advantages.

Background information, opinions, drama and music are also available for those who have time to listen or view. Gone, however, are many of the pleasures that come from community participation and creation of their own amusement.

In thas connection, the island produced four musical families, the Swanneys, Cutts, Thomsons and Tullochs, who formed the backbone of both church choirs during the major part of last century and the first quarter of the present one.

Outstanding amongst these singers was Hugh, Swanney, Nether Linnay, who could without difficulty rise from a low bass to a high tenor note. The quality and range of Hughie's voice was so impressive that the island schoolmaster, Mr. Mackenzie, never tired of trying to persuade him to have it properly trained, but time went by without this happening.. The last tribute to Hughie's voice was made by the minister conducting his burial service in 1922, when he compared it to those of the "Sweet Bards of Israel."

Hugh Thomson, Peckhole, also had a fine tenor voice, while Samuel Cutt, Stenabreck, combined an excellent ear with perfect control of his fiddle bow. After hearing a new tune either hummed or whistled, he would accompany it on his fiddle and thereafter play it on request. Visitors to the island, on getting to know about Samuel's ability, often made a point of testing him. Although he never failed to produce the tune, the secret of how it was done died with him.

The island's medical service of today is probably the most appreciated of all the improvements which have taken place. There was no resident doctor before 1914, and the pain and suffering arising from this want is indirectly shown in official records. Pre-1914 death certificates, for instance, frequently gave the cause of death as 'unknown, no doctor in attendance.'

It was due to the combined efforts of the two island ministers, the Rev. Robert Grieve of the Parish Kirk and the Rev. William MacPherson of the Free Kirk, and Mr Traill, that the island got a trained nurse in December, 1900. Nurse Noble stayed for about two years and was releived by Nurse Sandison, who held the post until the summer of 1905.

By that time, Miss Janet Tulloch, Upper Linnay, had completed her nursing training in St Helens and was due to return to her birthplace as a Queen's District Nurse. She proved to be an excellent choice, and served the island well over the next nine years.

When a government grant became available for providing doctors for isolated communities, it was again a minister, the Rev. William Forbes, who organised a successful application on behalf of the island. The vacancy was first filled by a young doctor, but he had held the post for a few months only before the 1914 war claimed him for what was considered as more important work. The replacement, Dr. Low, was an elderly man whose health did not allow him to stay for long.

Since then, the island has had over twenty doctors and each of them is credited with saving lives that would have been endangered had there not been a resident practitioner available. Several of them have also played a leading role in securing much needed improvements for the general welfare of the community. Dr. Ferguson, who was island doctor in the early twenties, obtained funds for converting the ferry-boat from sail to motor-power. He then followed this up by getting a further grant for a crane with which she could be launched from, or lifted on to, the island pier.

These initial improvements, although important in their day, are by comparison rather dwarfed by the advances of the last quarter-century. Anyone now requiring an urgent operation, or other specialised treatment, is flown to a Kirkwall or Aberdeen hospital by the air ambulance service.

The period following the second world war has

brought the island many overdue amenities. Roads, especially those to the farms, have all been brought up to a good standard. School children are now taken to and from school by car instead of having to walk there by the indifferent roads and cart tracks of former days. The pier has been lengthened and almost rebuilt. This enabled the Orkney Islands Shipping Company's vessels to be properly berthed and to maintain a regular weekly service. An airfield with the necessary buildings and equipment has been provided. It has been operational since 1967, and Loganair now flies passengers and mail to Kirkwall every Monday, Wednesday and Friday. A piped water supply, installed some years ago, now brings the sparkling waters of 'Charlie's Spring' to almost every household in the island.

While it is unlikely that such an imposing list of further improvements will either be necessary or obtainable in the near future, there is still one important amenity missing—a public supply of electricity. It will be another big step forward when all the small individual generators can be replaced by the national grid. This will naturally be held up until yet another government grant covering most of the cost is obtained. It is also unfortunate that the longer this is delayed the higher will be the ultimate cost. This upward tendency was well illustrated by the pier extension of the mid-sixties. The original structure cost £1,600 in 1901 and the alteration cost over forty times as much!

If a completely modern telephone service can be taken as an indicator of future trends, there should be no reason for despondency. A new exchange with all the automatic equipment required for direct dialling has just come into service. It seems reasonable to assume that this investment anticipates an increase in the island's seventeen telephone subscribers!

The way in which the stillness of the night can now be suddenly broken by the hum of a motor-generator starting up whenever a telephone receiver is lifted can be just as alarming as the ghosts of former times.

Even if this sort of fright is confined to the road

corner in the immediate vicinity of the exchange building, it still shows how the push-button technique is invading this island, which has so far managed to preserve as much of the past as can be found anywhere in Orkney.

Appendix 1

... a list of North Ronaldsay words which were in regular use beyond the end of last century, but are now less frequently heard and in some danger of being forgotten ...

Aber (v)—to thresh lightly, removing only part of the grain from a sheaf.

Aache (int)—expressing impatience, or contemptuous dismissal.

Aafu (adj)—Awful.

Aff-tak (n)—an interval or lull during rough weather.

Aicher (n)—an ear of bere (barley).

Aisins (n)—eaves, the projecting stones on which the roof of a house rests.

Aithken (n)—a sheepmark; an earmark denoting the ownership of N.R. sheep.

Aloor (excl)—exclamation of disgust.

Amas (adj)—in need of help; worthy of assistance.

Amers (n)—embers.

Andoo (v)—to keep a boat stationary by means of the oars when fishing.

Anteran-ane (n)—an odd one.

Arknae (n)—a beast of large size, especially a seal.

Arro-egg (n)—an under-sized egg. ?

Arvo (n)—common chickweed (stellaria media).

Assie-pattle (n)—child, person who lies about the hearth.

Atfares (n)—behaviour, especially misbehaviour; ongoings.

Ava (n)—none at all.

Aval (n)—helpless; prostrate; lying and unable to get up.

Avar (pred adj)—to be wary of; exercising caution (O.N. varr).

Axe (n)—an island sheepmark, showing ownership.

Backlins (v)—esp. to walk backwards.

Bafflin (n)—the flattening and entangling of crops by wind and rain (O.N. Baffin).

Band (n)—knotted straw for tying sheaves; carrying strap on a kaysie.

Bangry (n)—to obtain "a lion's share."

Baut (n)—boat.

Beeiran (adj)—captious, fault-finding.

Bees-milk (n)—the first milk of a new-calved cow.

Bees-will (int)—be as it will.

Beltane (n)—old Celtic festival and Scottish quarter day; reckoned in N.R. to be 13th May.

Benlins (n)—the wide part of a stack where thatch is fixed.

Beuld (n)—stall for animals; also sometimes used for an animal shelter.

Biggin (n)—cluster of houses set close together.

Bilge-cod (n)—protective strip placed on the widest part of a boat's side.

Bir (n)—strength; power; force.

Birt (n)—bearing on a tide-movement.
Biss (n)—bristle.
    (v)—to "set up the biss" is to display ill-temper.
Bist (v)—must.
Bits (n)—an island sheepmark; earmark denoting ownership.
Blash (n)—continual rain.
Blatho (n)—butter-milk.
Blide (adj)—well pleased.
Blindered (v)—dazzled.
Blooro (n)—tiff; slight quarrel.
Booa (n)—a pimple.
Bogle (n)—call made by cattle, or seals.
Bokey (n)—bogey; source of terror.
Boolsey (adj)—bow-legged.
Booney (v)—to tidy up.
Bovval (V)—to thresh or beat.
Brachans (n)—Hames for work-ox.
Brait (v)—to roll up sleeves or trouser legs.
Braithe (v)—process of melting fish livers into oil.
Bresso (n)—charlock; wild mustard.
Brigsteens (n)—stone pavements.
Brime (v)—to draw a boat slightly out of the water.
    (n)—salt liquid.
Brisk (n)—cartilage or gristle.
Bruck (n)—rubbish, any worthless material.
Brulye of heat) (adj)—used to describe overcoming sudden heat.
Brumplo (n)—bergal, fish of the wrasse family.
Buddo (n)—child (term of endearment).
Builwans (n)—dockweed (Rumex).
Brucksey (adj)—untidy, slovenly worker.
Bursteen (n)—meal made from scorched grain.
Busslin (n)—sheep's intestine used as covering skin for meal
          pudding.
By-geen (adj)—former; bygone.
Calm-sough (n)—silence; saying little.
Cantankerly (adj)—perverse in temper, cross-grained.
Ceul (n)—cold.
Ceul o' wind (n)—puff of wind.
Ceuts (n)—ankles.
Chaa (egg) (n)—infertile egg.
Chabble (n)—waves in a tideway.
Chaddy (n)—stomach of a pig.
Chalder (n)—oyster catcher (O.N. tjaldr).
Cheekily (adj)—off the straight.
Childer (v)—to bump, or jolt.
Cholder (v)—to shake-up liquid.
Chow (n)—quid of tobacco.
    (v)—to chew.
Chuffsy (adj)—full-faced.
Cla (v)—to scratch.
Claik (n)—cackle of a hen; woman addicted to idle talk.
Claikan (v)—to carry tales; gossiping.
Claps (n)—jaws.
Clashan (n)—scandal-mongers meeting for gossip.
    (adj)—given to tattling.
Clepo (n)—slight blow or slap.
Cleuks (n)—hands.
Climmer (v)—climb.
Clows (n)—cloves.

Contar (y)—to go against, an argument.
Cose (v)—exchange,
Cother (v)—to show affection, or friendliness.
Couped (v)—capsized.
Cra (1, n)—crow.
   (2, v)—boastful talk.
Greg (n)—throat.
Craiter (n)—creature.
Croopan (v)—to assume a bent-back posture.
   (n)—a hunchback.
Crous (adj)—brisk, cheerful.
Cruggle (v)—to crouch, or draw the body into a hunched-up posture.
Cruik (n)—sheepmark; island earmark.
Cungling (v)—indulging in noisy argumentive or debate.
Daffo (n)—a sloppy meal given to sick animals.
Dammle (v)—to fill a vessel by pressing down in water until it is brim-full.
Davesum (adj)—to deafen by excessive noise.
Deil-dor (adj)—a mild expletive.
Dell (n)—a heavy dunt.
   (v)—to delve.
Dilder (v)—to move things about in a noisy, jolting fashion.
Ding (n)—slight blow on any article.
Diss (n)—small stack.
Dister (n)—light shower.
Dive (n)—a noisy argument.
Dolder (v)—to walk clumsily.
Dooless (adj)—listless; unenergetic.
Domaless (adj)—slow and shiftless.
Doon (n)—chaff of oats.
Doop (n)—buttocks; doup (Scot.).
Doose (v)—to strike with the head as a ram.
Dore (v)—to annoy by boring repetition.
Dorty (adj)—easily offended, like a child
Drawn Bits or Hemlins (n)—sheep earmarks of N.R. sheep.
Dringle (v)—to loiter or trail behind.
Drivas (n)—powerful thump delivered with great force, such as by a large wave.
Drugger (n)—strongly-built boat for carrying cattle or other heavy cargoes.
Dugged (adj)—dogged or obstinate.
Dunder (n)—loud thump, or heavy bang.
Dunter (n)—eider duck.
Edgean (adj)—restless; eager to start.
Eek (v)—unite; join.
Eggel-on (v)—encourage a quarrel.
Elsin (n)—awl.
Emmer Goose (n)—great northern diver.
Ennis (adj)—sometimes said of a poor uncomfortable dwellinghouse.
Ersland (n)—part of parish set apart as a unit for the purposes burial.
Eum (n)—odour; smells and fumes produced by cooking, or burning.
Fain (adj)—eager; anxious.
Fang (n)—getting a catch in buying; extra special bargain.
Feefly (adj)—clumsy, feeble at work.
Fenty-t'ing (n)—nothing at all.
Ferty (adj)—agitated or excited.
Feesked (adj)—mouldy.
Fest (v)—the action of hammering down the stake to which the animal was tethered.

Fey—uncannily knowing before-hand.
Fierdy (adj)—substantial; of good physique.
Un-fierdy (adj)—of poor physique, or not in proper trim.
Fla (n)—Flaw or fault.
Flakie (n)—straw-mat.
Fleester (v)—to strip off a layer, as thatch from a roof.
Flegg (v)—to frighten.
Fleep (n)—stupid, lazy fellow.
Flix (v)—to scare; frighten.
Flyte (v)—to scold; argue noisily.
Footer (v)—to bungle.
Fordal (v)—slow and unwilling; lagging behind.
       (n)—a spare person or article.
Freck (n)—carprice.
      (v)—to have foolish fancies.
Fornaint (adj)—opposite; face to face.
Fouth (n)—abundance; fill.
Frootery (n)—witchcraft or sorcery.
Fuggus (n)—atmosphere laden with fumes and smoke.
Gafter (n)—loud, silly laugh.
Gaggles (n)—a mess, such as a muddy patch.
Galder (n)—burst of loud laughter, or barking.
Gamfer (n)—ghost, apparition.
Gams (n)—gums.
Gamsmyre (n)—clamour, pandemonium.
Gant (v)—to yawn.
Gappis (n)—silly person; one who is prone to foolish actlon;
      (gaupus, Scot.).
Gettlin (n)—a kitten.
Gibby (n)—male cat.
Gillie (n)—term of address, e.g. "Are thoo gaan tae the kirk, gillie?"
Gingle (n)—shingle or gravel.
Glafter (n)—loud, uncontrolled laughter.
Glaiked (adj)—giddy and foolish.
Glaip (v)—gulp; eat ravenously.
Glam (v)—grab or snatch.
Glamsy, or Glamsie (adj)—having a scared look.
Glaur (n)—soft mud, mire etc.
Gled (adj)—as glowing fire.
Glett (n)—lull; temporary stoppage of rain or snow.
Glisk (n)—a brief glimpse.
Glomer (v)—to grope about in bad light.
Glose (v)—to stun with a violent blow.
Gluffie (n)—rash person, doing silly things.
Gokk (n)—a practical joke. (gowk's errand, Scot.), as on 1st April.
Golt (n)—galt; male pig.
Gouster (n)—sharp outburst of speech.
Gowk (n)—foolish person.
Gowl (v)—growl; to speak in a rough, surly voice.
Grabbit (adj)—vexed, for having missed something.
Grind (n, O.N.)—gate.
Grope (n)—lightly ground grain where the husk is broken, but not
      removed.
Grotty-Buckie (n)—cowrie shell.
Grue (n)—cold shiver of danger.
Gumeral (n)—projecting lower-jaw.
Gump (n)—hump; the hind part of an animal's back (O.N. gumpr).
Guppon (n)—handful; generally the amount of grain that can be
      scooped up by using both hands. (c.f. goupan, Scot.).

Haffits (n)—temples: the sides of the head above the cheekbone.
Hallan (n)—space above the ceiling used for storage.
Hamsy (adj)—slovenly in appearance, or dress.
Hansel (n)—gift; present given for luck.
Hark (v)—whisper.
Harns (n)—brains.
Hemlin (n)—sheepmark of North Ronaldsay sheep.
Hent (v)—collect or gather, e.g. potatoes in harvest.
Hesp (n)—hank of worster yarn.
Hould (n)—middle of the night.
High-how (adj)—unplanned.
Himlest (adj)—Hindmost; last one (e.g. hinmaist, Scot.).
Hirpling (v)—limping.
Hix (v)—to hiccough.
Hoast (v)—to cough.
Hoolan (n)—very strong gale.
Honkers (v)—to squat on the haunches with the hams resting on the legs near the heels.
How (adj)—hollow, i.e. how-sound is that produced by rapping an empty barrel etc.
Ill-at (adv)—to go ill-at; means to experience bad luck or misfortune.
Ill-best (n)—the best of a bad job.
Ill-divized (adj)—of an unprepossessing expression.
Ill-haversed (adj)—untidy in person.
Ill-minted (adj)—tricky and mischievous.
Ill-twarted (adi)—cross-grained.
Ill-venyied (adj)—ill-disposed; disagreeable.
Ill-ways (v)—to malinger; to feign sickness.
Ilty-fu (adj)—full of evil or malice.
Ime (n)—soot.
Inkling (v)—slight warning beforehand.
Iper (n)—liquid outflow from byre or stable drains.
Ithy (n)—eddy on the edge of a tideway.
Jewed (v)—cheated.
Jookery-packery (v)—trickery; roguery (c.f. joukery-pawkery, Scot.).
Jubish (adj)—dubious; of doubtful validity.
Jupsie (adj)—large-headed
Kaff (n)—chaff.
Kamshell (n)—skeleton of a cuttlefish.
Kat (n)—undersized; insignificant.
Kattannow (n)—caterwaul; also applied to a noisy brawl by a group of people.
Keltar (n)—home-woven cloth.
Kil rusket (adj)—over-dried on a kiln (c.f. roustit, Scot.).
Kitpoch (n)—stomach of a fish.
Kittlan (v)—tickling; to tickle.
Klam (n)—mussel; sometimes also used for other shell-fish.
Klett (n)—flat rock.
Klink (n)—slap; slight blow with the open hand.
Klo-gang (n)—section of the beach where the native sheep find their food and claim as their own territory.
Klocks (n)—foliage, or leaves on the upper end of tangles.
Kloor (v)—scratch.
Klurt (n)—big, clumsy person.
Kniff (adj)—agile; nimble.
Knock (n)—bundle of carded wool.
Koom (n)—roughage; refuse of grain.
Kruttle (n)—noise in the throat and chest caused by opposed breathing.

Kuisarie (v)—undue favouritism to one's relatives, as in the bestowal of patronage.

Ku-kwacks (n)—cold, blustery weather; cold spell of May. (Gabs of May).

Kungles (n)—large, rounded, sea-polished stones.

Kwarr (v)—to wheeze, or breathe noisily like a person suffering from asthma.

Kye-on (v)—to show or make manifest.

Lach (v)—laugh.

Langsum (adj)—lengthy; tedious; long-drawn-out.

Lappert, milk (adj)—curdled milk.

Lanyied (adj)—striped across the back (description applied to animals).

Laufen (n)—some abatement in the weather.

Lavero (n)—skylark.

Leepsy (adj)—lop-sided; ill-balanced.

Leet (v)—pay attention; take heed. ("never leet" means ignore).

Leeth-fu (adj)—steady and conscientious good worker.

Leufer (n)—some abatement in the weather.

Leevan-lane (adj)—quite alone.

Ley (n)—deep crack between rocks, or in the sea-bed.

Liftan (v)—raising a weak animal on to its feet; lifting sheaves in harvesting.

Lith (n)—the natural division between the old and new fleece which is made use of in sheep-clipping.

Lithy (n)—lull; period of calm in a storm.

Looping (v)—when native sheep jump the Ness dyke.

Loot (v)—bend downwards.

Lorried (adj)—besmattered; soiled.

Lowe (n)—a flame.

Lue (adj)—lukewarm.

Luiffs (n)—palm of hands.

Lunder (n)—heavy, noisy blow.

Lye (n)—sea grass.

Lygeese (n)—barnacles.

Madrum (n)—anger, fury, rage.

Main (n)—willpower; self-control; patience.

Mak-a-doo (n)—pretense.

Matlo (n)—house-fly.

Maundom (n)—god physical qualities of a man.

Meil (n)—old weight. (A meil of kelp, also called " a weigh of kelp," weighed around two hundredweight).

Melder-corn (n)—corn dried on a kiln.

Meeth (n)—a fishing spot, with two cross-bearings.

Melr (n)—sandbank; leading to a geo (O.N.).

Merter (v)—to injure, hurt severely.

Minnwit (n)—shrewd commonsense.

Mirk (n)—darkness, or poor light.

Mirkan (adj)—getting dark.

Mirr (v)—throb.

Mittle (v)—to hurt; to interfere; or to damage.

Moags (v)—to trudge; walk with effort through mud or snow.

Moor (n)—blinding snowstorm.

Moorit (adj)—dusky, reddish-brown colour of wool.

Mose (n)—mould; a woolly or fluffy growth of small fungi due to dampness.

Mudge (v)—move (corr. of budge), e.g "He would na mudge."

Muffles (n)—half-gloves.

Muggaty-fou (adj)—saturated with moisture, as foggy light rain.

Mullar (n)—gravelly beach.
Mulls (n)—soft lips and muzzle of an animal.
Mullyo (n)—bundle of bere tied together with straw.
Munyo (n)—pith; power; vigour.
Murled (adj)—having a white patch on the face.
Murry (adj)—fine, drizzling rain.
Nabal (adj)—deceitful and mean.
Nacket (adj)—small and insignificant.
Nain (adj)—own; i.e. "me nain" means my own.
Neester (v)—squeak; to give forth a high-pitched sound.
Neirs (n)—kidneys. Name also in use in North Germany—Capt. Wm.
     Tulloch.
Neves (n)—clenched hands as used in fisticuffs.
Nibbet (adj)—scant measure or weight.
Nibsy (adj)—vigorous (generally applied to sturdy boys).
Nick (n)—pain of wreched muscle.
Nidder (v)—to dwindle away.
Niest (n)—small fire starved for fuel.
Niled (adj)—mouldy.
Nile-hole (n)—opening for "nile-plug" which allows bilge-water to
     be drained off when the boat is drawn ashore.
Nirped (adj)—cross-grained; stingy.
Noodan (adj)—almost asleep, with the head falling forward.
Noddle (n)—head.
Norn (n)—the Old Norse tongue of Orkney.
Norran (adj)—persistent, useless arguing.
Nory (adj)—ill-tempered wrangling over triffles.
Noust (n)—a landing place and boat stance.
Nowt (n)—ox or other cattle.
Nudgan (v)—to poke (gently).
Ober (n)—sense of responsibility.
Oddle (n)—drain for byre or stable effluent.
Omo (n)—helpless disorder, confusion.
Onca (on call) (adj)—occasional, "onca wark."
Oot-by (n)—name used for the part of an old island house furthest
     from the fireside.
Ootfaa (v)—to flow out.
     (n)—inferior, i.e. light grain and seeds separated by
     winnowing. ("ruthe" O.N. hrjoda).
Ootmocht (v)—exhausted, tired-out.
Oottak (n)—lasting power and quality.
     (adj)—very durable.
Ootwails (n)—residue after the best has been removed; leavings.
Ossigar (n)—moult. "In ossigar" means casting feathers.
Owse (v)—to ladle liquid out of one container into another container;
     to bale water out of a boat.
Paal (n)—holdfast; foothold enabling extra pull to be exerted.
Paalo (n)—porpoise.
Paddle (n)—lumpsucker (a fish).
Pattle (v)—walk with quick, short steps, like a child.
Pech (v)—breathe quickly; to pant.
Peedie (adj)—small.
Pellet (n)—pelt; sheep's hide with wool left on it.
Pickaterno (n)—Arctic tern.
Pidro (n)—slight touch; the game of tig (O.N. fidro).
Pivvcr (v)—to quiver, to vibrate.
Plank (n)—regular division of land replacing run-rig system.
Planti-creus (n)—circular enclosures for cabbage plants.
Pleed (v)—whine; to complain in an unmanly way.

Plink (n)—home-brewed ale of very low strength.
Ploots (n)—feet.
Pocky (n)—snall bag; paper cone.
Poort (n)—cry-baby.
Pooshan (n)—poison.
Poosted (adj)—without vigour; lacking bodily power.
Pootie (n)—small red-ware codling.
Powl (v)—to howl with pain, or in rage.
Praam (n)—punt, usually flat-bottomed.
Preeve (v)—to test for fish at likely land-marked positions.
Prinky (n)—concented fellow; show-off.
Pudyan (n)—small gluttonous person.
Puggy (n)—stomach.
Pugsy (adj)—stout; large-bellied.
Pund (Poind) (n)—sheep-pen.
Punder (n)—the head.
Pundler (n)—weighing beam (O.N.).
Puther (v)—to potter about.
Quern (n)—handmill for grinding grain (O.N. kvern).
Queyo (n)—heifer.
Quake (v)—to quake, or quiver, as in fear.
Queasy (adj)—affected with nausea.
Raffle (v)—to entangle.
Raim (n)—curdled cream.
Rake (v)—to stretch for; to hook by jerking up the flshing-line.
Rallied-tongued (adj)—foul-mouthed.
Rally (v)—to sway drunkenly.
Ramist (adj)—confused by drink; ill-rested from broken sleep.
Ramp (v)—to romp round noisily.
Ramse (adj)—rancid.
Rann (n)—herring roe.
Ransel (v)—to search for stolen property (O.N. reynsla, to search).
Ravsee (adj)—ragged and tattered.
Reddins (n)—fatty layer covering animal intestines.
Red-tap (n)—red-headed.
Reepan (n)—slippery, decaying seaweed.
Reested (adj)—cured by smoking near kitchen chimney, usually
applied to mutton or fish.
Reevis (n)—gale of such strength as to make it necessary to "reef " or
reduce sail.
Renye (v)—to wrench; with force.
Reveligo (n)—rash, uncouth person.
Rickle (n)—a rickety, ramshakle structure; a loose heap (Scot.).
Ridyan (n)—a rowdy; especially rude, quarrelling woman (term of
abuse.)
Ridyie (n)—a ridge of rocks running into the sea.
Rif (n)—submerged rocks; as Reef Dyke.
Rift (v)—to belch.
Riggin (n)—ridge; also used for backbone of an animal.
Rime (v)—to clear up after rain or snow; sky-clearance.
Rind (v)—melt suet.
Rip (n)—Sheepmark; earmark denoting ownership.
Risso (n)—a big stout girl.
Rivlin (n)—one-piece mocassin made of untanned skin.
Roo (v)—to make piles of hay, seaweed, etc.
Roose (v)—to praise highly.
Roost (n)—a tidal race (O.N. röst).
Routh (n)—arguments and disagreements.
Rowo (n)—roll of carded wool.

Ruckle (n)—(1) very thin person, or animal; (2) also a shrug.

Ruffy (adj)—having rough, unkempt hair.

Rugg (n)—(1) fine, close drizzle; (2) a sharp tug.

Ruggy (adj)—clumsy in dress, or loutish in appearance.

Ruithe (n)—inferior grain and small seeds separated by winnowing (O.N. hrjoda).

Rullye (n)—heaped-up formations of stones left by the sea.

Rumse (v)—to rummage; to ransack.

Runge (n)—a commotion responsible for an uproar in the sea.

Rusks (n)—protruding tufts of straw sticking out of a sheaf or stack.

Sab (v)—to soak; saturate.

Sae (n)—water tub, designed for a "sae tree" to enable it to be slung between the shoulders of two carriers.

Sand-greemy (n)—mixture of black earth and sand.

Sandwort (Arenaria Norvegica) (n)—a rare plant once found in North Ronaldsay.

Sanlo (n)—ringed plover.

Scarf (n)—cormorant.

Scrunty (adj)—very mean.

Segs (n)—wild iris.

Settin (n)—weight measure; about one-sixth of a meil (O.N.).

Sha (me) (v)—show me.

Shackle (n)—(1) after-birth of cow etc.; (2) a leg-band for preventing native sheep louping over the sheepdyke.

Shear (n)—sheepmark; earmark denoting the ownership of island sheep.

Shilpet (adj)—sour tasted.

Skate-fu (adj)—voracious, gluttonous.

Shoos (n)—the awns of bere.

Siar (n)—strainer.

Sile (n)—very young herring.

Sillo (n)—sillock; first-year coal-flsh.

Sindry (adv)—torn apart.

Sipe (v)—to drain.

Sirpan (adj)—saturated with water.

Skaff (v)—eat greedily (Eng. scoff).

Skarr (adj)—timid or shy.

(v)—to loath unappetising food.

Sgair (Skjaer) (v)—increase the length of a rope of a boat.

Skelder (n)—layers of flagstone that are too thin to be of any use.

Slapp (n)—a gate.

Skert (n)—sheepmark.

Skirter (Sgerter) (n)—coarse seaweed.

Skibal (skoibal) (n)—indecent exposure.

(adj)—of indecent appearance or behaviour.

Skoo (n)—drying place (O.N. skja).

Skoom (n)—scum, top layer.

Skow (n)—fragmenls, or other broken material.

Skra-fish (n)—dried cuithes (small coal-fish).

Skreek (n)—shriek.

Skruff (n)—scurf; an incrustation.

Skrunt (n)—stunted person; also a mean niggardly person.

Skurber (n)—barren soil, or a bare patch.

Skurt (n)—whatever can be carried in the encircling arms.

Skuttles (n)—empty egg-shells.

Slagg (n)—heavy sea-swell.

Slaver (n)—spittle running from the mouth.

Slokk (v)—to quence (a flame). (O.N. slokkva).

Slushy (adj)—slovenly, untidy in dress.

Smeer (v)—as to spread butter on bread (O.N. smjor).
Smero (n)—natural clover.
Smook (n)—smoke.
Smoly (v)—to wheedle (term of disdain).
Smoor (v)—to drown, or suffocate.
Sneet (v)—to blow one's nose.
Snitter (n)—a noose, or running-loop employed for holding open an animal's mouth so that medicine may be administered.
Snorrie (adj)—cross, bad-tempered.
Snye (n)—white spot, or star on forehead of a horse.
Spenye (n)—bamboo canes, as used for fishing rods.
Stair axes (n)—sheepmark; earmark denoting ownership.
Scart & Hole (n)—as above.
Stoo & Bits (n)—as above.
Stoo & Rips (n)—as above.
Stuian (n)—boat noust (O.N.).
Synsin (n)—the coot.
Sooko (n)—call-word for cow or calf.
Sookan (adj)—slow, lacking in drive. (n)—twisted straw puttees.
Soonan (pres. par.)—faint with hunger.
Souple (n)—the lower division of a flail, supple.
Sove (adj.)—a smart blow by the hand.
Sowany (n)—a ram with only one (descended) testicle.
Spaiter (v)—to use with care.
Spelkie (v)—to apply a splint.
Spret (n)—a spurt.
Sproosti (adj)—mottled.
Spurtan (v)—liquid spurting out.
Staint (v)—stint; avoid waste; use sparingly.
Steeth (n)—foundation.
Stiggle (n)—short, thin, starved crops of corn or oats.
Stiggley (adj)—of unsteady gait.
Stime (n)—haze; also condensation on window panes.
Stimmy (n)—slight mist.
Stoo (n)—sheepmark; showing ownership.
Stoor (n)—dust.
Stoop (stoup) (int.)—shut up! Stow (v)— halt!! or stop!
Stowers (n)—flags and water-reeds.
Strood (n)—suit of clothes, or sails.
Stunder (v)—to walk as if half asleep.
Stundery (adj)—moody and unpredictable.
Sturken (v)—to congeal; to change from liquid to solid form.
Styven (styven of cold) (v)—to be numbed with cold.
Sucky (adj)—messy; untidy.
Suddle (v)—to dirty or soil.
Sugg (n)—(1) boggy ground; (2) an easy-going woman.
Swalty (n)—a drink of considerable proportion (generally used in connection with home-brewed ale).
Swander (v)—to reel or stagger.
Swap (n)—a gust of wind.
Swee (n)—a stinging pain in any wound.
Swedge (n)—stretch and rest, after a heavy meal.
Swevel (v)—moving off the straight (O.N. sveifla).
Swill (n)—a homemade swivel made from wood.
      (v)—to wash
Swilter (v)—to spill or cause an overflow.
Sworl (n)—a knot, or fault in timber.
Tachy (adj)—slightly damp.
Taik (n)—thatch (thak, Scot.).

Taing (n)—small cape or point jutting into the sea.
Tano (n)—the shag.
Taivers (n)—tatters; rags.
Tangie (n)—a mythical being; a will-o'-the-wisp—actually
       phosphorescent.
Tarf (adj)—rank in smell or taste.
Tat (n)—a tuft of wool left on.
Teebro (O.N. **tidbra**) (n)—an apparent shimmer running over the
       ground on a hot day.
Tem (v)—to stretch a pelt on a pole or frame in order to air-dry.
Terran (adj)—headstrong, irritable.
Tiflin (pres. p.)—rummaging through spares, etc, for something to
       complete the job on hand.
Tirl (n)—a sudden bout of bad weather.
Tirry (n)—a fit of ill-temper.
Tirve (v)—to strip bare; the removal of thatch, etc. (orig. the
       stripping of turf).
Titter (v)—to shiver with cold or fear.
Tise (v)—to persuade.
Tollan-him (phr)—act to his advantage.
Too-fa (n)—a lean-to shed, built on the end or side of a house.
Toom-bit (n)—sheepmark; an earmark denoting ownership of a
       North Ronaldsay.
Tooltery (adj)—easily knocked down (said of an ill-built wall or
       other erection).
Tow-lowsin (n)—a quick or violent thaw.
Toomal (O.N. **Tun-valla**) (n)—the in-field nearest to the farm
       dwelling, generally the best soil.
Trabound (v)—rebound.
Traik (v)—wander idly.
Trebb (n)—an earthen rampart marker.
Trink (n)—a narrow cleft or crevice in rock.
Trip (n)—a dividing march.
Trowey (adj)—feebly and sickly.
Tulfers tn)—floor-boards in a boat.
Tuo (n)—small mound or hillock.
Twerny (adj)—awkward and difficult to please.
Tyoll (v)—to labour under a heavy burden.
Ugg-bone (n)—bone behind the gills of a fish.
Uncan-news (phr)—strange, unknown tidings.
Undeemin (adj)—of enormous size or quantity.
Unstowly (adj)—wild and blustery; unsettled weather.
Unwanden (adj)—unexpected.
Urm (n)—undersized potatoes; coal dust, etc.
Urter (n)—pastures that are bare and barren.
Vashal (n)—barrel, tub, vat or similar container.
Veill (n)—mischief maker.
Vildro (n)—confuse. (To "go vildro" means to go astray).
Vellye (n)—a forceful character, and one who is generally disliked.
Voar (n)—Norse Spring, seed-time.
Wain (v)—hope, or expectation.
Waffle (v)—to tangle.
Waft (waff) (n)—a signal, some article on the top of a pole.
Wap (n)—(1) a light blow; (2) the handle of a threshing mill.
Warp (v)—a stroke of the oar in rowing.
Warsie (adj)—having a feeling of faintness, and bad taste in the mouth.
Wart (n)—a former warning beacon; these hill-top positions are
       sometimes now marked by a cairn.
Weeks (n)—the corners of the mouth.

Weel-willed (adj)—kindly disposed.
Wheesk (v)—whisper, smallest rumour.
Weigh of kelp (phr)—measure of kelp weighing about two
        hundredweight.
Whaar (v)—to make wheezy sounds.
Whamsey (adj)—out of sorts; suffering nausea or sea-sickness.
Whar-on (n)—resources of money and property.
Wheesan (v)—taking short, quick breaths.
Whinner (n)—a sharp blow.
Whome (n)—a temporary finish to a partly-built stack.
Whumble (v)—to empty by turning over the container.
Will (v)—to stray; to become lost and bewildered.
Wint (n)— wont; habit.
      (v)—to be accustomed.
Wupped (adj)—bound with cord.
Wurry (v)—to choke; to strangle.
Wurs (adj)—pertaining or belonging to us.
Wusp (n)—a matted bundle of straw or other material.
Yackel (n)—a molar tooth.
Yard-sook (v)—a strong dry breeze that dries the stacks.
Yark (n)—the instep.
Yarm (n)—the cry of a lamb.
Yatlin (n)—a flat iron plate for baking bannocks (girdle, Scot.,
        griddle, Eng.).
Yeesp (n)—slightest squeak.
Yin (man) (adj)—as applied to yon man.
Yole (n)—a small undecked boat.
Yowe (n)—a ewe.
Yowling (n)—the sound made in yelling or barking.
Yuk (yuck) (v)—to itch.

LOCAL NAMES FOR SEASHORE WRACK AND WEED

Drooer—sea-lace, cat-gut etc (Clorda filum).
Dulse (Rhodymenia palmatic). Sou-Söll—sheep's weed in Norway.
Skerter (Laminaria saccharna).
Snue—collected from several accumulations of fine drift weeds.
Tangle, Oarweeds (Laminaria).
Tang-Yellow, Knotted Wrack (Ascophyllum nodosum).
Tang-Cow (Pelvetia canabiculata).
Tang-Paddy, Bladder Wrack (Facus vesiculosus).
Ware (Laminaria digitata).

Appendix 2

... many names in the following list have already been published by the late Dr. Hugh Marwick in his booklet "The Place-Names of North Ronaldsay" (1923) ...

Abutt—a former quoy, below Leean, north-east of Upper Breck.
Aby—The name of a district.
Backakelday—A natural spring and former house site. O.N. bakka-kelda—a slope and spring well.
Bannowatten—Small low bog, near West Sound.
Belyegrate—Ridge of rocks and stones sheltering the Stuin of Garso.
Blggin—Cluster of houses sited together; applies mainly to the Senness Biggin.
Boat-Geo—name of a deep cleft or channel near the middle of the Seal Skerry.
Boin Skerry—Outlying rocks north of Dennis Taing.
Breck—(O.N. brekka, a slope, house name.) Many houses have Breck included in their name, e.g. Craesbreck.
Buckakeith—An enclosure near North Manse.
Buistie-Tun—(1633 Val.) (O.N. bústaör), farm settlement.
Burgars Pow—A rocky pool east of Finnin Geo.
Burrian—(O.N. borgin), site of Brough
Burrigar—(1733 Rentals), old house on Howar's ground.
Clett Roos—A big rock in Gue Geo.
Conglibist—a house site and O.N. kǫngla-bústaör, a farm.
Corsegatc—a former grass-pathway, leading from Cross Kirk to Grind.
Cring-a-may—Lands east of Longar. O.N. a circle.
Cruyertus—An ancient house site.
Dennis Ness—Applied to the sheep-run outside the Ness Dyke.
Denmark Geo—Near Neven's House.
Dennis Taing—The south-easterly point of the North End.
Disher—(O.N. dysjar), a mount, a nineteenth-century house site.
Dog Geo—A landing place below Stenabreck; former name Hesta Geo.
Donald's Stripe—A partly-closed ditch, east of Garso, used [or draining Garso and Senness Lochs..
Dubhall—Former name of Phisligar.
East-Breed—The tide eddies east of Seal Skerry.
Enyan—(O.N. engin), the meadowland south of Ancum Loch.
Fairasibby—Small bay inside the Green Skerry.
Fairy Brae—A slight rise on the left-hand side when passing out through Andrew's Gate into Turrieness Hill.
Feerless—a rock at the entrance to the Noust of Howar.
Finyarhouse—(O.N. vinjar-hús), a brae and former dwelling north of Waterhouse.
Furvo—A boundary dyke terminating at Doo Geo.
Galtie Rock—Rock in mid-Linklet Bay, covered at high tide.

Garso—(O.N. garðs-haugr), garth-mount, house name,

Gerback—Old name for Gerbo, 1733 Rentals. O.N. garð-bolkr, a dividing-wall.

Geyro—(O.N.). Name applied to special pasture lands.

Girnavald—(O.N. grœnivollr), green-field, now named Greenwall.

Gravity (Grev-ite)—(O.N. grafar), a hollow or depression, house name.

Gri'ö—(O.N.). Applied to Cross Kirk, meaning Peace, Sanctuary, Security.

Grutcheen Loch—(O.N. grjót-tjorn, stony loch). Situated in Holland's Loch Park.

Haan—Beach and small geo east of Burrian.

Hangie—High black rocks forming the two Geos of Hangie.

Haskie Taing—A taing south-east of Hooking.

Hooking—1798 R. O.N. á[r]kvern, Millburn, house name.

Hole-o-Brue—A fishing place inside the Altars of Linnay.

Holland—(O.N. hó-há-land), high land.

Hoe-Skerries—A stretch of flat tidal rocks near Crewgather.

Howback—A sloping brae near the beach-head S.W. of Quoybanks.

Hoyn—A small brae above the Eastbanks, name still in use in Denmark. (per Captain William Tulloch).

Hasmire—A former wet mire located north of Howar.

Husnabie—A small ware-beach S.E. of Sandback.

Hyan—A former house site and well.

Kirbest—(O N. Kirkju-bolstaðr, Kirk-Farm). (Busta 1595, R.), still house name.

Klett-Sweyn—(O.N.), a tidal rock off Burrian Point.

Kirk Taing—The taing below the Old Beacon with a supposed Chapel somewhere near. The accuracy of the Chapel theory is now considered doubtful, and it is thought that the Kirk part of the name is more likely to refer to the Cross Kirk, while the whole North End of the island fits into the description of a " Taing."

Knowe of the Enyan—Situated south of Ancum Loch.

Knowe of Link's Park—Situated in south-east corner of park.

Knowe of Samisland—A knowe to the south of Hooking Loch, also lands southwards of this hillock are given the name "Samislands."

Kruger—A small patch of pasture above Burgess Pow where the rare wildflower Skull-Cap (Scutellaria galericulata) was last seen.

Kuter's Mire—Low mirey land below Upper Linnay, which has now been drained.

Landward Ley—A shoal extending outwards from the most northerly point of the Seal Skerry.

Lashan—Flat rocks at the entrance to the Geo of Rue.

Leean—Sloping ground north of Upper Breck.

Leeatangie—A fishing-crag at the West Beach.

Lensmire—Low ground above Lenswick Beach.

Ley—One example is the deep channel cutting into the Seal Skerry.

Linklet—Arable land between Ancum Loch and Finyarhouse; 1595 an urisland (18d land).

Lint-Lus—Rigs of land in the Toon o' Senness.

Lity-Well—Old well for the Senness Biggin, situated between Lochend and Sandback.

Matches-Crag—A fishing-crag at Himero Geo.

Mayback—Mound near Grind, may have been a house site.

Messigate—Formerly a path to Old Kirk; now part of the main road. O.N. messu-gata, mass-road.

Mursie—Part of the beach east of Skaiver.

Muckle Well—A fishing spot inside west end of Seal Skerry.

Musapol—Wet pasture land along Senness Loch, near Lochend.

Ness-tun—(O.N. nes) a headland.

Neeoquoy—An enclosure at Westness.

Nockan—A fishing-ground in outer Linklet Bay.

Nouster—O.N. naustar), nousts.

Noust—A landing-place for boats, such as the Noust of Howar, Noust of Sandback, etc.

North-yard—(O.N. norð-garð).

Oot-Kletts—Outlying rocks of Hangie.

Packhouse—Once a storehouse for shipwrecked seamen, located on western part of Trinley.

Pickadike—A ridge of loose stones enclosing a pool inside Scottigar Taing.

Pool—A deep rock-depression in the ebb near Westness, which holds a large salt-water pool throughout ebb tide.

Rif—Short for Reef Dyke.

Rimmers—A stretch of flat rocks to the westward of Bewan Pier.

Roor—A rock at the entrance to Swin Geo.

Roy's Well—A well formerly located in the land of Purtabreck and used to provide the water needed for building at the Free Church and Manse.

Saedar—The highest rocks of the Seal Skerry.

Sanlogate—An old track, now part of the main road from Sandback up to Senness Biggin.

Sholtis-skoo—(O.N. kvi—enclosure: skja—a drying place). Present name Sholtisquoy.

Senness (Sailness 1595, 1733)—Sailness and Sander-be-north, together comprised 24d lands.

Skett-o'-Fincus—Land near the Cross Kirk (Skatt land O.N.).

Skett Holter—(O.N. offshore rock), Ires Taing, North End.

Skeet-Mill—A pointed rock south of Fairasibby, covered at high tide and bearing about north-east from Westness.

Sketherus—May have been a house site, now part of Purtabreck's land.

Sodlis Geo—An old name for Roof Geo.

Sowluran—An outlying rock on the west side of Twinyas Point.

Stenabreck—(O.N. stein-brekka), stony slope.

Stevan—A low, wet hollow west of Hooking Loch, and including the Stevan Road.

Steven o' Papy—An outlying rock below the Brae of Howmie.

Stripe o' Sangar—A ditch leading from Ancum Loch to Linklet Bay.

Stoot's Well—A well between Burray and Longar, located on the land of Brigg.

Sugarhouse (Suggarhous 1653)—O.N. suðr-garð-hús, south garth-house.

Summer Ayre—a high ridge of stones stretching along the beach east of Burgos Pow and having swampy ground on the southern side.

Surtos of Sangar—Dark patches of seaweed and rocks in Linklet Bay, opposite Sangar.

Suthinasus—Old arable land, south of Ness Houses.

Tinkigar—Once a quoy near Cross Kirk.

Tootsin—A fishing-ground in Linklet Bay.

Trunky-gate—A narrow path leading through Linklet

Tunlins—Rigs of arable land in the Toon o' Senness.

Tunlands—Old arable land north of Ness Houses.

Tungy—The dangerous west-point of the Seal Skerry.

Vacles—Rocks leading into the Stuian of Garso.

Verhoose (Verus)—The School Brae and adjoining ground to the southwards.

Vincoin—(O.N. vin), green pasture.

Westhouse—West Senness, 1733 R.

Westness—Vestness, 1733 R. (O.N. nes, headland).

Whunderless—A house-site in Busta-tun, Kirbest.

Appendix 3

From the 1733 Rental of North Ronaldsay

Summary of the surnames of the house-holders in the island of North Pconaldsay 1733

Tulloch 18; Swanney 7; Thomson 5; Muir 4; Kelday 3; Cutt 2; Hay; Moar; Borrow; Fea; Walls; Martln (a miller); Torfinson (Turfus); one of each of the last seven names, 46 households.

Population of North Ronaldsay 1791 onwards

1791-420, 1801-411; 1811-384; 1831-522; 1836-443; 1851-536; 1861-532; 1871-539; 1881-547; 1891-501; 1901-442; 1911-436, 1931-283.

Summary of the surnames of the house-holders in the island of North Ronaldsay 1801

Tulloch 20; Swanney 8; Thomson 7; Kelday 6; Cutt 5; Muir 4; Scott 2; Turfus 2; Martin; Walls; Donaldson; Manson; one of each of the last four names, 58 households.

Summary of the surnames of the house-holders in the island of North Ronaldsay 1901

Tulloch 24; Swanney 12; Thomson 11; Muir 7; Cutt 9; Scott 3; Kelday; Seatter; Laverty; Knight; Grieve; Campbell; McAdie; McPherson; McFadyan; McKay; one of each of the last ten names; 76 house-holds.

Summary of the surnames of the house-holders in North Ronaldsay, 1973

Swanney 12; Tulloch 11; Thomson 7; Muir 4; Scott 4; Knight 2; Seatter; Laverty; Deyell; Cutt; Gray; Edwardson; Young; Jamieson; Broadhurst; one of each of the last nine names, 49 households. Population approximately 128.

Distribution of island surnames during the seventeenth, eighteenth and nineteenth centuries

North End: 17th century—Tulloch, Muir, Walls, Torfinson (Turfus).
18th century—Scott, Swanney.
19th century—Thomson, Cutt.

South End: 17th century—Swanney, Thomson, Kelday, Cutt, Martin.
18th century—More, Tulloch, Turfus.
19th century—Seatter, Knight.

Mlddle of island Linklet:
17th century—Thomson, Swanney, Tulloch, Kelday.
18th century—Turfus, Donaldson, Cutt, Mwr.
19th century—Scott, Laverty.

Since this book went to press, it has been proved that the largest exodus of people from the island was between 1831 and 1836, amounting to about eighty persons. Many went to the island of Eday, some to other North Isles, and others much further afield.

Appendix 4

"The Biggin o' Senness" has figured so often in the story of North Ronaldsay that it would be interesting to introduce yet another branch of this Tulloch family, a family which taken over all, were never far away when adventure was abroad!

This particular episode originated out of what is generally referred to as "the Cutt family being warned out of their house at Disher." A daughter of Senness called Mary, together with her husband, Robert Cutt, finding themselves without any home, had no alternative but to return to Senness.

Upon this happening, William Tulloch, the elder son of Senness, decided that the croft did not offer much prospect for both his sister and himself. So William, along with his wife (formerly Mary Muir from Burray) and their young family cleared out in order to start life afresh in Kirkwall.

There, he soon established himself as a boatman and fisherman and was reasonably successful for many years, before being involved in a boating accident. This happened while he was ferrying naval sailors back to their ships during a visit of the British Home Fleet to Kirkwall, and it cost him his life.

Of his family of six sons and two daughters, most of the boys took to the sea. Robert was lost with the "Julia," a Kirkwall schooner, and Martin too was drowned while on a deep-sea voyage.

John, another of the sons, also took up a seafaring life and served on the Clippers engaged in the wool and guano trade. He sailed for some years along with two cousins from North Ronaldsay. These were John Muir of Burray, and Hugh Muir of Midhouse. John Tulloch himself eventually married and settled down in Southampton, where his wife belonged.

The pull of the sea was evident in their family too, and one of John's sons, serving as a Senior Officer on a British Cruising Liner, was present at the Agadir incident of 1910-11. His thoughtful and well-considered evidence at the Court of Inquiry is credited as an important contribution in helping to smooth over the quarrel, which at that time looked like blowing up into an international crisis.

So it seems that this Southampton branch of the Senness family had become diplomatic as well as adventurous. This is further borne out by the practical evidence that one of John's daughters was for many years employed as private secretary to a top official of the British Foreign Office.

The last member of the Tulloch family of Senness, mentioned above, was Mr Thomas Tulloch, Seaside, who died in December 1939 at the advanced age of 92 years.

―――

During the process of writing "A Window on North Ronaldsay" I tried to get full information regarding the very early teachers who served at North Ronaldsay school. I could get no trace of the early Log Book either at the Education Office, Kirkwall or at the North Ronaldsay school. The Log Book, however, was still intact at the North Ronaldsay school during the time Mr Donald MacInnes served as head teacher, and until such time when he left the island in 1955. After considerable research at different souces, I did, eventually, get the necessary information needed for inclusion in the chapter on Education contained in the book.

―――

Addenda

In the chapter "Going to the Wars" John Thomson of Howatoft was omitted. He served as a Flight Sergeant in R.A.F. Bomber Command.

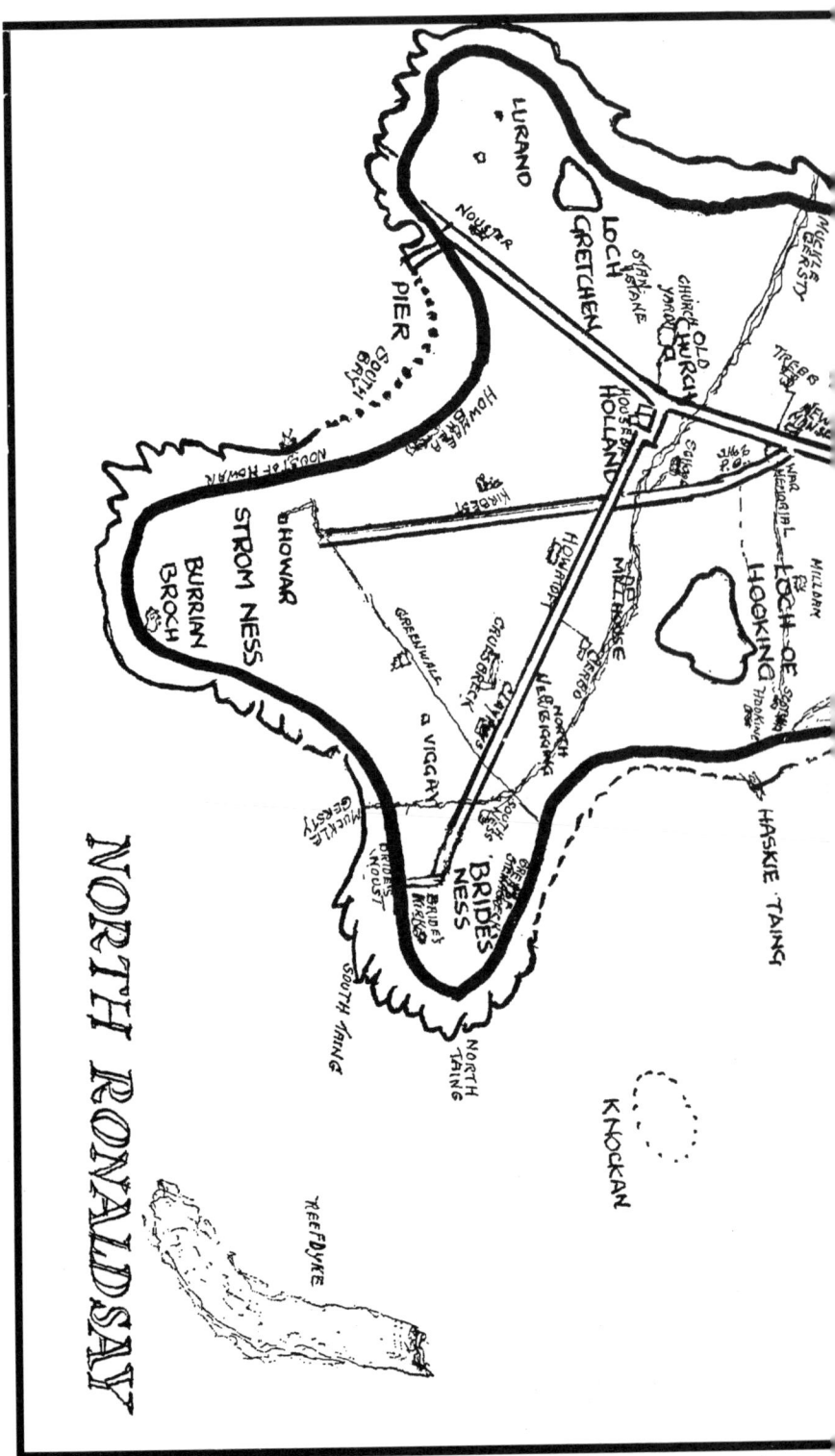

NORTH RONALDSAY